REVISE PSYCHOLOGY

FOR **AS** LEVEL

BARTON PF

R   RODY
(Brighton and Hove Sixth Form College, UK)

DIANA DWYER
(South Nottingham College, UK)

PSYCHOLOGY PRESS
ALERE FLAMMAM
Taylor & Francis Group

Published in 2002 by Psychology Press Ltd
27 Church Road, Hove, East Sussex, BN3 2FA

http://www.psypress.co.uk
http://www.a-levelpsychology.co.uk

Simultaneously published in the USA and Canada
by Taylor & Francis Inc
29 West 35th Street, New York, NY 10001

Psychology Press is part of the Taylor & Francis Group

British Library Cataloguing in Publication Data
A catalogue record for this book is available from the British Library

Library of Congress Cataloging-in-Publication Data

ISBN 1-84169-325-1

Cartoons drawn by Sean Longcroft, Beehive, Brighton, East Sussex
Cover design by Hurlock Design, Lewes, East Sussex
Cover illustration: Copyright © Science Photo Library
Typeset in the UK by Facing Pages, Southwick, West Sussex
Printed and bound in Italy by Legoprint

Roz Brody

*For my dad for always giving me the courage
to be myself, John for his wit and wisdom,
Tommy for his unconditional love,
and of course my mother for making me
the person I am.*

Diana Dwyer

*This book is dedicated to Alan Woodcock
(and his wine cellar) with great love, Di.*

Contents

Preparing for the Exam

Okay, so you have the date of the exam and you are sitting or lying down thinking about revising. This is the hardest part—starting revision.

It's no good putting it off any longer. The exam date is looming and you want to feel confident that you will perform well. This revision guide will help you to do so, without overwhelming you with unnecessary information. Although this guide has been written for use alongside Michael Eysenck and Cara Flanagan's *Psychology for AS Level*, if you have been using another AS psychology textbook in class, then this book should still help you to revise effectively.

Time is of the essence, and you need to focus your energy so that you gain the most amount of knowledge in the least amount of time.

No more excuses, and no more delays—now you HAVE to start revising!

REVISION TECHNIQUES

Remember that you need time to revise thoroughly. Even if you don't feel in the mood to revise, you know you need to, so just begin. Stick with it for 30 minutes. Go somewhere that you can't be distracted and do these two things:

**First, think about how you learn information.
Use the diagram below to work out the strategies that will suit you:**

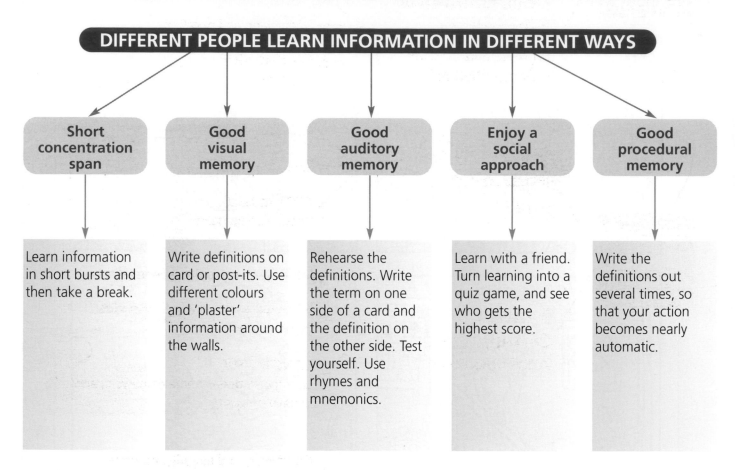

DIFFERENT PEOPLE LEARN INFORMATION IN DIFFERENT WAYS

Short concentration span	Good visual memory	Good auditory memory	Enjoy a social approach	Good procedural memory
Learn information in short bursts and then take a break.	Write definitions on card or post-its. Use different colours and 'plaster' information around the walls.	Rehearse the definitions. Write the term on one side of a card and the definition on the other side. Test yourself. Use rhymes and mnemonics.	Learn with a friend. Turn learning into a quiz game, and see who gets the highest score.	Write the definitions out several times, so that your action becomes nearly automatic.

Second, list what you need to know for the exam:

The AS psychology exam is divided into three units:

UNIT 1   Cognitive Psychology and Developmental Psychology

UNIT 2   Physiological Psychology and Individual Differences

UNIT 3   Social Psychology and Research Methods

Each topic in each unit is broken down into three subsections. So check the following unit map and make sure that you are clear about which topics are covered in each unit.

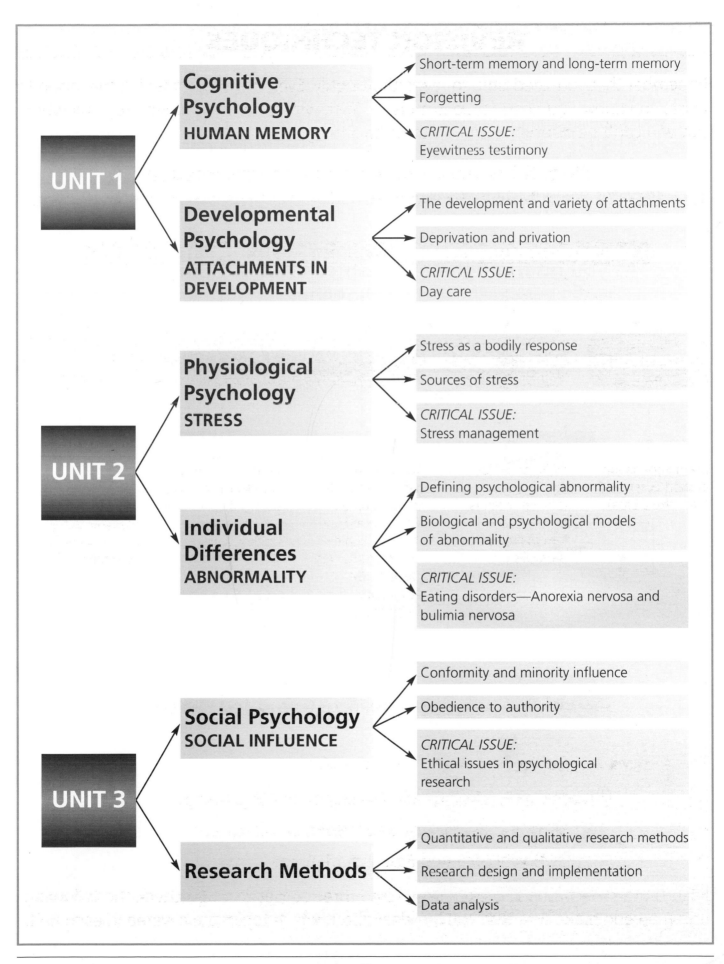

UNIT 1

Cognitive Psychology
HUMAN MEMORY

- Short-term memory and long-term memory
- Forgetting
- *CRITICAL ISSUE:*
  Eyewitness testimony

Developmental Psychology
ATTACHMENTS IN DEVELOPMENT

- The development and variety of attachments
- Deprivation and privation
- *CRITICAL ISSUE:*
  Day care

UNIT 2

Physiological Psychology
STRESS

- Stress as a bodily response
- Sources of stress
- *CRITICAL ISSUE:*
  Stress management

Individual Differences
ABNORMALITY

- Defining psychological abnormality
- Biological and psychological models of abnormality
- *CRITICAL ISSUE:*
  Eating disorders—Anorexia nervosa and bulimia nervosa

UNIT 3

Social Psychology
SOCIAL INFLUENCE

- Conformity and minority influence
- Obedience to authority
- *CRITICAL ISSUE:*
  Ethical issues in psychological research

Research Methods

- Quantitative and qualitative research methods
- Research design and implementation
- Data analysis

It might look like a lot to learn, but remember that there are only six topics, and you will get a choice of questions. Each of the topics is covered in this book, and each chapter gives you guidelines on the *key studies* you will need to know for the exam (see Appendix), along with the *key terms and concepts* that you will need to define or explain (see Glossary). The chapters also give you an overview of each of the subsections (in the main textbook they are called sections) together with positive and negative evaluations of both theories and research, so DON'T PANIC.

As you go through each chapter make sure that you do the following:

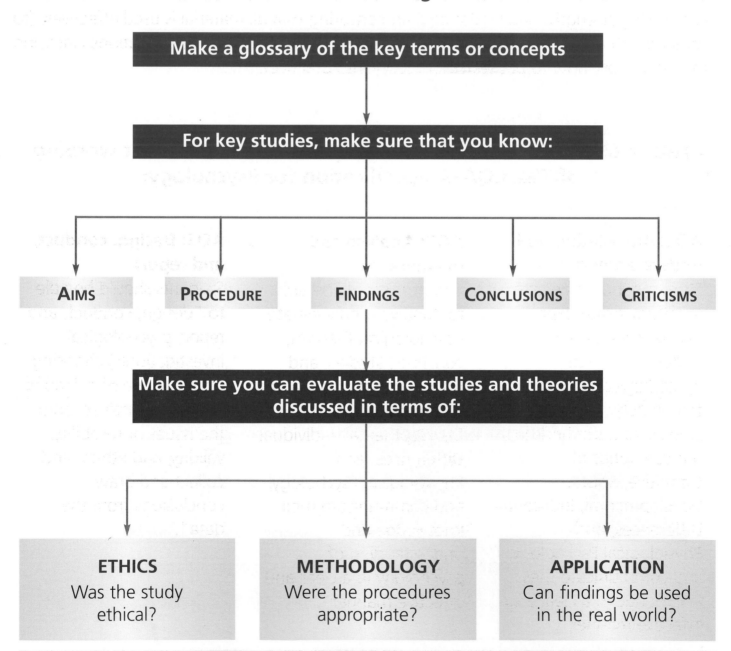

Make a glossary of the key terms or concepts

For key studies, make sure that you know:

| AIMS | PROCEDURE | FINDINGS | CONCLUSIONS | CRITICISMS |

Make sure you can evaluate the studies and theories discussed in terms of:

ETHICS
Was the study ethical?

METHODOLOGY
Were the procedures appropriate?

APPLICATION
Can findings be used in the real world?

HOW YOU WILL BE ASSESSED

In the AS exam there are three main skills that are examined: **AO1**, **AO2**, and **AO3**.

AO1 is concerned with *knowledge* and *understanding*.

AO2 is concerned with *analysing* and *evaluating*.

AO3 is concerned with *designing*, *conducting*, and *reporting* psychological investigations [this is only assessed in the Research Methods question].

In a nutshell, AO1 requires you to provide facts—information that is indisputable; AO2 involves analysing (breaking the question down into component parts), evaluation (identifying strengths and limitations) and ensuring that all material is used effectively (to construct an argument); and AO3 is concerned with conducting investigations (showing that you know how to put research theory into practice).

Let's look at these in more detail by looking at the exact wording of The AQA–A Specification for Psychology:

AO1: Knowledge and understanding
Students should be able to demonstrate their "knowledge and understanding of psychological theories, terminology, concepts, studies, and methods in the core areas of Cognitive, Social, Developmental, Individual Differences, and Physiological Psychology, and communicate their knowledge in a clear and effective manner".

AO2: Analyse and evaluate
Students should be able to "analyse and evaluate psychological theories, concepts, studies, and methods in the core areas of Cognitive, Social, Developmental, Individual Differences, and Physiological Psychology, and communicate their knowledge and understanding of psychology in a clear and effective manner".

AO3: Design, conduct, and report
Students should be able to "design, conduct, and report psychological investigation(s) choosing from a range of methods, and taking into account the issues of reliability, validity, and ethics, and collect and draw conclusions from the data".

WHAT EXACTLY ARE THESE AO THINGS?

AO means assessment objective. This means that when a question is asked, the examiner requires you to show the skills involved in AO1, AO2, or AO3 and your marks (assessment) depend on how well you demonstrate these skills. Each question (except those on Research Methods) consists of three parts:

Part (a) is out of 6 marks and examines **AO1**.

Part (b) is out of 6 marks and examines **AO1**.

Part (c) is out of 18 marks; 6 marks for **AO1** and 12 marks for **AO2**.

Here are some examples of **AO1** questions:

Outline **two** assumptions of the biological (medical) model of abnormality.	(3 marks + 3 marks)
Explain **one** psychological approach to stress management.	(6 marks)
Describe the procedures and findings of **one** study on attachments in development	(6 marks)
Give **two** criticisms of this study.	(3 marks + 3 marks)
Outline **two** explanations of forgetting in short-term memory.	(3 marks + 3 marks)
Outline **two** ways that personality may modify the effects of stressors.	(3 marks + 3 marks)
Outline the conclusions of research on obedience to authority.	(6 marks)
Describe **two** explanations of why people yield to majority influence.	(3 marks + 3 marks)
Describe findings of **one** study of minority influence and give **one** criticism of this study.	(3 marks + 3 marks)
Outline Bowlby's maternal deprivation hypothesis.	(6 marks)
Outline **three** clinical characteristics of bulimia nervosa.	(2 marks + 2 marks + 2 marks)

So, for each of these questions, all you need to do is *provide information*. You do not need to evaluate or assess their worth. Just to emphasise the point, for 'Describe **one** explanation of forgetting in short-term memory', you simply need to describe the theory without giving any good or bad points. You therefore need to be able to describe the theory in sufficient detail to get all the marks for the question in that one description.

AO2 questions require you to evaluate, assess, consider, and so on. **AO2** can include several aspects, and it's worth being familiar with these so you can think about them as you revise.

- **Applications**. Can the research or theory be applied to real life? Obvious examples are theories of memory (or forgetting) being applied to eyewitness testimony, or theories of attachment being applied to day care practices.
- **Empirical evidence**. Is the theory supported by research? If so, briefly use it to establish the value of your explanation.
- **Commentary**. Can you comment on the meaning of a particular theory or research? For example, you could say "this theory implies that a person's attitude, as well as biological factors, can strongly influence the effect stressful situations have on him or her".
- **Analysis**. Can you outline clearly the separate strands of an argument so as to point out the value of a theory? Analysis refers to breaking things down into constituent parts and can be demonstrated by working out several arguments to answer the question.

INTRODUCING AN **AO2** POINT IN AN ANSWER

Don't risk leaving it to the imagination of the examiners to spot that you are making an evaluative point. Examiners aren't allowed to use their imagination (much as they'd love to). SPELL IT OUT. Use expressions such as:

"Although these studies support the theory, others contradict it. For example..."

"There are, however, serious limitations to this approach. For example..."

"Although this implies that children are better off if they stay with their mothers full-time, other studies would lead to quite different conclusions..."

"However..."

"This strongly implies that..."

"This research has important implications in the real world..."

"This suggests that..."

"On the other hand..."

"Later research confirmed these findings. For example, ..."

"Such research has important applications..."

EVALUATING PSYCHOLOGICAL STUDIES

It is not unusual for exam questions to ask you to evaluate or criticise a key study. You may be surprised to learn that, with a bit of thought, you can do this for yourself. Honestly, you do not need to learn an evaluation of every study from a textbook, but you can learn to write your own evaluations. Just follow these guidelines:

1. What method was used? Whatever the method, there will be at least one (usually two) positive points about it, and at least one (usually two) limitations. What is more, the advantages of one method tend to be the disadvantages or limitations of another method. Chapter 7 (Research Methods) covers the advantages and disadvantages of each method. Let's take an example and see how it works. If the study was an experiment, it will have the advantage of the careful control of all the variables, enabling conclusions about cause and effect to be made. The study will be replicable (able to be repeated in exactly the same way), so its reliability (the consistency of the results) can be tested. However, as experiments are usually conducted in very controlled and artificial conditions (not corresponding to real life), the study in question is likely to lack ecological validity, and therefore the findings do not necessarily tell us much about everyday behaviour.

2. What about the number and type of participants? You can usually make at least one evaluative point—either positive or negative—concerning the participants. For example, if a large number of participants was used, and as long as the sample was not too biased (so participants did not all come from one particular group), then the results can be broadly generalised. However, the sample of the participants is often biased. In many studies, only students were used. Although there's nothing wrong with students—they are a wonderful bunch of people—they are not *representative* of the general population. They tend to be young, middle-class, and well educated. Think about other possible biases, such as whether the participants were all male. This was the case in Friedman and Rosenman's study of heart disease (see E&F p.141), where using only males enabled them to gain a valuable insight into the relationship between personality type and coronary heart disease. Nevertheless, their findings do not tell us much about heart disease amongst women. Another bias can be race, so consider whether the participants were all from one ethnic group. If a study used animals (such as Brady's 'executive monkey' study, see E&F p.124), then we must be cautious about using the findings to formulate theories that apply to humans. That is not to say that the findings are not useful as they provide information that can provide the basis for further research, but we need to be cautious in their application.

3. How important are the findings in terms of their application? Some studies only really provide fairly trivial and/or obvious information, whereas others involve important findings that can be of considerable use. If we return to Friedman and Rosenman's research study, this has provided important testable hypotheses about the causes and prevention of coronary heart disease. Likewise, Loftus and Palmer's research on leading questions (see E&F p.65) has provided essential information about interviewing eyewitnesses of crime, and Czeisler et al.'s study of shift work (see E&F p.138) has given employers guidelines for the best shift patterns for their workers.

4. Was the study ethical? There are some studies in which there is unacceptable cruelty, especially to animals, but try to give a balanced view when writing about such research. In fact, always introduce an ethical point by saying that all research is a balance between costs (such as embarrassment, deception, distress in humans, pain and suffering in animals) and the benefits gained. Then go on to outline these costs and benefits in a reasoned way. Remember that the specification asks that you "communicate your knowledge in a *clear and effective* manner".

Experimental research can be both pointless and unethical.

WHAT NOT TO SAY IN EXAMS

There are certain inappropriate comments that any experienced teacher comes across time and again. They are inappropriate because they are either inaccurate, ill-informed, sweeping, or judgemental in an uninformed way. Let's consider a few of these.

Don't say this!	Why not?
"I don't think this was a very good study because..."	Don't express personal opinions. If the study wasn't a good one, give a clear explanation as to why not. It would be better to say "This study can be criticised on the grounds that..."
"This proves that..."	Psychology is not an exact science in which theories can be proved, as they can in physics or maths. Be cautious and say things like "This indicates that..."
"This explanation is a load of rubbish..."	Does this one need to be spelt out? Every point should be well argued.
"This research was dead unethical. They shouldn't have done it."	Well, maybe 'they' shouldn't have, but the language is colloquial, there's no balance, and there's no explanation.
"Freud was wrong because he was obsessed with sex."	Well, maybe he was, but this is not a balanced or reasonable comment. You should be discussing Freud's theory, not him. By all means mention the considerable emphasis on sex in his theory, but give an informed commentary with appropriate support.
"This study was definitely unethical."	Okay, there are a few studies that could reasonably be said to be unethical, but for the vast majority it is better to say that they were 'ethically dubious', thus implying that there are ethical problems with them, but then go on to consider their worth. Maybe you will feel strongly that the study should not have been conducted on ethical grounds, but you should always give clear reasons, rather than starting (and possibly ending) with a black-and-white judgement.
"This study was immoral because it upset the children."	The term 'immoral' is not the same as unethical, so be careful with your use of language.

THE EXAM FORMAT

In each of the core areas of the AQA–A AS level psychology specification (Cognitive Psychology, Developmental Psychology, Physiological Psychology, Individual Differences, Social Psychology, Research Methods), *two* questions will be set and you have to answer *one* of these. Each question is in several parts, so it is essential that you read through *all* parts of *each* question before deciding which one to attempt.

THE FORMAT OF THE QUESTIONS

Each question is in several parts, labelled (a), (b), and (c):

Part (a) is out of 6 marks and examines **AO1**.

Part (b) is out of 6 marks and examines **AO1**.

Part (c) is out of 18 marks; 6 marks for **AO1** and 12 marks for **AO2**.

In Chapters 2–7 inclusive, we have provided examples of part (a) and part (b) questions with some of them answered in a way that would gain the full 6 marks. In Chapter 8, we have included complete questions—parts (a), (b), and (c)—and provided guidance on how they could be answered, along with sample answers, and examiner's comments.

Typical complete questions may be as follows:

(a) Explain the terms 'memory' and 'forgetting'   (3 marks + 3 marks)

(b) Outline findings from Loftus' research on eyewitness testimony   (6 marks)

(c) "The duration of long-term memory is unmeasurable."
Outline explanations of forgetting in long-term memory and consider
what such explanations tell us about memory.   (18 marks)

(a) Describe **two** sources of stress in the workplace.   (3 marks + 3 marks)

(b) Describe the aims and findings of **one** study into the
relationship between stress and cardiovascular disorders.   (6 marks)

(c) To what extent can stress be explained in terms of
physiological responses?   (18 marks)

We have used the last question on the previous page to illustrate some important points.

Part (a) is marked as 3 marks + 3 marks. You will therefore get a maximum of 3 marks for describing each source of stress in the workplace, and no more. It is therefore pointless to write lots on one work stressor and very little on another. Treat it as if it were 2 separate questions, each worth 3 marks. There is also the possibility that a question will be 2 marks + 2 marks + 2 marks (usually requiring 3 short definitions). Treat this in the same way.

Part (b), however, is different in that there is a total of 6 marks. In this case you need to describe both the aims and findings, but there is less need for balance. You can write more on one than the other and still gain the full 6 marks. Obviously, your answer should not be too unbalanced, e.g. if you write *only* about aims or *only* about findings, you will get a maximum of 4 marks. In essence, be reasonably balanced, but do not worry about giving 2 perfectly equal parts to the answer.

Part (c) is a combination of AO1 and AO2, so ensure that you think in these terms when answering the question. The danger is to launch into a lot of AO1 material and lose track of the AO2 part, so you happily write the required amount, but it does not address the issues and you barely get more than 6 marks out of the potential 18 marks. In the case above, for the AO2 part, you need to carefully consider the advantages and limitations of considering stress only in terms of physiology.

When answering questions, stick to the idea of A MARK A MINUTE. This provides a very convenient way of splitting up your time. Obviously if a question is worth 6 marks, you should not spend more than 6 minutes answering it, but don't forget about thinking time. In total, any one question should take half an hour, and no longer.

Passing the exam is less about intelligence and memory and more about exam strategies.

EXAM TECHNIQUE

So you know what each unit is about and how you will be assessed, you now need to think about exam technique.

Passing the exam is less about intelligence and memory, and more about applying exam strategies.

Before you even start writing in the exam you need to THINK and ASK YOURSELF some questions that might help to guide you.

Have I chosen the right question?

Sometimes in the first moments of sitting in the exam room, you are so pleased that you can answer part (a) that you fail to read on and then realise that you will find it difficult to answer parts (b) and (c). Therefore READ ALL THE QUESTIONS CAREFULLY before you put pen to paper.

Which question can I get the most marks for?

Always remember that part (c) on each unit—apart from Research Methods—is worth 18 marks so it is more sensible to choose the question with a part (c) that you can answer well.

What is the question asking me to do?

Underline the KEY WORDS in the question so that if you are asked to describe the *aims* and *findings* of a research study, you don't waste time by describing the *procedures* and *conclusions*.

Am I answering the question set?

There is a great temptation in exams to write down everything you know about a topic in the hope that the examiner will select the most relevant parts of your answer. This is referred to as the 'vomit on the page' approach and will get you very few marks, so don't do it.

What about timing?

Once you have chosen the question you want to answer, you then need to consider the issue of timing. You have 30 minutes to answer each question. Make sure that the time you spend on each question is proportional to the number of marks you can get. To spend 15 minutes answering a question that will only give you 3 marks is a waste of time, so be aware of this.

Also, PLAN YOUR ANSWER carefully. Just take a few moments before you start writing to think through the key points you want to make. This will help you to be succinct and prevent you from falling into the trap of repeating the same point. 'Analysis' is an AO2 criteria.

Perhaps one of the best ways to think about exam technique is to analyse how people fail and become determined not to fall into making the same mistakes. The following list contains most of the strategies that you can use if you definitely want to fail an exam.

Take note and don't do any of these things in the exam.

TEN WAYS TO FAIL EXAMS

1. Don't answer the question that has been set, but the one you wanted to come up.

2. Write down everything you know about the topic, preferably using your own personal experiences.

3. Repeat the same point and same study over and over again, so that the examiner thinks you only know one study from the whole of the course.

4. Don't plan your answer at the outset, but just let it meander and develop in its own time.

5. Miss out a question, or decide to answer all the questions on the paper.

6. Fall asleep in the exam due to having stayed up all night trying to revise.

7. Tell the examiner that you haven't revised the topic and you were taught very badly.

8. Spend 20 minutes answering a question that will only give you 3 marks.

9. Launch in and start writing as soon as you sit down, so that you only realise that you can't answer the rest of the question when you have finished part (a).

10. Forget to turn over the page, thereby finishing half an hour early, or losing out on the choice of questions.

Finally, you need to get yourself in the right frame of mind when taking exams.

BEFORE THE EXAM

Ban all negative thinking, such as:

Replace these thoughts with the following:

IN THE EXAM

The most important thing that you can do when you turn over the exam paper is to AVOID PANIC, so ban phrases like:

Instead, use your knowledge of psychology to help you in your time of need...think of the concept of context dependent memory and imagine yourself back in the classroom or reading your textbook or revision guide. Something *will* come back to you.

Remember that it's not what you know, but how you use the knowledge, that counts. Can you use the information you have to support a viewpoint or argue against it?

It is very important that you remember how to evaluate and criticise, and do this wherever you are asked to.

AFTER THE EXAM

Different people handle the after-exam experience differently.

Some people like checking everything they think they've written, but don't forget the findings of Bartlett's work on reconstructive memory that suggests that our memories aren't always 100% accurate.

Others prefer to discuss their answers with their friends, teachers, and anyone who is willing to listen. If this is your preferred course of action and it makes you feel better, fine—you've earned it!

But for many people it's great to think it's all over and there's nothing that you need to do until the results come out.

Good luck!!!

Cognitive Psychology

HUMAN MEMORY

What's it about?

Cognitive psychology focuses on how we interpret the world around us. It includes exploring perception, thinking, language, attention, and memory.

Cognitive psychologists try to help us understand why we remember some things and not others, why our perception of the world is not always accurate and why we think about the world in the way we do.

Cognitive psychologists were strongly influenced by the computer revolution and often use models to help aid our understanding of how we acquire, store, and retrieve information.

What's in this unit?

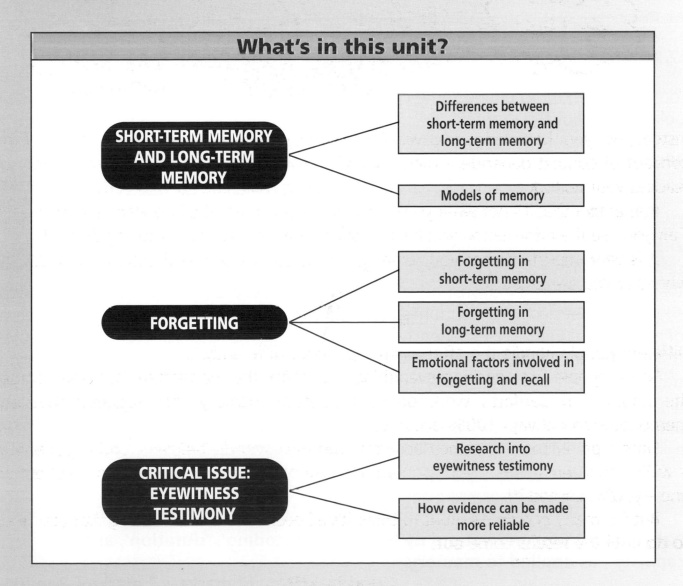

SHORT-TERM MEMORY AND LONG-TERM MEMORY

- Differences between short-term memory and long-term memory
- Models of memory

FORGETTING

- Forgetting in short-term memory
- Forgetting in long-term memory
- Emotional factors involved in forgetting and recall

CRITICAL ISSUE: EYEWITNESS TESTIMONY

- Research into eyewitness testimony
- How evidence can be made more reliable

DEFINING KEY TERMS AND CONCEPTS

You will need to be able to define and explain the key terms listed in blue below. The other concepts listed in black will aid your understanding of human memory. Make a list of definitions of the following key terms and if you get stuck, go to the glossary at the end of the book.

Capacity	Short-term memory	Proactive interference
Duration	Reconstructive memory	Rehearsal
Encoding	Repression	Retrieval
Eyewitness testimony	Working memory model	Retroactive interference
Flashbulb memory	Acoustic coding	Schema
Forgetting	Articulatory-phonological	Semantic coding
Levels of processing	loop	Serial reproduction
Long-term memory	Chunking	State dependency
Memory	Context dependency	Trace decay
Memory for faces	Cue-dependent forgetting	Visual spatial coding
Multi-store model	Displacement	Visuo-spatial sketch pad

You may be asked to define some of these key terms in the exam. To give you an idea, look at the following example.

What do you understand by the terms 'flashbulb memory' and 'repression'?
(3 marks + 3 marks)

Flashbulb memories describe long-lasting vivid memories formed at a time of intense emotion. These memories may be of a significant public or personal event. For example, people often have a vivid memory of what they were doing and where they were when they heard about the terrorist attack on the World Trade Center. Cahill and McGaugh suggested that flashbulb memories might serve a useful biological function as release of hormones during such experiences may aid our response to similar events in the future.

Repression is a term used by Freud to explain why people have difficulties in recalling traumatic experiences. For Freud, repression was a defence mechanism, which prevented any information that disturbed the good image people want to have of themselves from emerging into their consciousness. Thus, any information that causes us fear or distress is likely to be hidden from our conscious awareness.

OVER TO YOU

Explain what you understand by the terms 'encoding', 'duration', and 'capacity', as applied to memory.

(2 marks + 2 marks + 2 marks)

DESCRIBING AND EVALUATING KEY STUDIES

One kind of AO1 examination question is described as the 'APFCC' question. In this question you are asked to describe the aims, procedures, findings, conclusions, and give criticisms (APFCC) of a study into a named topic. In any question you will be asked for one or two of these, for example, 'aims and conclusions' or 'findings and conclusions'. There is not a requirement that these are given in balance as the question is marked out of 6 marks (for example, if you provide findings only then you may receive a maximum of 4 marks). You may be asked for the 'findings plus one criticism', in which case the question is marked as '3 marks + 3 marks'.

You may also be asked questions about research more generally, rather than about a specific study. In this case the question will say 'Describe the findings of research into…' (6 marks). You may also be asked about 'conclusions'. In such questions you may describe the findings/conclusions from one study, or from several studies, or even from a theory (which is a form of research).

If the question asks for 'procedures and findings', any other material will not receive credit, such as information relating to aims or conclusions. Make sure you understand the difference, for example, between a finding (the facts) and a conclusion (what the findings show us).

For the module on Cognitive Psychology you need to know the following APFCC studies:

KEY STUDY TOPICS	EXAMPLE	WHERE TO FIND IT	OTHER RELATED RESEARCH
Encoding in STM	Baddeley (1966)	Appendix	Conrad (1964, see E&F p.36) Posner (1969, see E&F p.36)
Capacity in STM	Jacobs (1887)	Appendix	Miller (1956, see E&F p.34) Simon (1974, see E&F p.34)
Duration in STM	Peterson and Peterson (1959)	Appendix	Glanzer and Cunitz (1966, see E&F pp.33–34)
If asked to give information on a study of short-term memory, you can use either the encoding in STM, capacity in STM, or duration in STM studies listed above.			
Encoding in LTM	Baddeley (1966)	Appendix	
Duration in LTM	Bahrick et al. (1975)	Appendix	Shepard (1967, see E&F pp.38–39)
If asked to give information on a study of long-term memory, you can use either the encoding in LTM or duration in LTM studies listed above.			
Flashbulb memory	Conway et al. (1994)	Page 30 and Appendix	McCloskey et al. (1988, see E&F pp.58–59) Johnson and Scott (1978, see E&F p.63)
Repression	Levinger and Clark (1961)	Page 29 and Appendix	Myers and Brewin (1994, see E&F p.57)
If asked to give information on a study of emotional factors in forgetting, you can use either the flashbulb memory or repression studies listed above.			
Reconstructive memory	Bartlett (1932)	Appendix	Sulin and Dooling (1974, see E&F p.61) Cohen (1981, see E&F p.62) Bransford and Johnson (1972, see E&F p.62)
Eyewitness testimony	Loftus and Palmer (1974)	Appendix	Follow-up research by Loftus and Palmer (1974, see E&F p.65) Loftus and Zanni (1975, see E&F p.65)
Memory for faces	Young et al. (1987)	Appendix	Bruce and Young (1986, see E&F p.67) Bruce and Valentine (1988, see E&F p.67)

OVER TO YOU

You need to be able to write for three minutes on aims, procedures, findings, conclusions, and criticisms. In order to do this well in the examination it might help to identify key words and concepts to recall. You only need a few for each of the APFCCs (in other words a few key concepts for the aims and a few for the procedures—a maximum of five). Do this for each study listed above.

SHORT-TERM MEMORY AND LONG-TERM MEMORY

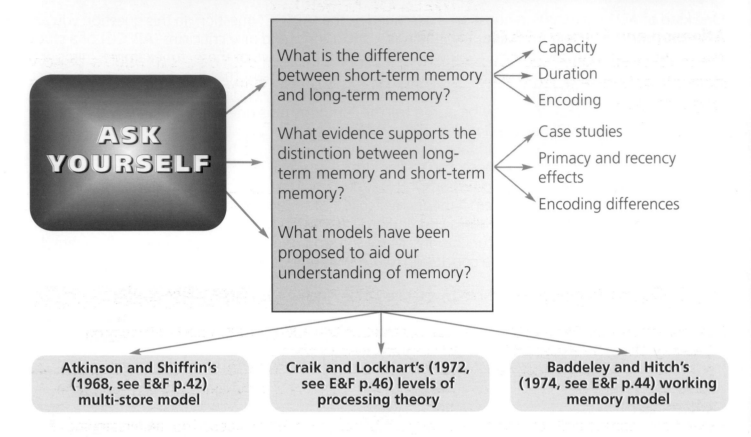

ASK YOURSELF

What is the difference between short-term memory and long-term memory?

→ Capacity
→ Duration
→ Encoding

What evidence supports the distinction between long-term memory and short-term memory?

→ Case studies
→ Primacy and recency effects
→ Encoding differences

What models have been proposed to aid our understanding of memory?

| Atkinson and Shiffrin's (1968, see E&F p.42) multi-store model | Craik and Lockhart's (1972, see E&F p.46) levels of processing theory | Baddeley and Hitch's (1974, see E&F p.44) working memory model |

Some of the alleged differences between short-term memory and long-term memory are shown below.

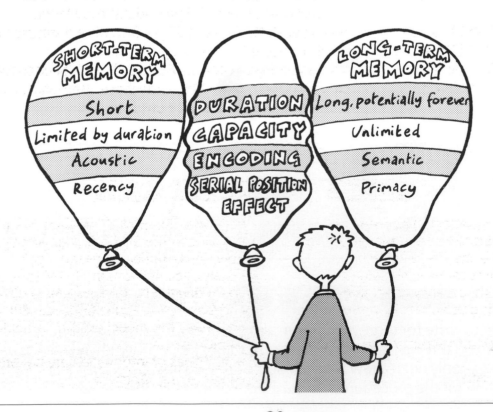

MODELS OF MEMORY

Atkinson and Shiffrin's Multi-store Model

The multi-store model (see E&F p.42) suggests that incoming data passes through a sensory store into a short-term store. If rehearsal takes place, the information is then transferred to the long-term store.

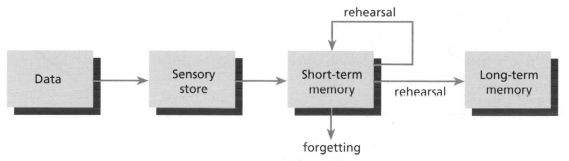

SUPPORTING STUDIES

Differences between STM and LTM:
- Capacity: Miller (1956, see E&F p.34) determined that people can remember 7 +/− 2 chunks of information.
- Duration: Peterson and Peterson's (1959, see E&F p.35) study revealed that a memory has approximately an 18-second duration in STM.
- Encoding: Baddeley (1966, see E&F p.36) found that STM relies mainly on acoustic coding, whereas LTM relies mainly on semantic coding.

OTHER SUPPORTING RESEARCH

- Glanzer and Cunitz's (1966, see F&F pp.33–34) study on primacy and recency effects.
- Bahrick et al.'s (1975, see E&F p.38) research into recognition of classmates after 35 years, and the concept of very-long-term memory (VLTM).
- Tulving (1972, see E&F p.39) broadened our understanding of the LTM store, by dividing it into semantic memory and episodic memory.
- Cohen and Squire (1980, see E&F p.41) made a distinction between declarative and procedural knowledge.
- Tulving et al. (1982, see E&F p.40) made a distinction between implicit and explicit memory.
- The case study of HM (see E&F p.37), who failed to form any new long-term memories, and whose attempts at trying to reconstruct memories were unsuccessful.

EVALUATION

In support

- Primacy and recency effects. First items are recalled from LTM, having been rehearsed, and last items are still being held in STM.
- Glanzer and Cunitz's research showing the disappearance of the recency effect if an interference task is given after the presentation of the list.
- Baddeley's research into acoustic and semantic coding.
- Case studies, e.g. HM.

Problems and limitations

- Rehearsal does not always lead to storage.
- If coding in the STM is predominantly acoustic, how do we understand language?
- Initial oversimplification of LTM store, but this was redressed by Tulving (semantic/episodic), and Cohen and Squire (procedural/declarative).
- How does this model explain flashbulb memories?
- Some types of information are not amenable to rehearsal, e.g. smells.

Baddeley and Hitch's Working Memory Model

This model (see E&F p.44) suggests that our memory consists of a central executive, which is a limited capacity, modality-free attentional system that has overall control, along with two slave systems. The central executive allocates attention and directs the operation of the slave systems. One slave system—the phonological loop—is an articulatory control system that is responsible for acoustic coding. It acts like an inner voice and an inner ear, and is primarily concerned with our perception and production of speech. The other slave system—the visuo-spatial sketch pad—is an inner eye, and is responsible for visual spatial coding. It is a bit like a writing pad for remembering visual data, such as how to get back to where the car is parked.

Articulatory-phonological loop that holds information in a speech-based form

CENTRAL EXECUTIVE

Visuo-spatial sketch pad (inner eye) that is specialised for spatial and/or visual coding

rehearsal   rehearsal

SUPPORTING STUDIES

These often involve using the dual-task technique: This technique assumes that the slave systems have a limited capacity and therefore if people are asked to perform two tasks that use the same slave system, their performance on one or both will be affected. One of the most common techniques used to test this hypothesis is getting the participants to repeat meaningless words like 'the' or recite a list of digits, whilst trying to read information or do a verbal reasoning task.

- Baddeley and Lewis (1981, see E&F p.44) found that articulatory suppression led to difficulties in reading and understanding texts.
- Hitch and Baddeley (1976, see E&F p.45) found that participants' performance on a verbal reasoning task was slowed down when they were required to repeat a random string of digits at the same time as doing the verbal reasoning task.
- Gathercole and Baddeley (1990) found that children with reading problems had an impaired memory span and had difficulties saying whether words rhymed, perhaps suggesting that there is a phonological loop deficit.

EVALUATION

In support

- Broadens the role of the STM store, by emphasising its importance in active processing as well as storage.
- The central executive links memory with attention.
- The notion of slave systems is an insight. The phonological loop is implicated in a range of activities such as verbal reasoning, mental arithmetic, reading, and planning.
- The model has practical applications in helping children to read by suggesting that the difficulties may reside in deficits with the phonological loop.

Problems and limitations

- Not a great deal is known about the central executive.
- Perhaps it is oversimplistic to have a single central executive.
- The visuo-spatial store has not been explored in as much depth as other slave systems.

Craik and Lockhart's Levels of Processing Theory

This model (see E&F p.46) focuses on how incoming information is processed, rather than exploring memory stores. Three main levels of processing are discussed:

- **Physical processing**. Shallow processing that analyses information in terms of its physical qualities. For example, CAT—is the word written in capitals?
- **Phonemic processing**. This processing attends to the sound of the information. For example, CAT—does the word rhyme with bat?
- **Semantic processing**. Semantic processing, sometimes known as deep processing, analyses the information in terms of its meaning. For example, CAT—does the word describe an animal?

Craik and Lockhart's theory suggests that information that is processed at a deep level is more likely to be recalled than information that has been processed at a shallow level. However, the term 'deep processing' was thought to be simplistic and so other forms of processing have been included:

- **Elaboration**. Elaboration of processing can lead to greater recall, and it benefits LTM. Recall can be twice as high for words accompanying complex sentences.

- **Organisation**. Organisation creates a lasting memory, yet no conscious processing needs to take place. It is a necessary condition for memory.

- **Distinctiveness**. Memory traces that are distinctive or unique in some way will be more memorable than those that resemble other traces. It depends in part on the context in which a stimulus is presented.

SUPPORTING STUDIES

- Hyde and Jenkins (1973, see E&F p.43) rated words for pleasantness, frequency of use in the English language, occurrence of certain letters, what part of speech the word was, and whether the word fitted the sentence. They found that deeper processing led to higher recall.
- Craik and Tulving (1975, see E&F p.47) gave participants shallow, phonemic, and semantic processing tasks and found that recognition was higher for semantic processing.
- Bransford (1979) demonstrated the effectiveness of distinctiveness by comparing participants' recall of the sentence 'A mosquito is like a racoon because they both have hands, legs, and jaws' (elaborative processing) with 'A mosquito is like a doctor because they both draw blood' (distinctive processing). Recall was higher for distinctive processing.

EVALUATION

In support

- Recognises encoding as active.
- Has practical applications.
- Links memory, attention, and perception.
- Emphasises that recall is influenced by how information is encoded.

Problems and limitations

- A vague and circular theory.
- Places too much emphasis on acquisition thereby ignoring other determinants of the LTM, such as retrieval cues.
- Doesn't really *explain* why semantic processing is better.
- Does processing only take place at the level prescribed? Participants may process the word PIG at a semantic level, even when asked about the physical characteristics of the word.
- Might be confusing effort with depth.

To give you an idea of the type of question you might be asked:

Describe three differences between the short-term memory and the long-term memory. **(2 marks + 2 marks + 2 marks)**

Differences between the long-term memory and short-term memory focus on duration, capacity, and encoding.

Whilst the duration of the short-term memory is thought to be seconds (18 seconds according to Peterson and Peterson's research), the duration of the long-term memory is forever.

The capacity of the short-term memory is limited to 7 +/– 2 chunks (Miller), whilst the capacity of the long-term memory is thought to be unlimited.

Finally, research by Baddeley has suggested that encoding in the short-term memory is predominantly acoustic, whilst encoding in the long-term memory focuses on meaning and is predominantly semantic.

Describe the working memory model. **(6 marks)**

Baddeley and Hitch's working memory model emphasises the active nature of memory; it is known as the 'working' memory model as it is the area of memory that is used while working on things. This model draws our attention to the central executive. The central executive is modality free and has overall control of how resources are allocated when we encode incoming information.

In addition to the central executive, Baddeley proposed there are two 'slave systems' that support the central executive. These are the articulatory-phonological loop, which is concerned with both our production and perception of speech and holds information in a speech-based form, and the visuo-spatial sketch pad, which processes data visually and is specialised for spatial and/or visual coding. The visuo-spatial sketch pad explains how we manage to remember information such as the layout of our bedroom or how the food is arranged in our kitchen cupboards.

OVER TO YOU

Describe Craik and Lockhart's levels of processing model of memory.

(6 marks)

FORGETTING

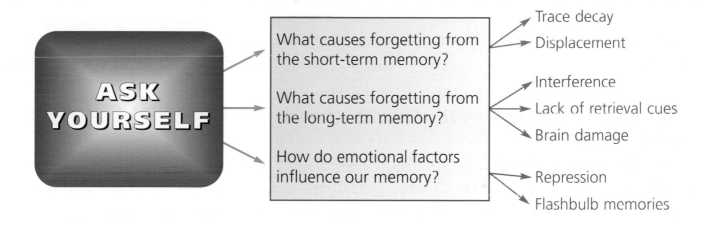

ASK YOURSELF

What causes forgetting from the short-term memory?
- Trace decay
- Displacement

What causes forgetting from the long-term memory?
- Interference
- Lack of retrieval cues
- Brain damage

How do emotional factors influence our memory?
- Repression
- Flashbulb memories

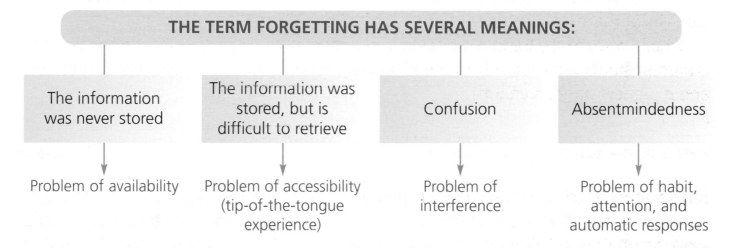

THE TERM FORGETTING HAS SEVERAL MEANINGS:

The information was never stored	The information was stored, but is difficult to retrieve	Confusion	Absentmindedness
Problem of availability	Problem of accessibility (tip-of-the-tongue experience)	Problem of interference	Problem of habit, attention, and automatic responses

Confusion can occur when new information interferes with the information we are trying to remember.

EXPLANATIONS OF FORGETTING

All memory experiments rely on retrieving information from memory and they assume that if it cannot be retrieved, then it must be forgotten. The concept of 'forgetting' suggests that something has disappeared from memory, so it is not available. Or it could be that the memory has been mislaid in some way, and therefore is not accessible.

Research has tried to establish whether forgetting from STM and LTM is due to lack of accessibility or lack of availability. The following diagram deals with some of the theories and supporting research.

FORGETTING FROM:

Short-term memory

Trace decay. Spontaneous disappearance of the memory trace. Peterson and Peterson (1959, see E&F p.35) found that memories were held in STM for approximately 18 seconds, after which they disappeared via trace decay. This occurs when the memories are not rehearsed.

Retroactive interference. New information displaces or pushes out old information from the memory store. Reitman (1971, see E&F p.51) gave participants either a syllable detection task or a tone detection task during the retention interval and found that those in the syllable condition had much lower recall than those in the tone condition, because syllables interfered more than tones.

Lack of consolidation. An injury to the head prevents the memory trace being stored.

Insufficient level of processing. Processing information at a shallow level prevents it from being stored.

Brain damage. Damage to the brain causes a variety of effects on performance. Warrington and Shallice's (1972, see E&F p.37) study of KF found that his short-term forgetting of auditory letters and digits (things that were heard) was much greater than his forgetting of visual stimuli, suggesting that the STM is not just a single store, but consists of a number of different stores.

Long-term memory

Trace decay. If a person does nothing during the time of initial learning and the retention interval, and they forget the material, it is probable that the memory trace has disappeared.

Retroactive interference. New information interferes with the recall of previous information stored.

Proactive interference. Old information interferes with the recall of new information.

Lack of retrieval cues. Cue-dependent forgetting takes place due to lack of accessibility of the memory. The memory will pop up when an appropriate cue is given.

Context dependency. You may need to be in the same context as learning took place to be able to recall information.

State dependency. You may need to be in the same emotional or physical state as you were in when learning took place to recall the information.

Repression. A defence mechanism that prevents emotionally threatening memories from being accessible to consciousness.

Brain damage. Depending on the damage, there can be various impairments to LTM.

FORGETTING RESEARCH

In the nineteenth century Ebbinghaus (1885, see E&F p.50) conducted studies that proved that we definitely do forget, and that forgetting increases over time. In his studies, Ebbinghaus was both the experimenter and the only participant, so the results were destined to be invalid and unreliable from the start, but his simple method has since been adapted for many other studies of forgetting over time. He learned a list of *nonsense syllables* until he could recall all of them. If he tested himself after a short period of time, his recall was good, but recall decreased as the retention interval got longer. There was a large increase in forgetting over the first hour after learning, after which forgetting increased more slowly. When he attempted to re-learn forgotten lists he needed less practise, suggesting that each time you learn something, some kind of trace is left which is not enough for complete recall but will make subsequent learning quicker.

FORGETTING FROM SHORT-TERM MEMORY
Trace decay: Peterson and Peterson
(1959, see E&F p.35)
Interference: Reitman (1971, see E&F p.51)
Diversion of attention: Watkins et al.
(1973, see E&F p.51)

FORGETTING FROM LONG-TERM MEMORY
Interference versus retrieval cues:
Tulving and Psotka (1971, see E&F p.54)
Retrieval cues—context dependency: Abernethy
(1940, see E&F p.56)
Emotional factors in forgetting—repression:
Levinger and Clark (1961, see page 29)

OVER TO YOU

Use your textbook to write down and learn the findings, conclusions, and criticisms of the memory key studies listed above, i.e. Peterson and Peterson (1959) and Levinger and Clark (1961). You need to be able to provide a brief outline of the significant points.

EMOTIONAL FACTORS AND MEMORY

Repression

The concept of *repression*, an unconscious process in which certain memories are made inaccessible, can be used to explain forgetting. It occurs when emotionally threatening material is held back from conscious awareness, and Freud (1915, see E&F p.56) suggested that material that caused anxiety is dealt with in a number of ways that will reduce one's feelings of anxiety. Thus, according to Freud, repression is one of the methods of *ego defence*.

CASE STUDIES

Case studies provide examples. Freud tells the case of a man who kept forgetting the line "With a white sheet". Free association revealed that the term 'white sheet' was associated with the sheet placed over a corpse. The man's friend had recently died from a heart attack and the white sheet was associated with death; this made him fearful since he was overweight and his grandfather had died of a heart attack.

It is hard to test Freud's theory, but there have been attempts to demonstrate the phenomena of repression, so let us consider one of these now (see Levinger and Clark's study of repression as an emotional factor in forgetting on the next page).

REAL-LIFE RESEARCH

Real-life research has tried to shed some light on the concept of repression. Taylor and Kopelman (1984) found that 30–40% of convicted criminals, in particular those convicted of homicide, are unable to recall the crime, especially when the victim is a close relative or a lover killed in a crime of passion. However, children who saw their parent killed do not support the theory of repression, for they recalled the incident frequently, even if they have tried to forget it.

DOES REPRESSION EXPLAIN FORGETTING?

The jury is 'still out' on whether repression does explain forgetting. Herman and Schatzow (1987, see E&F p.57) found that 28% of a group of female incest victims reported severe memory deficits from childhood. One major problem is that it is difficult to verify whether the repressed memory, once surfaced, is actually accurate.

PROBLEMS WITH REPRESSED MEMORIES

As it is difficult to verify whether a repressed memory that has surfaced is accurate or not, it is a particular cause of concern when looking at recovered memories from victims of child abuse. In some cases parents or other relatives have been accused of child abuse many years later, causing distress to both the victim and family as the courts attempt to verify whether the accusations are founded in truth.

AIMS	PROCEDURE	FINDINGS	CONCLUSIONS	CRITICISMS

Study: **Levinger and Clark's (1961) study of repression as an emotional factor in forgetting**

Aims: To investigate the effects of emotionally-charged words on recall under controlled laboratory conditions. The experiment sought to compare participants' recall of neutral words with those that were negative and emotionally charged. If negative emotionally-charged words are less easy to recall this would demonstrate repression because such words are more 'threatening'.

Procedure: Participants were tested in a repeated measures design. They were asked to produce word associations for a list of 60 words. Some of the words had neutral meanings (e.g. 'tree' or 'cow'), and some of the words had high negative emotional content (e.g. 'war' and 'fear'). The time taken to produce an association was measured. In addition, the participants' galvanic skin response (GSR) to each association was recorded. The GSR is a measure of a person's emotional arousal based on their sweatiness, which indicates increased arousal of the autonomic nervous system. Immediately after the first task of producing associations participants were given the cue words again and asked to recall their associations.

Findings: Participants were slower at producing associations to the negative emotionally-charged words. These words also produced a higher GSR. When asked to recall their associations, participants had more difficulty recalling the negative emotionally-charged associations.

Conclusions: These findings support Freud's concept of repressed memories. It was concluded that the greater difficulty in the recall of negative emotionally-charged words compared to neutral words was explained by repression. This was supported by the GSR data, which showed that the words created more emotional arousal, which may have led them to being repressed into the unconscious to reduce the anxiety. Thus, speed of recall was slower because the negative emotionally-charged words were made inaccessible due to their emotional threat. Thus, repression as an explanation of forgetting was supported.

Criticisms: One major concern with this study is that the levels of arousal may be a confounding variable and that higher arousal may inhibit immediate recall. This idea has been supported by Parkin (1993) who found that if participants were asked to recall their associations a week later (delayed recall condition) participants' level of recall improved. A second criticism relates to using emotionally-charged words to assess repression. Participants' recall (or not) of such words may be a rather artificial test of memory and thus not represent memory (and forgetting) in the real world. As such we would say that the study lacked external validity.

FLASHBULB MEMORIES

The term *flashbulb memory* describes a long-lasting vivid memory formed at a time of intense emotion, such as significant public or personal events.

FOR EXAMPLE: What were you doing on September 11th 2001?

Flashbulb memories do not have to be negative memories or concern international events; they can be 'photographic' images of happy events, such as a moment at a wedding or party, or the birth of a child. Brown and Kulik (1977, see E&F pp.57–58) suggest that a special neural mechanism might be responsible for flashbulb memories. Cahill and McGaugh (1998, see E&F p.58) argue that flashbulb memories are a useful biological mechanism, which are *adaptive*, and at times of high emotional arousal hormones are produced. Their effects are as follows:

- **Short-term effect**. Creates a sense of arousal and aids the response to the event.
- **Long-term effect**. Influences memory in that future responses to the same kind of event will be remembered well.

AIMS	PROCEDURE	FINDINGS	CONCLUSIONS	CRITICISMS

Study:	**Conway et al.'s (1994, see E&F p.59) investigation into flashbulb memory of Mrs Thatcher's resignation**
Aims:	To show that if an event has a distinctive meaning for the participant, it will be more memorable.
Procedure:	Conway compared UK participants' memory of Margaret Thatcher's resignation with participants' recall of the event from other countries. Two thirds of the participants were UK nationals, whilst the remaining one third were drawn from other nationalities; mainly North Americans. All the participants (923 of them) were tested a fortnight after Margaret Thatcher's resignation, and a subset of 369 of the participants were tested 11 months later.
Findings:	Assessment at 11 months indicated that 86% of the UK participants still had a flashbulb memory of the event, compared to 29% of the participants from other countries. The UK participants' memories were very detailed and were consistent over time.
Conclusions:	Important public events, which have a particular cultural resonance for the individual, are more likely to be recalled by individuals for whom the event is important than by other groups.
Criticisms:	One of the major concerns about research into flashbulb memories is whether the memory is an accurate depiction of what has happened, since it is difficult to ascertain whether a person was where they said they were if they were tested, say, a fortnight after the event. In addition, given that certain events are discussed publicly (e.g. the death of Princess Diana), recall may be influenced by listening to others *retelling* their experience. This may affect a person's memory of the actual experience as they saw and felt it.

To give you an idea of the type of question you might be asked:

Explain what is meant by 'flashbulb memory', 'repression', and 'reconstructive memory'. **(2 marks + 2 marks + 2 marks)**

Flashbulb memory is believed to occur when we recall a particularly dramatic or unusual event. The memory of such an event is believed to be detailed, vivid, long lasting, and accurate, and includes the emotion felt at the time.

Repression involves the assignment of unpleasant memories to the unconscious mind, so that they are forgotten. This concept was suggested by Freud. He considered repression to be a defence mechanism that protects us from the anxiety caused by harmful and distressing experiences or thoughts.

Reconstructive memory involves the distortion of the original memory by the individual's previous knowledge or expectations. Memories are not accurate representations of experiences and events because we do not store memories passively; instead we store them in terms of our past experience or schemas.

Describe the procedures and findings of one study of forgetting in short-term memory. **(6 marks)**

Peterson and Peterson wanted to find out how long it took to forget information from the short-term memory. They used trigrams, which are meaningless sets of letters, to test memory. They are meaningless so that they are not especially memorable for some people.

Participants were presented with a trigram (e.g. BVM or TCR) and asked to recall it after various time intervals: 3, 6, 9, 12, 15, or 18 seconds. In addition, participants were given an interference task between the initial presentation of the trigram and recall. The task involved counting backwards in threes from a three-digit number. This was done to stop the participants from rehearsing the digits.

Peterson and Peterson found that after 3 seconds participants were able to recall the trigrams, but they recalled fewer after 6 seconds, and after 18 seconds their recall dropped to 10%. This is a steady decline.

OVER TO YOU

Outline findings of research into the role of emotional factors in memory.
(6 marks)

CRITICAL ISSUE: EYEWITNESS TESTIMONY

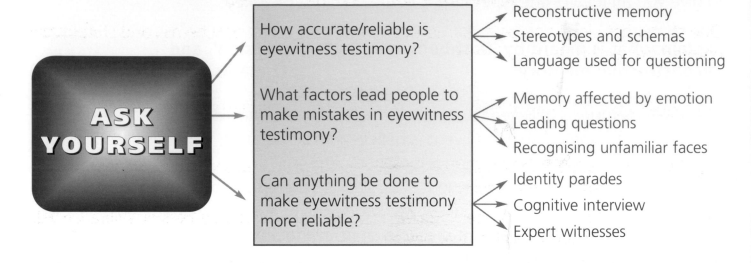

ASK YOURSELF

How accurate/reliable is eyewitness testimony?
- Reconstructive memory
- Stereotypes and schemas
- Language used for questioning

What factors lead people to make mistakes in eyewitness testimony?
- Memory affected by emotion
- Leading questions
- Recognising unfamiliar faces

Can anything be done to make eyewitness testimony more reliable?
- Identity parades
- Cognitive interview
- Expert witnesses

TOPICS TO AID YOUR REFLECTION:

Reconstructive memory
Bartlett (1932, see E&F p.61)

Research into leading questions
Loftus and Palmer (1974, see E&F p.65)

Research into memory for faces
Young et al. (1987, see E&F p.66)
Bruce and Young (1986, see E&F p.67)

Research into improving reliability
Cognitive interview techniques (Geiselman et al., 1985, see E&F p.68)
Photofits/Identikit pictures (Bruce & Valentine, 1988, see E&F p.67)

RECONSTRUCTIVE MEMORY

Using stories, Bartlett (1932, see E&F p.61) demonstrated that people's recall of information was influenced by schemas—frameworks for thinking about the world based on one's experience and culture. Bartlett's work demonstrated that participants' recall of information was not only influenced by how they interpreted the information, but also that their recall of the information often changed over time. One of his famous studies involved asking participants to read a Native American folk tale called 'The War of the Ghosts'. The participants were asked to recall the story several times up to one year later. He found the following factors influenced recall:

- **Omission**. Information considered to be irrelevant is often omitted from recall.
- **Transformation of order/detail**. Participants may change the order in which events occurred when retelling their story, or they might shift their focus of what is the most important aspect of the story.
- **Rationalisation**. In an attempt to make sense of the story, people may try and explain what happened in a way that makes sense to them and is coherent, even if this is not accurate.
- **Cultural shifts**. Both the style of the story and the content will be altered to be more appropriate to one's own culture.

Bartlett's work highlighted the importance of schemas and stereotypes. He demonstrated that humans often distort the information they receive to fit in with their own ways of looking at and understanding the world. He also clearly showed that we reconstruct our memories.

SCHEMAS AND STEREOTYPES

One study that clearly supports Bartlett deals with the effect of schemas and stereotypes on memory, and is detailed below.

Aims	Procedure	Findings	Conclusions	Criticisms

Study:	**Cohen's (1981, see E&F p.62) investigation into whether stereotypes influence memory**
Aims:	To see whether being told that a target person is a waitress or a librarian will influence recall of that person.
Procedure:	Participants were shown a 15-minute videotape of a man and woman eating a meal, and celebrating a birthday. The woman was described as either a waitress or a librarian. Later, participants were asked to describe the woman's behaviour, appearance, and personality. In one condition, the occupational information was provided before the videotape was shown, and in the second condition the occupational information was provided after participants had seen the videotape.
Findings:	Participants were more likely to recall information that was consistent with the stereotype of 'waitress' or 'librarian' than information that was inconsistent. It was found that receiving occupational information before the video was seen led to more accurate recall than if the participants were told the woman's occupation after they had seen the video.
Conclusions:	The pre-tape information served to generate expectations, and these expectations enhanced recall.
Criticisms:	Consistent traits for the waitress and librarian stereotypes had been established in a pilot study. Bartlett (1932) had argued that schemas affect the retrieval process rather than initial storage, but this study shows that schemas and stereotypes are important at both the initial storage and retrieval stages of memory. Schemas seem to direct attention and guide the encoding of schema-relevant information. However, this theory has negative implications, as shown in a real-life study of the witnesses called to the Oklahoma bombing trial. Memon and Wright (1999, see E&F p.62) showed how information received subsequent to a trial could influence the witnesses' recall of events. Two eyewitnesses who initially stated that there was only one man who came to a garage to hire a van changed their account when they heard another witness say that he definitely saw two men. Days after their initial statement they came to 'remember' the second man, showing that information received subsequent to the crime influenced their memory.

RESEARCH USING LEADING QUESTIONS

After witnessing an event, people are often asked questions about what they saw, who was involved, and what happened. Research, most notably by Loftus and colleagues, has shown that the language used when questioning eyewitnesses may alter what they remember. If the questions contain misleading information then the new information can influence the original memory. This may result in witnesses saying that they saw something or someone when in fact they did not. In some cases this is due to *post-event information,* where the person confuses information received outside the context of the witnessed event with the event itself. In other situations, *memory blending* occurs whereby details from various sources are combined with memories of the actual event.

An important study conducted by Loftus and Palmer (1974, see E&F p.65) investigated the effects of language on recall using a series of projected slides showing a car crash. They found that changing the description of how the cars went into each other resulted in participants perceiving the speed of the cars differently:

- "Smashed" led participants to estimate that the cars were going at 41 mph.
- "Collided" led them to say the cars were going at 39 mph.
- "Hit" reduced the perceived speed to 34 mph.
- "Contacted" reduced the perceived speed further to 32 mph.

More important than the initial speed assessment, there had been no broken glass, but a week later participants were asked if they had seen broken glass. In the "smashed" condition, 32% said they had, and in the "hit" condition 14% said they had, showing that at least some participants had been influenced by the initial wording used to describe the crash. However, if the misleading information is blatantly incorrect, it does not have the same influence.

EVALUATION

In support

- The research highlights the importance of asking the right questions when getting witness statements.
- It has led on to real-life research into eyewitness testimony.

Problems and limitations

- Baddeley noted that "the Loftus effect is not due to the destruction of the memory trace but due to interference with retrieval".
- The study lacks ecological validity as viewing a videotape is not the same as viewing a real-life crime, where flashbulb memories may make the memory particularly intense.

REAL-LIFE RESEARCH

One example of a real-life situation that has been studied was of a shooting outside a gun shop in Canada (Yuille & Cutshall, 1986). They examined witnesses recall of a real-life crime and suggested that:

- Important information in real-life crime is not easily distorted.
- People are more likely to be misled by insignificant details, and if there is a delay between the event and being given false information.
- There is a *weapons effect*, where people tend to focus on the weapon rather than other details.

MEMORY FOR FACES

Obviously eyewitness testimony is dependent on people's ability to recognise faces. Research into memory for faces has suggested that people tend to remember unfamiliar faces very poorly, have difficulties in providing verbal descriptions of people that they have seen, and are strongly influenced by their schemas and stereotypes. It might have been thought that with the growth of CCTV memory for faces would become easier, but this is not always the case. The quality of CCTV images is often unclear and fuzzy, and people often look different from different angles.

Research by Bruce and Young (1986, see E&F p.67) has suggested that our recognition of familiar faces may be dependent on *configural recognition*, whilst our recognition of unfamiliar faces may be dependent on *feature detection.* In addition, Bruce and Valentine (1988, see E&F p.67) note that one of the difficulties in trying to recognise faces from Identikit pictures is that the pictures lack movement, and movement can aid our recognition of someone's face. Factors that influence memory for faces are as follows:

Schemas and stereotypes. Harrower (1998) found that people's recall of criminals often reflected what they believed the criminal should look like, rather than how the criminal actually appeared. Brigham and Malpass (1985) found that people were better at recognising people from the same racial background.

Individual differences. Some people are more accurate at remembering faces than others.

Disguises. People's ability to recognise faces is strongly influenced by whether the person has remained similar to how they were at the time of the initial encoding. Baddeley and Peterson (1977) compared accuracy of recall of faces that had been disguised. Changes to the face led to poorer recognition (without a disguise there was 70% accuracy, with a wig there was 50% accuracy, and with a beard and wig there was 30% accuracy).

Similarity between faces. Identity parades require the police to choose people who are similar, but this can lead to confusion and make accurate recall more difficult.

Brain damage. *Prosopagnosia* results in people being unable to recognise the faces of people who were previously familiar to them.

Methods used to describe the wanted person. Verbal descriptions are quite difficult, as you'll see if you try to describe your own face. Artist's drawings have the same problem as verbal descriptions. Photofit and Identikit images tend to focus on individual features. This is not particularly helpful, as it is the configuration of features that is often crucial for facial recognition. In addition, facial recognition is often dependent on movement (Bruce & Valentine, 1988, see E&F p.67), so Photofit and Identikit images are not easily recognised.

IMPROVING THE RELIABILITY
OF EYEWITNESS TESTIMONY

Bartlett's research into reconstructive memory using *The War of the Ghosts* (see E&F p.61), and Loftus and Palmer's research into leading questions (see page 34) have clearly shown that eyewitness testimony may be prone to errors. Research by Cohen (1981) has demonstrated that schemas and stereotypes may lead to our interpreting information to fit our expectations (see page 33). Studies into memory for faces have similarly highlighted difficulties into obtaining accurate recall.

However, on a more positive note, we know that placing people back in the context where the event took place may aid their recall. This explains the use of reconstruction scenes in television programmes like *Crimewatch*.

Does Hypnosis Improve Recall?

Research into repression has also resulted in some police forces in America using hypnosis in an attempt to access repressed memories, but there is some debate as to whether hypnosis does improve recall.

In one study, Putnam (1979, see E&F p.64) studied whether hypnosis increased participants' accuracy of recall of an event. Participants were shown a videotape of an accident involving a car and a bicycle. They were then asked a series of questions, some of which contained misleading information. Some of the participants were asked these questions after they had been hypnotised, whilst the others were asked the questions without being hypnotised.

It was found that participants who had been hypnotised made more errors in their answers than the participants who were not hypnotised. The hypnotised participants were also more likely to be influenced by the misleading questions in that they were more suggestible.

Putnam concluded that participants were:

"...more suggestible in the hypnotic state and are, therefore, more easily influenced by the leading questions."

The findings do not support the view that hypnosis necessarily enables people to recall information that may have been hidden from their consciousness. However, the use of a videotape to test participants' recall lacks ecological validity in that participants may be more able to recall a personal traumatic event under hypnosis, if is has deeper significance for them. In addition, it has been suggested that if hypnotised people are warned that they may misremember information, the number of errors they are likely to make decreases.

To help prevent convicting innocent people, it is essential that steps are taken to improve the reliability of eyewitness accounts.

When considering identity parades, the following precautions should be taken:

- Place suspects in different places in the identity parade.
- Tell the witness that the suspect may not be in the identity parade.
- 'Fillers' in the line-up should resemble the suspect, but not too much.
- Use sequential line-ups.
- Avoid post-identification suggestions (e.g. "Yes, well done").
- Avoid contact of the witness with members of the identity parade beforehand.

When considering interview techniques:

- Ask open-ended questions.
- Avoid encouraging guessing, as it may consolidate a false memory.
- Do not prompt the witness, but allow them to volunteer information.
- Establish a rapport with the witness so they feel comfortable.

The Cognitive Interview Technique

These ideas have filtered into the *cognitive interview* technique that was developed by Geiselman (1985, see E&F p.68). With this approach the witness has to:

- Reinstate the context and recall everything they remember, whether they feel it is relevant or not.
- Recall details of the incident in various different orders.
- Recall the event from a different perspective, such as that of another witness.

Roy (1991, see E&F p.68) added some more recommendations for the basic cognitive interview technique:

- Avoid making judgmental and personal comments.
- Encourage the witness to speak slowly.
- Tailor the complexity of your language to suit individual eyewitnesses.
- Try to minimise distractions.
- Follow up each bit of information with an interpretive comment.
- Allow a pause between the response and the next question.
- Try to reduce eyewitness anxiety.
- Always review the eyewitness' description of events or people under investigation.

To give you an idea of the type of question you might be asked:

Describe the procedures and findings of one study of eyewitness testimony. (3 marks + 3 marks)

Loftus and Palmer (1974) showed participants a series of projected slides of a multi-car accident. They were asked a set of questions including one critical question about the speed that the car was travelling. In one condition participants were asked how fast the cars were going when they 'smashed' into each other. In the other conditions the word 'smashed' was replaced by the word 'collided', 'hit', or 'contacted'. Participants gave estimates of how fast they thought the cars were travelling.

Loftus and Palmer found that the language used to question participants about the speed of the cars influenced how they remembered the event. Their results showed that changing the description of the accident had a marked effect on participants' estimation of speed. When the term 'smashed' was used, the estimated speed was 41 miles per hour, whereas when the term 'collided' was used the estimated speed went down to 39 miles per hour. For 'hit', the estimated speed was 34 miles per hour, and for 'contacted' it was 32 miles per hour.

Describe two factors that influence memory for faces. (3 marks + 3 marks)

One important factor that influences memory for faces is whether the face is familiar or not. Studies by Bruce and Young have suggested that recognition of familiar faces is easier than recognition of unfamiliar faces. They suggest that the recognition of familiar faces is dependent on the configuration of the face (configural recognition), whereas the recognition of an unfamiliar face is dependent upon feature detection analysis, which is the method used to compile Identikit or Photofit photographs of criminals. Bahrick found that people could recognise their classmates after 35 years.

According to Brigham and Malpass, another important factor that influences memory for faces is whether the person to be recognised comes from the same ethnic/racial background as the witness. They found that participants' memory for faces was higher when presented with people from the same racial grouping, than when the people came from another racial group. This closely links with research on stereotyping.

OVER TO YOU

Describe two factors that influence the reliability of eyewitness testimony. (3 marks + 3 marks)

Developmental Psychology
ATTACHMENTS IN DEVELOPMENT

What's it about?

Developmental psychology (also known as lifespan psychology) is concerned with the changes that occur as humans move from infancy, to childhood, through adolescence, and on to adulthood. These changes include the development of thought processes, emotion, and social interactions. The changes that occur in the first 20 years or so usually result in behaviour being better organised, more complex, more competent, and more efficient.

What's in this unit?

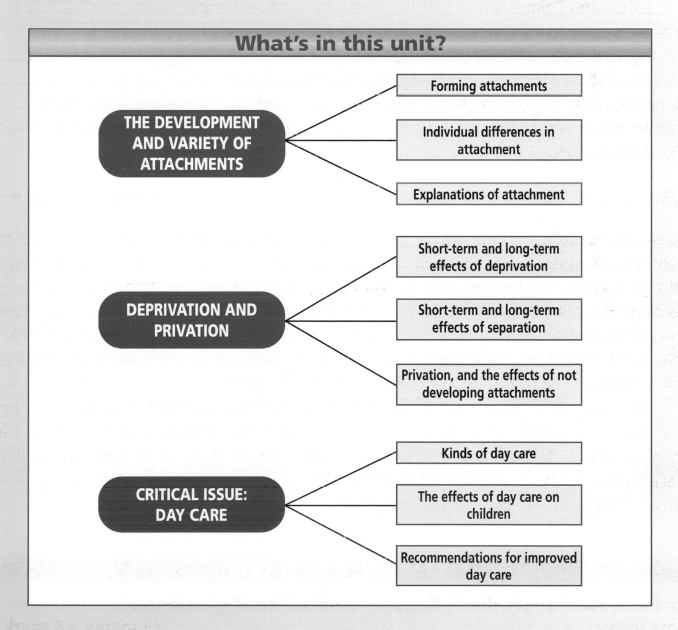

THE DEVELOPMENT AND VARIETY OF ATTACHMENTS
- Forming attachments
- Individual differences in attachment
- Explanations of attachment

DEPRIVATION AND PRIVATION
- Short-term and long-term effects of deprivation
- Short-term and long-term effects of separation
- Privation, and the effects of not developing attachments

CRITICAL ISSUE: DAY CARE
- Kinds of day care
- The effects of day care on children
- Recommendations for improved day care

DEFINING KEY TERMS AND CONCEPTS

You need to be able to define and explain the key terms listed in blue below. The other concepts listed in black will aid your understanding of attachments in development. Make a list of definitions of the following key terms, and if you get stuck, go to the glossary at the end of the book.

Attachment	Affectionless psychopathy	Ethological approach
Cognitive development	Anaclitic depression	Monotropy hypothesis
Cross-cultural variations in attachments	Avoidant attachment (type A)	Resistant attachment (type C)
Day care	Bond disruption	Secure attachment (type B)
Deprivation	Bonding	
Insecure attachment	Caregiving sensitivity hypothesis	Sensitive period
Maternal deprivation hypothesis		Separation anxiety
	Critical period	Separation protest
Privation	Deprivation dwarfism	Stranger anxiety
Separation	Disorganised attachment (type D)	Strange situation
Social development		Temperament hypothesis

You may be asked to define some of these key terms in the exam. To give you an idea, look at the following example.

Explain what is meant by the terms 'secure attachment' and 'deprivation' in relation to the development of attachments. **(3 marks + 3 marks)**

Secure attachment refers to the strong emotional attachment bond that a child has to its main caregiver. A securely attached child uses the caregiver as a safe base from which to contentedly explore the environment and is distressed if separated from the caregiver, but easily comforted by her (or him) when reunited.

Deprivation is the term used to describe the situation in which a young child is separated from its main attachment figure—usually the mother—for a considerable period or time, or repeatedly. It was an expression coined by Bowlby, who believed that maternal deprivation could have long-lasting adverse consequences for the mental health of the deprived child, possibly resulting in an inability to form long-lasting meaningful relationships.

OVER TO YOU

In the context of attachment, explain what psychologists mean by the terms 'separation' and 'privation'. **(3 marks + 3 marks)**

DESCRIBING AND EVALUATING KEY STUDIES

One kind of AO1 examination question is described as the 'APFCC' question. In this question you are asked to describe the aims, procedures, findings, conclusions, and give criticisms (APFCC) of a study into a named topic. In any question you will be asked for one or two of these, for example, 'aims and conclusions' or 'findings and conclusions'. There is not a requirement that these are given in balance as the question is marked out of 6 marks (for example, if you provide findings only then you may receive a maximum of 4 marks). You may be asked for the 'findings plus one criticism', in which case the question is marked as '3 marks + 3 marks'.

You may also be asked questions about research more generally, rather than about a specific study. In this case the question will say 'Describe the findings of research into…' (6 marks). You may also be asked about 'conclusions'. In such questions you may describe the findings/conclusions from one study, or from several studies, or even from a theory (which is a form of research).

If the question asks for 'procedures and findings', any other material will not receive credit, such as information relating to aims or conclusions. Make sure you understand the difference, for example, between a finding (the facts) and a conclusion (what the findings show us).

For the module on Developmental Psychology you need to know the following APFCC studies:

KEY STUDY TOPICS	EXAMPLE	WHERE TO FIND IT	OTHER RELATED RESEARCH
Secure/insecure attachments	Ainsworth et al. (1978)	Appendix	Main and Solomon (1986, see E&F p.88) Main and Weston (1981, see E&F p.89) Kagan (1984, see E&F p.89) Belsky and Rovine (1987, see E&F p.89)
Cross-cultural variation	Van IJzendoorn and Kroonenberg (1988)	Appendix	Sagi et al. (1991, see E&F p.90) Grossmann et al. (1985, see E&F p.91)
If asked to give information on a study of individual differences in attachments, you can use either the secure/insecure attachments study or the cross-cultural variation study listed above.			
Short-term effects of deprivation/separation	Robertson and Bowlby (1952)	Appendix	Barrett (1997, see E&F p.97) Robertson and Robertson (1971, see E&F pp.97–98)
Long-term effects of deprivation/separation	Bowlby et al. (1946)	Appendix	Bowlby et al. (1956, see E&F pp.100–101) Rutter (1981, see E&F p.101)
If asked to give information on a study related to Bowlby's maternal deprivation hypothesis, you can use the long-term effects of deprivation/separation study listed above.			
Long-term effects of privation	Hodges and Tizard (1988)	Appendix	Rutter (1981, see E&F p.101) Curtiss (1989, see E&F p.102) Freud and Dann (1951, see E&F pp.102–103)

OVER TO YOU

You need to be able to write for three minutes on aims, procedures, findings, conclusions, and criticisms. In order to do this well in the examination it might help to identify key words and concepts to recall. You only need a few for each of the APFCCs (in other words a few key concepts for the aims and a few for the procedures—a maximum of five). Do this for each study listed above.

THE DEVELOPMENT AND VARIETY OF ATTACHMENTS

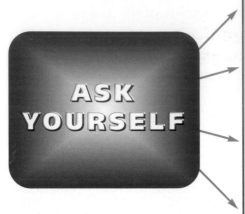

ASK YOURSELF

When you were a small child, who did you go to if you were hurt?

Can you remember how you reacted to separation from your mother (or main caregiver) on your first day at nursery or school?

How does your relationship with your mother differ from that with your father? If you have brothers and sisters, how does your relationship with each differ? Think of all the reasons why each of these relationships is distinct.

Do you think your childhood relationships with your parents have affected your adult relationships? If so, how?

The study of attachment in infancy and childhood is of particular interest to developmental psychologists because of the effect it is believed to have on later relationships. But first, let's consider how we can define attachment.

WHAT IS ATTACHMENT?

Attachments occur across the lifespan; they are a *reciprocal* emotional relationship in which both partners must be involved in order for a bond to be forged. Attachments depend on interaction rather than just two people being together.

Shaffer (1993) defines attachment as:

"A close emotional relationship between two persons, characterised by mutual affection, and a desire to maintain proximity [closeness]."

Maccoby (1980, see E&F p.74) lists the characteristics of infant–caregiver attachment as:

- Seeking proximity—wanting to be near each other.

- Separation anxiety (or distress) —a mutual feeling of upset if separated.

- Pleasure when reunited.

- General orientation towards the primary caregiver—the infant is always aware of the attachment figure and seeks reassurance that they are there.

BENEFITS AND CONSEQUENCES OF ATTACHMENT

According to evolutionary theory, all behaviour has evolved so as to propagate genes. How does this operate with respect to attachment?

Short-term Benefits

The evolutionary approach says that behaviour is shaped by survival of genes. When animals help their offspring to survive, they propagate their own genes. The caregiver provides:

- Food and care (warmth, etc.).
- Protection.
- Education in survival.

Long-term Benefits

Attachment shapes various important long-term relationships:

- **Sexual relationships**. These help to propagate genes. Attachment means that the father stays to help look after the young.
- **Attachment to infants**. This ensures their survival.
- **Friendships and close-knit communities**. Helps survival by mutual co-operation and reciprocal care (looking after each other).

Long-term Consequences

Bowlby (1969) hypothesised that the quality of early attachment relationships affects later ones. Evidence has been provided to support this theory:

- **Romantic relationships**. Hazan and Shaver (1987, see E&F p.76) found that security or insecurity in early relationships was reflected in security or insecurity of adult romantic relationships.
- **Friendships**. Grossman and Grossman (1991, see E&F p.75) found that quality of early attachment was reflected in quality of close friendships later in childhood.
- **Relationships with own children**. Quinton et al. (1988, see E&F p.75) found that poor or inadequate attachment in early life due to institutionalisation led women in later life to have poor attachments with their own children.

When you evaluate the influence of early attachments, you have to ask the following question:

IS ATTACHMENT THE ONLY MAJOR INFLUENCE?

OTHER EXPERIENCES

There are several other factors that shape our later relationships, which include other childhood experiences, e.g. divorce of parents, or moving school frequently. The adult experiences within the relationships experienced will also have an effect.

INDIVIDUAL DIFFERENCES

Some psychologists believe that *temperament* rather than experience affects our most fundamental relationships. Thus, a 'difficult' infant results in poor attachment, which results in poor later relationships, and vice versa. This shifts the emphasis from the caregiver to the infant.

STAGES OF ATTACHMENT

From their research, Schaffer and Emerson (1964, see E&F pp.77–78) list three stages in attachment:

Asocial stage (0–6 weeks)
Babies love human company but it makes no difference who the infant is with. When smiling begins (4–6 weeks), it is directed at anyone.

Stage of indiscriminate attachments (6 weeks–7 months)
The child happily goes to anyone and enjoys attention from people in general. However, he or she tends to smile more at familiar adults and children.

Stage of specific attachments (7–11 months)
The child typically, but by no means always, becomes attached to one individual, and this is the person who cares for them most of the time. The characteristics of this stage are:

- Distress if separated from that person, known as *separation protest*.
- Wariness and fear of people with whom they have had no contact at all, known as *stranger anxiety* or *stranger fear*.
- Formation of strong attachments to other familiar figures after about 10 months. Because of this, this stage is sometimes referred to as the stage of *multiple attachments*.

EVALUATION OF SCHAFFER AND EMERSON'S STAGE THEORY:

In support

Observations in real life, and especially during Schaffer and Emerson's (1964) research, have demonstrated that these stages definitely exist. The attachment to a specific individual is demonstrated by *separation protest*. Up to this point, the infant has not shown distress at the absence of anyone. *Stranger anxiety* has also been demonstrated in several studies, including the Strange Situation study (see E&F p.88). Both of these responses indicate that the infant has formed *schemas* of familiar and unfamiliar people.

Problems and limitations

There is evidence that behaviour during the asocial stage may not be as asocial as suggested, as babies *do* respond differently to familiar and unfamiliar people. Carpenter (1975, see E&F p.78–79) showed that even infants a few days old respond differently to their mother than to others. For example, they spend more time looking at her, so they must recognise her face and voice, and they can become quite distressed if the face and voice do not match (if the mother mouths words spoken by someone else). Similarly, Bushnell et al. (1989, see E&F p.79) found that babies only two days old show a preference for the face of their mother over a stranger's face.

CHARACTERISTICS OF ATTACHMENT

Is There a Critical Period for Bonding?

The biologically programmed, innate behaviour of imprinted geese occurs only during a *critical period* soon after birth. Is human attachment the same? Generally, researchers refer to a *sensitive period*, when attachment occurs most easily, but it is not the *only* time it can occur.

- Bowlby (1969, see E&F p.81) suggested a sensitive period that ends between 1 and 3 years of age, during which infants orient towards, and attach to, a single individual.
- Klaus and Kennell (1976, see E&F pp.81–82) suggested the *skin-to-skin hypothesis* in which there is a sensitive period immediately after birth when bonding occurs through skin contact.
- The hormone surge of mothers and infants around the time of birth may make them especially sensitive to bond formation (Klaus & Kennell, 1982, see E&F p.82) and although early skin-to-skin contact is not necessary for bond formation, it makes attachment easier.
- However, cross-cultural research suggests that the amount of early physical contact makes little difference to bonding (Lozoff, 1983, see E&F p.82).
- Chateau and Wiberg (1977, see E&F p.82) found that mothers who immediately suckled and had skin-to-skin contact with their babies after birth engaged in more kissing and embracing, and breastfed on average for 2½ months longer than 'traditional contact' mothers.

So, bonding may start with early skin-to-skin contact but attachments change over time. It is unlikely that any experiences immediately after birth can have irreversible effects in humans.

Is There One Attachment or Many?

The question arises as to whether infants become attached to one person or many people.

- Bowlby (1953, see E&F p.83) believed infants have one main attachment, referred to as the *monotropy hypothesis*, and that multiple attachments occur in a hierarchy.
- Schaffer and Emerson (1964, see E&F p.78) showed that the first main attachment occurred around 6–7 months, and this was followed by *multiple attachments*.
- Tronick et al. (1992, see E&F p.83) studied the African Efe tribe and found evidence of a primary attachment by 6 months of age, even though infants were cared for by many people.
- However, different attachments may serve different purposes. Thomas (1998, see E&F p.83) believes that multiple attachments are desirable as each relationship satisfies different needs.

Quality or Quantity of Attachments?

There is also the question of whether the strength of the attachment is due to how long someone spends with the infant, or how caring and sensitive they are.

- Fox (1977, see E&F pp.83–84) found that attachment in a kibbutz situation was usually still to the mother. Also, it has also been found that children in day care attach well to their mothers.
- In Harlow's (1959, see E&F p.85) study, the isolated monkeys 'attached' to cloth mothers, but they became maladjusted as the cloth mothers were unresponsive. Schaffer and Emerson (1964, see E&F p.78) showed that babies attach to those most sensitive to their needs.

It seems that quality of care is far more important than the amount of time spent with the infant. Babies attach to those who are responsive to their needs, and who offer them love and attention.

INDIVIDUAL DIFFERENCES IN ATTACHMENT

There are considerable differences in the *type* of attachment that infants make. These have been investigated by Ainsworth and her colleagues (Ainsworth & Bell, 1970, see E&F p.88) using the Strange Situation set up. The Strange Situation set up uses a *controlled observation study* to see how infants, normally aged between 12 and 18 months, respond to various situations in unfamiliar circumstances (see E&F p.87 for procedure). Measurements made in the Strange Situation are as follows:

- **Separation protest**. The response the child makes when the mother departs.
- **Stranger anxiety**. The reaction of the child to the stranger.
- **Reunion behaviour**. How the child behaves when the mother returns.

Types of Attachment

From her Strange Situation studies, Ainsworth observed three different types of attachment behaviour. Later, Main and Solomon (1986, see E&F p.88) argued that a small number of infants display a fourth type of behaviour that they called disorganised and disoriented attachment (Type D). Most infants seem to fit into one of these attachment types.

Secure Attachment (Type B)
Infants explore freely when their mother is present and use her as a secure base when the stranger appears. They show distress when she leaves and greet her warmly when she returns. They are readily comforted by her, soon returning to a state of contentment, and show a clear preference for her over the stranger. This is the optimum form of attachment, and is present in about 70% of infants.

Anxious/Resistant Attachment (Type C)
Children do not explore the new toys with such confidence. Compared to secure infants, they remain closer to their mother, showing signs of insecurity even in her presence. They become very distressed when she leaves. When she returns they may cling to her but show ambivalent reactions, such as hitting her while still clinging. They are clearly angry and anxious. She does not provide a secure base.

Anxious/Avoidant Attachment (Type A)
Children show little or no concern when the mother leaves, and show little pleasure when she returns. There is no indication of stranger anxiety and the children show little preference for the mother over the stranger, often avoiding both.

Disorganised/Disoriented Attachment (Type D)
There are a few infants who lack any coherent strategy for coping with the Strange Situation and their behaviour is a confusing mixture of approach and avoidance. The children show no set pattern of reaction when the mother departs or when she returns (hence 'disorganised'). This kind of behaviour is associated with abused children or those whose mothers are chronically depressed.

CROSS-CULTURAL VARIATIONS IN ATTACHMENT

When considering attachment types, it is important to remember that findings from studies conducted in one country might not generalise to other cultures. There have been a number of studies that have looked at how children outside the USA have reacted to the Strange Situation, and a summary of the results was reported by Sagi et al. (1991, see E&F pp.90–91).

- **American children**. Findings were similar to those reported by Ainsworth and Bell, in that 71% were secure, 12% were anxious/resistant, and 17% were anxious/avoidant.
- **Israeli children**. The Israeli children were raised in a kibbutz and therefore saw few strangers but were used to separation from the mother. Secure attachment was shown by 62%, with 33% being anxious/resistant, and only 5% being anxious/avoidant. The fact that they were not used to the presence of strangers may account for the high percentage of resistant attachment, where their anxiety was shown not when the mother left but when the stranger entered.
- **Japanese children**. The Japanese children showed similar attachment styles to the Israeli children, but probably for very different reasons. Secure attachment was shown by 68%, 32% were anxious/resistant, and there were no anxious/avoidant children. Japanese children are rarely left by their mothers, so the Strange Situation may have been particularly stressful when the mother leaves. Such children are likely to show avoidant behaviour. The Japanese children's anxious/resistant attachment behaviour was more likely to be due to the mother leaving rather than a stranger arriving.
- **German children**. The German children showed a different pattern of attachment from the other children. Only 40% were securely attached, but 49% were anxious/avoidant, and the remaining 11% were anxious/resistant. German children are encouraged to be independent and not clingy, and the relatively high percentage of avoidant infants may reflect the ethos of encouraging independence (Grossman et al., 1985, see E&F p.91).

EVALUATION OF CROSS-CULTURAL VARIATIONS:

Results of Strange Situation studies from eight different countries were analysed by Van Ijzendoorn and Kroonenberg (1998, see E&F p.91), and some interesting points were made:

- **Inter- and intra-cultural differences**. Variations *within* cultures were found to be 1½ times greater than variations *between* cultures. In every culture there are liable to be several sub-cultures, so we must be cautious of generalising, and be aware that cross-cultural comparisons may lack validity.
- **Sample sizes**. Although there were many children studied overall, some sample sizes were too small to make safe generalisations. For example, only 36 Chinese children were used—not a representative sample from a population of hundreds of millions!
- **The methodology**. The Strange Situation set up assumes that reactions to separation indicate secure or insecure attachment, which is an American interpretation. The Israeli and Japanese children show that this is not the case, as behaviour does not always have the same meaning in all cultures, and is therefore an invalid measuring tool. The use of a technique developed in one culture to study another is known as an *imposed etic*, and it makes the methodology inherently flawed.

EXPLANATIONS OF ATTACHMENT

The Psychodynamic Approach

- The first major stage of psychosexual development is the oral stage. The mother is the primary love object because she feeds the child.
- Freud saw this first relationship as the foundation of all others. If it was loving and caring, the child developed the ability to give and receive love. If not, relationships in adulthood would be unsatisfactory.

Learning Theory

- All behaviour is learnt, either by association (classical conditioning, CC) or consequences (operant conditioning, OC).
- By CC, the pleasure of feeding becomes associated with the person who feeds the infant and this person becomes a source of pleasure even when there is no feeding.
- Because the mother (or caregiver) is associated with positive reinforcement she becomes a *secondary reinforcer.*
- The attachment is not just one way; mothers are reinforced positively by smiles and general development, and reinforced negatively by cessation of crying.

Social Learning Theory

- Babies learn by imitation as well as by direct reinforcement.
- Hay and Vespo (1988, see E&F p.93) believe that parents deliberately teach their children to love them, e.g. by modelling affection.

EVALUATION

Psychodynamic Approach
- Harlow's (1959, see E&F p.85) study demonstrates that 'cupboard love' is not a valid explanation for infant attachment behaviour—babies do not always attach to the person who feeds them. The attachment need is separate from the need for food.
- Schaffer and Emerson's (1964, see E&F p.78) study also showed that 39% of babies attached to someone other than the person who met their everyday needs.

Learning Theory
- This approach emphasises the role of 'cupboard love' so it has the same problems as the psychodynamic approach. Studies by Harlow (1959) and Schaffer and Emerson (1964) support this criticism.
- If this theory were correct, you would expect the attachment process to be gradual and steady, whereas the stage of specific attachment and the accompanying separation protest occur suddenly. This suggests a *maturational process* rather than a learning process.
- Later learning theorists emphasised the role of attention and affection rather than food as a positive reinforcer. There is more support for this but it does not get over the previous criticism of suddenness.

Social Learning Theory
- Durkin (1995, see E&F p.94) pointed out that it is doubtful that strong emotions can be entirely learned.
- There is still the problem of timing (suddenness).
- However, it provides a much better model of parent–child interaction.

Bowlby's Theory

When looking at Bowlby's theory it is useful to recall the functions of attachment (see E&F p.95 and page 43 of this guide). Bowlby was greatly influenced by evolutionary theory and believed that attachment behaviour was an innate, adaptive response. The different phases that he proposed are detailed in your textbook (see E&F p.94).

Bowlby's theory of attachment is based mainly around the evolutionary perspective that attachment serves to promote survival. Here are his main points:

- Babies are born with certain *social releasers*—actions that release a social response in adults, such as smiling and crying.
- Attachment behaviour is *reciprocal* (two-way), and mothers or carers are pre-programmed to respond to the infant's needs.
- Attachment does not need to occur until about 7 months as it is synchronised with crawling. Before that, the baby cannot move far from the carer. It is as if a physical 'stay-close' mechanism is replaced by a psychological one.
- The bond made with the main carer is a very special one that is different from all other attachments. The tendency to bond with one main person is called *monotropy*.
- The first attachment serves as an *internal working model* that is the basis of all expectations and rules regarding relationships in later life.
- In the short term, babies use the attachment figure as a *secure base* from which they can explore. If the attachment is poor, exploration will not occur as the child will not move far from this base.
- The consequences of poor attachment are *dire* and possibly *irreversible*.

EVALUATION

In support

- Bowlby's theory has formed the basis of a large body of research into the care of children.
- The theory has certain important practical applications.

Problems and limitations

- Correlations between the quality of a child's various relationships are actually quite low (Main & Weston, 1981, see E&F p.96), so attachment is not necessarily the template for future relationships, and where a positive correlation exists it may be simply because some infants are better than others at forming relationships.
- Schaffer and Emerson's (1964, see E&F p.78) study indicates that attachment may not be monotropic. Most babies attach to more than one person and some psychologists believe that although these attachments may be different, no single one is more important than another.
- The evolutionary approach appears on the surface to be sensible and valid, but the arguments are *post hoc* (after the event). They are based on observing behaviour and then proposing a survival function to account for it. The problem with this is that any behaviour can be explained in this way (could you think of an advantage of *not* being attached to one person, but being quite content to be with anyone?). The evolutionary explanation is plausible but there's no proof that it's correct.

To give you an idea of the type of question you might be asked:

Describe the procedures and findings of one study of attachment. (6 marks)

Harlow (1959) placed 8 newborn rhesus monkeys in separate cages. In each cage there were 2 models: a wire structure 'mother', and a cloth 'mother'. In 4 of the cages a feeding bottle was attached to the wire structure and in the other 4 it was attached to the cloth model.

The findings were that, regardless of where the feeding bottle was placed, the monkeys spent most of their time clinging to the cloth 'mother'. They ran and clung to the cloth model when a fearful stimulus was introduced into the cage. In unfamiliar surroundings they used the cloth model as a 'safe base'.

In general the monkeys showed signs of severe developmental disturbance as a result of their experiences. Those isolated for 6 months would typically spend hours rocking, and would bite themselves. After a year they reportedly became 'semi-animated vegetables'.

Outline two criticisms of this study. (3 marks + 3 marks)

One criticism of the study is that the monkeys were deprived in several ways: they were not only deprived of their mother (hence suffering maternal deprivation) but they were also deprived of the company of all other monkeys. Since they spent most time in a single cage, they were also deprived of stimulation. It is therefore impossible to isolate the effects of maternal deprivation from other deprivation effects, and we cannot conclude that a lack of mother love was the sole cause of their extremely disturbed behaviour.

The second criticism is an ethical one. Monkeys are naturally sociable creatures that live in groups, and they are also intelligent animals. It is therefore highly probable that the experience of isolation was very distressing for them, as indicated by their extremely disturbed behaviour and the great fear they showed. Although at the time these studies were probably justified on the grounds that the benefits of investigating attachment processes outweighed the harm done to the monkeys, it is unlikely that such studies would be conducted today because of the stricter guidelines governing research using non-human animals.

OVER TO YOU

Describe one research study that has investigated cross-cultural variations in attachments. (6 marks)

DEPRIVATION AND PRIVATION

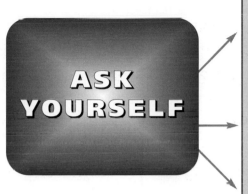

ASK YOURSELF

Imagine you are a psychologist interested in the long-term effects of secure and insecure attachment. How would you go about researching them? What methodological problems are you likely to encounter?

If the mother of a 2 year-old child had to go into hospital, what measures could be taken to minimise the upset for the child?

If a 3 year-old child had to go to hospital, what measures could be taken to minimise the upset?

WHAT YOU NEED TO KNOW:

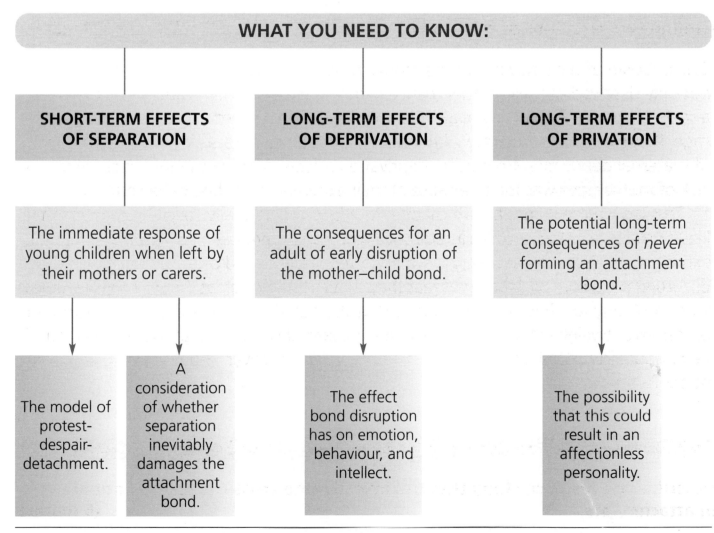

SHORT-TERM EFFECTS OF SEPARATION	LONG-TERM EFFECTS OF DEPRIVATION	LONG-TERM EFFECTS OF PRIVATION
The immediate response of young children when left by their mothers or carers.	The consequences for an adult of early disruption of the mother–child bond.	The potential long-term consequences of *never* forming an attachment bond.

| The model of protest-despair-detachment. | A consideration of whether separation inevitably damages the attachment bond. | The effect bond disruption has on emotion, behaviour, and intellect. | The possibility that this could result in an affectionless personality. |

SHORT-TERM EFFECTS OF SEPARATION

Robertson and Bowlby (1952, see E&F pp.97–98) documented the protest-despair-detachment (PDD) model. This model, also known as the syndrome of distress, consists of three stages that a child goes through when separated from its main caregiver:

Protest

The child attempts to follow the mother, cries and screams, and does everything he or she can to recover her. This lasts for a long time after she has gone.

Despair

The child sobs in a desperate, helpless way. He or she shows a distinct loss of hope.

Detachment

The child appears calm and settled. However, the calm masks underlying distress. There is emotional flatness, a lack of response, and a lack of curiosity (which could have effects on cognitive development). There may be occasional spats of temper, revealing the underlying desperation.

EVALUATION AND APPLICATION OF THE PDD MODEL:

ARE ALL CHILDREN EQUALLY AFFECTED?

A criticism of the PDD model is that it does not take into account individual differences in coping (Barrett, 1997, see E&F p.97). Insecurely attached children may be far more affected than securely attached children, or may reach the protest and despair stages almost immediately and become quite disorientated.

IS SEPARATION INEVITABLY HARMFUL?

In the 1950s it was not uncommon for children to go into hospital and be visited only briefly, or for children to be placed in a residential nursery whilst their mother went into hospital (e.g. to have another baby). Robertson and Robertson made amateur films to highlight the children's distress and indicate the damage done to attachment. They also showed how it could be avoided.

MINIMISING THE EFFECTS OF SEPARATION

Robertson and Robertson were instrumental in putting psychological theory into practice and took separated children into their home to try and establish the best way to minimise the effects of separation. They recommended:

- Children should be introduced to their new home before the separation in order to be familiar with their new surroundings.
- Children need to be given a daily routine as close as possible to their familiar one.
- The carer should talk to them about their mother.

The separated children the Robertsons cared for fared much better than children who were not given such care.

LONG-TERM EFFECTS OF DEPRIVATION

Prior to the development of Bowlby's (1969) theory of attachment he proposed a version called the *maternal deprivation hypothesis* (1953, see E&F p.98), which focused more on the effects of deprivation rather than the benefits of attachment. The hypothesis states that children have an innate need for a warm, continuous relationship. If the main attachment bond is broken in the early years then it will have an adverse effect on the child's emotional, social, and cognitive development. If many separations are experienced, behaviour patterns such as detachment or despair may persist into future life and develop into psychopathy or depression. Research showed that maternal deprivation of this kind can have the following effects:

* Emotionally disturbed behaviour such as bed-wetting (*enuresis*).
* Physical underdevelopment in children; a condition known as *deprivation dwarfism*.
* Depression.
* Intellectual retardation.
* An inability to make relationships; a condition known as *affectionless psychopathy*.

EVIDENCE SUPPORTING THE MATERNAL DEPRIVATION HYPOTHESIS:

Institutionalisation

Many of the important studies on institutionalisation and its effect on attachment behaviour were conducted during the 1940s, around the time of the Second World War. All the research pointed to the fact that early separations were associated with severe consequences:

* Bowlby's (1946, see E&F p.99) study found that maternal deprivation can lead to a lack of emotional development and *affectionless psychopathy*.
* Spitz (1945, see E&F p.98) found that some deprived orphanage children developed *anaclitic depression*.
* Spitz and Wolf (1946, see E&F p.98) found that many hospitalised children were seriously depressed, and that if they were in hospital for more than 3 months, complete recovery was unlikely.
* Goldfarb (1947, see E&F p.99) found that orphanage children fostered after 3 years were lower in IQ, less socially mature, poorer at language skills, more likely to be aggressive, and had poorer relationships than children who had been fostered before 3 months.
* Rutter (1998, see E&F pp.99–100) found that Romanian orphans who were adopted at age 2 showed marked improvement by age 4, but those adopted later in life fared less well.

All these effects could have been caused by poor physical care. However, Widdowson (1951, see E&F p.100) demonstrated the importance of emotional care. Children in an orphanage run by a harsh, uncaring supervisor suffered *deprivation dwarfism* until a more humane person took over, despite there being no change in diet.

Hospitalisation

Children experience separation as a result of being hospitalised, and when children are hospitalised for prolonged periods it may lead to the breaking of attachment bonds and later maladjustment.

* Douglas (1975, see E&F p.100) analysed data from the National Survey of Health and Development on 5000 children born in 1946. The longer they had spent in hospital, the more intellectual and behaviour problems they had.
* Quinton and Rutter (1976, see E&F p.100) found that repeated hospitalisation was associated with later problems, but single admissions rarely had later difficulties.

However, Clarke and Clarke (1976, see E&F p.100) argue that it may not be separation that is the problem but another factor such as general home problems. Perhaps children from disadvantaged homes are more likely to need hospitalisation because of poor living conditions. Also, the experience of being in hospital is likely to create anxiety and the lack of caregiving at such a critical time may lead to long-term problems. However, Bowlby et al. (1956, see E&F pp.100–101) studied children hospitalised due to TB who were visited by their families every week so bond disruption was minimised and found few differences between them and their school peers in terms of intellectual and emotional development. It would therefore appear that hospitalisation does not inevitably have harmful effects, so long as bond disruption is minimised.

EVALUATION OF THE MATERNAL DEPRIVATION HYPOTHESIS:

In support

Problems and limitations

- The studies of hospitalisation and institutionalisation that appear on the previous page are generally in support of the maternal deprivation hypothesis.
- Likewise, Harlow's (1959, see E&F p.85) study of infant monkeys supports this theory.

- The hypothesis is similar to the concept of imprinting and is therefore subject to the same criticisms.
- There may be a sensitive period for attachment formation but it is unlikely that there is a critical period. Clarke and Clarke (1976) propose that early childhood is no more important than middle or later childhood. However, the work of Goldfarb (1947) and Rutter (1998) indicates that early life *is* more crucial than later childhood.
- The damage caused by deprivation may be reversible, and with very good care, children can recover.
- The work of Rutter and his colleagues (presented in more detail on the next page) is essential to any evaluation of the maternal deprivation hypothesis. His work recognised the importance of the hypothesis, but extended and modified it. Rutter (1972, see E&F p.101) pointed out that Bowlby had assumed that all experiences of deprivation were the same whereas in fact there are differences, and he led on to introduce the distinction between *deprivation* and *privation*.

Applications of the Maternal Deprivation Hypothesis

Bowlby's maternal deprivation hypothesis has led to some important real-life applications:

- **A positive change in attitudes towards infant care**. Bowlby's ideas were quite revolutionary. At the time he started publishing his work, physical care was considered to be the only important factor in rearing children. Back in 1928, J.B. Watson's recommendation to parents was that affection should be avoided. Bowlby's work changed attitudes for the better, and child-care manuals started to strongly recommend plenty of love.
- **Humanising child-care practices**. The theory led child-care practices to be reviewed and improved. The care in orphanages was improved to take account of emotional needs. Wherever possible, fostered children were kept in one foster home rather than being moved around. In maternity units mothers spent more time with their babies. Finally, provision was made for parents to stay in hospital with young children and much longer visiting time was allowed.
- **Controversial applications**. The most controversial interpretation of Bowlby's work was that mothers were encouraged to stay at home with children under 5 years of age. In fact this was not a direct recommendation from Bowlby, but an interpretation made by the government who may have wished to discourage women from working outside the home once the war was over and jobs were required for returning soldiers. Nevertheless, even if the advice did not come direct from Bowlby, he thought that very young children were better off spending most of their time with their mother or primary caregiver.

LONG-TERM EFFECTS OF PRIVATION

The Work of Rutter

Rutter pointed to key differences in separation experiences, and distinguished between:

- **Deprivation**, where a bond is formed and broken, usually through separation.
- **Privation**, where no bond is ever formed, as with many institutionalised children.

Rutter argued that the effects of privation are far worse than those of deprivation. He believed that many of the delinquents studied by Bowlby had experienced so many changes of home and carer that no bond had ever formed. It was these children who were liable to become *affectionless psychopaths*, but these later problems were probably due to privation.

Studies of Privation

A few researchers have looked at the effects of very extreme privation and isolation on children, and it is surprising how resilient the children that were studied seemed to be:

- **The Koluchová twins**. Koluchová (1976, 1991, see E&F p.102) studied twin boys who suffered severe privation (locked in a cellar, beaten) until age 7, who had virtually no language skills. They were fostered into a loving home at age 9. By 14 their behaviour and intellect was normal, and by 20, they were of above average intelligence and had excellent loving relationships with members of their foster family. Note that in this instance, the boys had each other during the early years of their lives, and their foster family (two sisters) was extremely supportive and loving.
- **Genie**. Curtiss (1989, see E&F p.102) studied the case of Genie who suffered very severe abuse (kept in one room, isolated, beaten, malnourished) until age 13½. She was then given intensive education. Her language skills never developed fully, but other skills improved considerably, and many perceptual skills were near normal. Rymer (1993, see E&F p.102) reported lack of interest in other people. Note that Genie was rescued at a very late age, and had been kept completely on her own before that, and she had not been given good psychological and nurturing care after she was rescued, as she had a series of difficult relationship with carers followed by an abusive foster home.
- **The concentration camp children**. Freud and Dann (1951, see E&F p.102) studied six war orphans who spent their first three years in a concentration camp, with no continuous adult care. They were strongly attached to each other and very fearful of being separated. Initially they showed hostility towards adults, but once rescued managed to attach to their adult carers and eventually developed normal social and intellectual skills. As adults, the group as a whole was within the normal range of development. Note that the outcome for these children was generally good. They did have the opportunity to attach in early life, like the Koluchová twins, and unlike Genie.

OVER TO YOU

Why do the studies by Tizard and colleagues (see E&F p.105) provide a better body of evidence than case studies by which to judge the effects of deprivation and privation?

CONCLUSIONS ABOUT SEPARATION, DEPRIVATION, AND PRIVATION

Taking Account of the Reasons for Deprivation

As well as distinguishing between the effects of deprivation and privation, Rutter (1972) proposed that the *circumstances* of separation could be very important. Separations can occur in stressful or relatively non-stressful circumstances. Rutter proposed that it was the amount of stress in the family that caused the later problems, not the separation itself.

Most children from a stable home can survive a brief separation without too much harm being done. If they come from a stressful home with lots of upheaval and uncertainty, then they are far more likely to experience long-term pathology.

The Isle of Wight Study

Rutter et al. (1976, see E&F p.104) conducted large-scale research of over 2000 boys on the Isle of Wight to study the relationship between separation and delinquency. They found that if separation was due to physical illness or death of the mother, there was no relation to delinquency. If it was caused by family friction or psychiatric illness, the boys were four times more likely to be delinquent. Delinquent boys also came from homes where there was no separation but a great deal of conflict.

Cockett and Tripp (1994, see E&F p.104) found that family discord was related to low self-esteem and that this could increase the likelihood of problems, especially delinquency, in later life.

The Different Effects of Separation, Deprivation, and Privation

Rutter believed that there were distinct effects from different deprivation experiences:

- Privation (failure to form bonds, such as in institutional care) was associated with *affectionless psychopathy*.
- Family discord and lack of secure attachment was associated with *delinquency*.
- Lack of stimulation and necessary life experiences resulted in *intellectual retardation*.

The question arises as to whether children can recover from extreme adverse early experiences. Research evidence indicates that children can recover if given a good home environment with plenty of love and individual attention. The longer the deprivation, the more uncertain the recovery, but even later in life children can make reasonable progress (Dennis, 1973).

An Increase in Vulnerability

Rutter's main conclusion was that maternal deprivation *increases a child's vulnerability* to becoming disturbed but it does not necessarily mean that maladjustment is inevitable.

To give you an idea of the type of question you might be asked:

Describe the findings and conclusions from one study investigating the short-term effects of separation. **(6 marks)**

Robertson and Bowlby (1952) documented three stages of reaction that children typically pass through when separated from their main carer. These are known as the syndrome of distress, or the protest-despair-detachment model.

The first stage is protest in which the child screams, cries, and does everything he or she can to recover contact with his or her carer. The second stage is that of despair during which the child is very miserable and apathetic, and takes no interest in his or her surroundings. The third stage is that of detachment. The child now appears settled, but still takes little interest in anything. If the mother returns, the child's immediate reaction is disinterest in her.

The main conclusion of this research was that even short-term separation can cause insecurity and anxiety. The child becomes more vulnerable to upset from stressful circumstances. A further conclusion was that if separation was inevitable, it could be planned in a way that minimised the adverse effects. Before the separation, children should be introduced to their new surroundings and the person who will care for them. If possible, the substitute carer should be one person. The overall conclusion is that separation does not need to cause unhappiness and long-term harm if managed properly.

Describe the findings and conclusions of one study that has investigated the effect of privation on the development of attachment. **(6 marks)**

Tizard et al.'s longitudinal study of 65 children showed that at age 8 years, the adopted children had formed strong attachments to their adoptive parents but did not get on as well with their peers as did other children. When investigated at age 16, this group still showed strong attachments that were no weaker than those of a comparison group from a similar background who had experienced a family upbringing. Only half of the children who had been returned to their natural families showed strong attachments at age 16.

Tizard et al. concluded that the first two years have an important influence on later relationships, and therefore spending these years in an institution does have an effect. This may have been the cause of some of the behavioural problems shown by these children, but the fact that they had formed attachments offers little support for Bowlby's belief in a 'critical period' for attachment formation. Early institutionalisation is not necessarily irreversibly damaging but such children probably need a great deal of love and support afterwards in order to develop favourably.

OVER TO YOU

Give two criticisms of this study. **(3 marks + 3 marks)**

CRITICAL ISSUE: DAY CARE

ASK YOURSELF

What does Bowlby's maternal deprivation theory imply about using day care for pre-school children?

What are the advantages and disadvantages of using day care for both the child *and* the mother?

Consider the differences between childminding and day nurseries, taking into account the types of social experiences and play activities the children may be exposed to, and the kind of people who would be caring for the children.

WHAT YOU NEED TO KNOW:

Studies of the effect of day care, both childminding and day nurseries.

The effect of day care on children's social development and how they relate to other children and adults.

The effect of day care on children's cognitive development.

The ways in which day care can be improved.

IS DAY CARE HARMFUL OR BENEFICIAL?

Is it harmful?	Is it beneficial?
In 1951 the World Health Organisation stated that day nurseries would cause "permanent damage to the emotional health of a future generation". They used Bowlby's research and theory of maternal deprivation to support this view.	In America in the 1960s day care schemes were instigated to improve the pre-school opportunities for disadvantaged children so they could start school on a par with their peers. The best known was a large-scale programme called Headstart.

Kagan et al. (1980) suggested a double standard was being applied: day care is good for lower-class children (it improves cognitive abilities), but not for middle-class children (due to maternal deprivation).

STUDIES OF DAY CARE

The main forms of day care are for pre-school children in either day nurseries or with childminders. There are some important studies that involved day nurseries:

- Kagan et al. (1980, see E&F p.106) compared 33 nursery children with a control group of 'home' children. The children were about 3½ years old and were assessed for 2 years. No significant differences were found in attachment, cognitive abilities, or general sociability. The use of a control group meant that the effects of day care could be reliably measured, and the study concluded that day care is not harmful.
- Andersson (1992, see E&F p.108) studied 100 Swedish children to investigate the long-term effects of day care. Some of the children had spent their pre-school years in day nurseries and were assessed at ages 3, 4, 8, and 13. Those in day care, especially those starting before 1 year old, performed better in school. The worst school performers were those who had no day care. However, children who started nursery before 1 year of age were from the highest socio-economic groups, and this may have caused them to perform better at school.
- Headstart (see E&F p.107) was not a 'minding' service but intended to improve opportunities for disadvantaged children. Those attending these 'enrichment' programmes were cognitively more advanced when starting school than their counterparts from similar backgrounds, but by age 11 these differences had disappeared. Lazar and Darlington (1982, see E&F p.107) found that by adolescence fewer Headstart children were on welfare, more were in college, and fewer were delinquent. It is difficult to evaluate the findings because the programme was so large and varied, but it showed no detrimental effects of intensive pre-school education.

Childminding is another form of day care that some feel is preferable because it is apparently more similar to home care. However, studies have proved that this is not always the case:

- Mayall and Petrie (1983, see E&F p.107) studied London childminders and found that care was often not very good. Many children were exposed to an unstimulating environment and failed to thrive. As there was no control group, maybe children at home would be equally deprived.
- Bryant et al. (1980, see E&F p.107) studied childminders in a middle-class Oxfordshire area. They found that 75% of the children were passive and detached, and 25% were disturbed and had bad speech. Bryant believes that these behaviour patterns are not an inevitable consequence of childminding, but some of the minders were untrained, and did not view it as part of their job to stimulate the youngsters in their care.

EFFECTS OF DAY CARE ON SOCIAL DEVELOPMENT

Day care can have a positive effect on children so that they become more active, sociable, outgoing, playful, and less aggressive:

- Shea (1981, see E&F pp.107–108) used videotapes of children in day nurseries to assess them on aggression, rough-and-tumble play, frequency of peer interaction, distance from teacher, and distance from the nearest child. They found that children became more sociable over time. This was greater for those attending nursery five days a week than those attending two days a week, indicating that it was the nursery setting rather than normal maturation that was producing the changes.
- Clarke-Stewart et al. (1994, see E&F p.109) observed 150 children from Chicago, aged 2–3 years. They found that the day care children had more advanced peer relationships and could negotiate with them better than children brought up at home. They also learnt how to cope in social situations earlier than the home group.

However, Pennebaker et al. (1981, see E&F p.108) emphasised that children are individuals and some react differently to the day care setting, and when children are shy and unsociable then nursery school can be very frightening and make them even more withdrawn.

Day care can also affect emotional development, sometimes in a negative way:

- Belsky and Rovine (1988, see E&F p.109) found that there was an increased risk of an infant developing insecure attachments if they were in day care for at least 4 months and if this had begun before 1 year of age, but there were no negative effects on children who started after they were 1 year old.
- Stroufe (1990) believed that the first year of life was vital for mother–child attachment and day care should be delayed until the second year.

However, there is also evidence to the contrary:

- Clarke-Stewart et al. (1994, see E&F p.110) investigated the relationship between time spent in day care and quality of attachment in over 500 children, and found that 15-month-old children who had experienced 'high intensity' child care (30 hours or more a week from 3 months onwards) were equally distressed when separated from their mothers in the Strange Situation as 'low intensity' child care (less than 10 hours a week). This suggests that attachment was not affected by the experiences of separation.
- Roggman et al. (1994, see E&F p.110) compared infants who were cared for at home with those who attended day care before the age of 1, and both were equally securely attached when assessed by the Strange Situation set up.

EFFECTS OF DAY CARE ON COGNITIVE DEVELOPMENT

There is evidence that day care has a positive effect on cognitive development for all children:

- Burchinal et al. (1989, see E&F p.109) found that day care children had a higher IQ on entering school than those who stayed at home.
- Broberg et al. (1997, see E&F p.109) used a sample of 146 Swedish children and compared those at day nurseries with those being minded and those staying at home. At age 8, the day nursery group was better in verbal and mathematical ability and the childminder group performed worst.
- Andersson's (1992, see E&F p.108) longitudinal study of Swedish children assessed at ages 8 and 13 showed that children who had begun nursery before 1 year old did better at school than those starting nursery later. The home group was the worst performing.
- Clarke-Stewart et al. (1994) found that day care was of cognitive benefit, as long as children did not stay longer than 6 hours a day.

However, Tizard (1979, see E&F p.109) compared mother–child conversations with nursery teacher–child conversations and found that the latter were less complex than the former. This could well have an effect on later cognitive development.

IMPROVING DAY CARE

The two crucial variables that affect day care are *consistency* and *quality*. The less consistent the care and the poorer the quality of care, the more harmful the experience is for the child. Consistency refers to minimising the number of changes a child has to experience both in terms of carers and conditions. Quality of care is difficult to define but there are some recommendations that can be made to maintain good quality care:

Recommendations

With respect to consistency
- Minimal turnover of staff to ensure consistency.
- One staff member assigned to each child.
- Consistent routines.
- Consistent physical environment.

With respect to quality
- Low child-to-carer ratio.
- Carers sensitive to the children's needs.
- A good number of toys and activities.
- Regular discussions with parents.

Howes et al. (1998, see E&F p.111) gave carers minimal training in sensitively handling children and found an improvement in the children's security and general happiness.

General conclusions

Individual differences
It is possible that the question "Does day care harm children?" is misleading because children have different temperaments and therefore they may not all react in the same way. Some children may benefit from day care while others may be harmed by it. For example, Egeland and Hiester (1995, see E&F p.110) found that day care had a negative effect on secure children and a positive effect on insecure ones.

Type of care
The National Institute of Child Health and Human Development (1997) longitudinal study of over 1000 children in America concluded that the family environment more strongly links to children's development than the type of child care they experience.

To give you an idea of the type of question you might be asked:

Outline two factors that can explain how day care affects a child's cognitive and/or social development. **(3 marks + 3 marks)**

One factor that affects a child's social and cognitive development is the warmth of the staff and how responsive they are to the needs of the children in their care. For example, there should ideally be a reasonable amount of one-to-one verbal interaction between the carer and child. Howes et al. (1998) showed that training aimed at improving sensitivity of carers did improve the attachment security of the children over a 6-month period compared to a control group who received no training.

A second factor that particularly affects social development is the consistency of care experienced by the children. It is advisable to have a low staff turnover and for the children to be assigned to one specific individual who feels responsible for the child. The children will not then be made insecure or anxious by constant changes.

Describe the procedures and findings of one research study that has investigated the effects of day care on children's cognitive development. **(6 marks)**

Andersson (1992, 1996) conducted a longitudinal study of more than a hundred children from both lower-class and middle-class homes who had been in good quality preschool day care in Sweden. The families were first contacted when the children were aged between 3 and 4 years, when their early child-care arrangements were recorded along with the age they first started day care. The children were assessed at ages 8 and 13 by means of IQ tests and teacher ratings. Their progress was compared with that of a control group who had been looked after full-time by their mothers.

It was found that those children who had begun day care before they were one year old were rated most highly on school performance at 8 and 13 years, and received more positive ratings from teachers in terms of socioemotional development. Children who started day care after the age of one year were rated less well. School performance was worst in those children who did not attend any day care programme.

OVER TO YOU

Outline the findings of research on the effects of day care on children's social development. **(6 marks)**

Physiological Psychology

STRESS

What's it about?

Physiological psychology focuses on the biological causes and explanations of behaviour. Human behaviour is so complex that very little can be explained by physiology alone. Instead, we have to look at how psychological and social factors interact with physiology. Explanations that consider this interaction offer a biopsychosocial approach.

The topic areas of interest in the physiological approach include the way the nervous system, including the brain, operates; how hormones affect our body and how our bodily rhythms affect our mood and what we do. It also includes the topic area of this section; what constitutes stress and the effects it has on us.

What's in this unit?

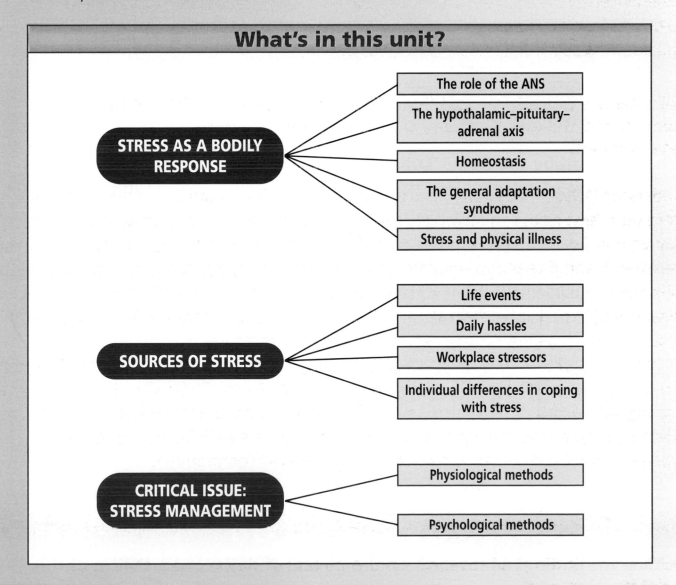

STRESS AS A BODILY RESPONSE
- The role of the ANS
- The hypothalamic–pituitary–adrenal axis
- Homeostasis
- The general adaptation syndrome
- Stress and physical illness

SOURCES OF STRESS
- Life events
- Daily hassles
- Workplace stressors
- Individual differences in coping with stress

CRITICAL ISSUE: STRESS MANAGEMENT
- Physiological methods
- Psychological methods

DEFINING KEY TERMS AND CONCEPTS

You need to be able to define and explain the key terms listed in blue below. The other concepts listed in black will aid your understanding of stress. Make a list of definitions of the following key terms, and if you get stuck, go to the glossary at the end of the book.

Cardiovascular disorders	Stressor	Hardiness
Control	Workplace stressor	Homeostasis
General adaptation syndrome (GAS)	Adrenal glands	Hypothalamus
	Adrenaline	Noradrenaline
Immune system	ANS (autonomic nervous system)	PNS (peripheral nervous system)
Life changes		
Physiological approaches to stress management	Barbiturates	Psychoneuroimmunology
	Benzodiazepines	Set point
Psychological approaches to stress management	Biofeedback	Stress inoculation training
	Burnout	
Stress	CNS (central nervous system)	System variable
Stress management	Endocrine system	Type A personality

You may be asked to define some of these key terms in the exam. To give you an idea, look at the following example.

What is meant by the terms 'stressor' and 'stress management'?

(3 marks + 3 marks)

A stressor is an event that triggers the stress response. A stressor throws the body out of balance and forces it to respond. For example, life changes, daily hassles, lack of control, noise, and temperature are all stressors.

Stress management is the attempt to cope with the negative effects of stress. This may be done by using physiological methods (such as biofeedback or anti-anxiety drugs) or psychological methods (such as stress inoculation training or hardiness training).

OVER TO YOU

Outline the general adaptation syndrome and describe one criticism of this model.

(3 marks + 3 marks)

DESCRIBING AND EVALUATING KEY STUDIES

One kind of AO1 examination question is described as the 'APFCC' question. In this question you are asked to describe the aims, procedures, findings, conclusions, and give criticisms (APFCC) of a study into a named topic. In any question you will be asked for one or two of these, for example, 'aims and conclusions' or 'findings and conclusions'. There is not a requirement that these are given in balance as the question is marked out of 6 marks (for example, if you provide findings only then you may receive a maximum of 4 marks). You may be asked for the 'findings plus one criticism', in which case the question is marked as '3 marks + 3 marks'.

You may also be asked questions about research more generally, rather than about a specific study. In this case the question will say 'Describe the findings of research into…' (6 marks). You may also be asked about 'conclusions'. In such questions you may describe the findings/conclusions from one study, or from several studies, or even from a theory (which is a form of research).

If the question asks for 'procedures and findings', any other material will not receive credit, such as information relating to aims or conclusions. Make sure you understand the difference, for example, between a finding (the facts) and a conclusion (what the findings show us).

For the module on Physiological Psychology you need to know the following APFCC studies:

KEY STUDY TOPICS	EXAMPLE	WHERE TO FIND IT	OTHER RELATED RESEARCH
Stress and cardiovascular disorders	Friedman and Rosenman (1959, 1974)	Appendix	Matthews et al. (1977, see E&F p.141) Ganster et al. (1991, see E&F p.141)
Stress and the immune system	Kiecolt-Glaser et al. (1984)	Appendix	Cohen et al. (1991, see E&F p.126) Riley (1981, see E&F p.127) Schliefer et al. (1983, p.128)
If asked to give information on a study of stress and physical illness, you can use either the stress and cardiovascular disorders study or the stress and the immune system study listed above.			
Life changes	Rahe et al. (1970)	Appendix	Holmes and Rahe (1967, see E&F p.132) Rahe and Arthur (1977, see E&F p.133)
Workplace stressors	Marmot et al. (1977)	Appendix	Shirom (1989, see E&F p.137) Czeisler et al. (1982, see E&F p.138) Matteson and Ivancevich (1982, see E&F p.138)

OVER TO YOU

You need to be able to write for three minutes on aims, procedures, findings, conclusions, and criticisms. In order to do this well in the examination it might help to identify key words and concepts to recall. You only need a few for each of the APFCCs (in other words a few key concepts for the aims and a few for the procedures—a maximum of five). Do this for each study listed above.

STRESS AS A BODILY RESPONSE

WHAT IS STRESS?

There are several definitions of stress. Selye (1950) provided a general definition of stress:

"The non-specific response of the body to any demand."

A more specific definition of stress was provided by Statt (1981):

"Physical and psychological strain, usually lasting for a period of time, which threatens the ability of a person (or animal) to go on coping with a given situation."

The stress response originally evolved to help animals (including humans) react QUICKLY.

FOR EXAMPLE: When a mouse sees a cat, the sequence of events goes like this:

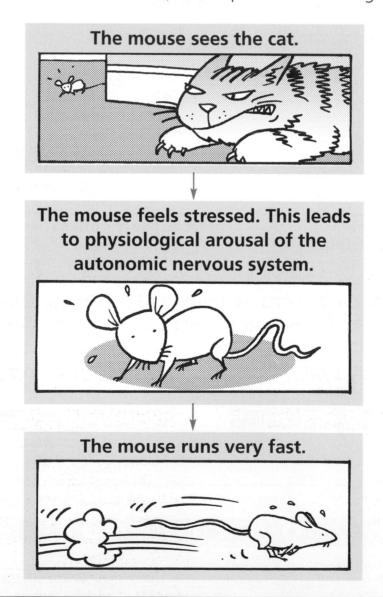

The mouse sees the cat.

The mouse feels stressed. This leads to physiological arousal of the autonomic nervous system.

The mouse runs very fast.

NOTE: Stress is an *innate*, *defensive*, *adaptive* reaction that promotes survival.

THE NERVOUS SYSTEM

The nervous system is a complex network:

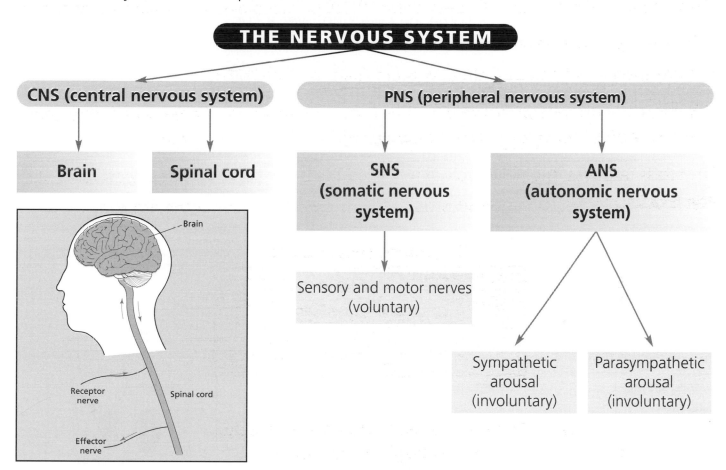

The central nervous system (CNS) consists of the brain and spinal cord. Receptor nerves transmit information to the brain via the spinal cord, and instructions from the brain are sent via the effector nerves. The autonomic nervous system (ANS) plays a vital role in stress:

ACTIVITIES OF THE AUTONOMIC NERVOUS SYSTEM:

Sympathetic branch	Parasympathetic branch
• Increases heart rate. • Reduces stomach activity. • Inhibits saliva production. • Pupils become dilated (expanded). • Bronchi of lungs relax. • Glucose is released. • Expends (uses) energy. • Acts as a troubleshooter ('fight or flight' response).	• Decreases heart rate. • Increases stomach activity. • Increases saliva production. • Pupils become contracted (smaller). • Bronchi of lungs constrict. • Glucose is stored. • Conserves (saves) energy. • Acts as a housekeeper ('test and digest' response).

THE HYPOTHALAMIC-PITUITARY-ADRENAL AXIS

Higher brain centres (the cortex, etc.) respond to changes in the environment—even mild but unexpected ones such as someone knocking over a cup, or a door slamming hard. The stress response originates in the hypothalamus, which is the first link in a chain that also includes the pituitary and adrenal glands. Jointly, this *hypothalamic–pituitary–adrenal axis* is responsible for arousing the ANS in response to a stressor.

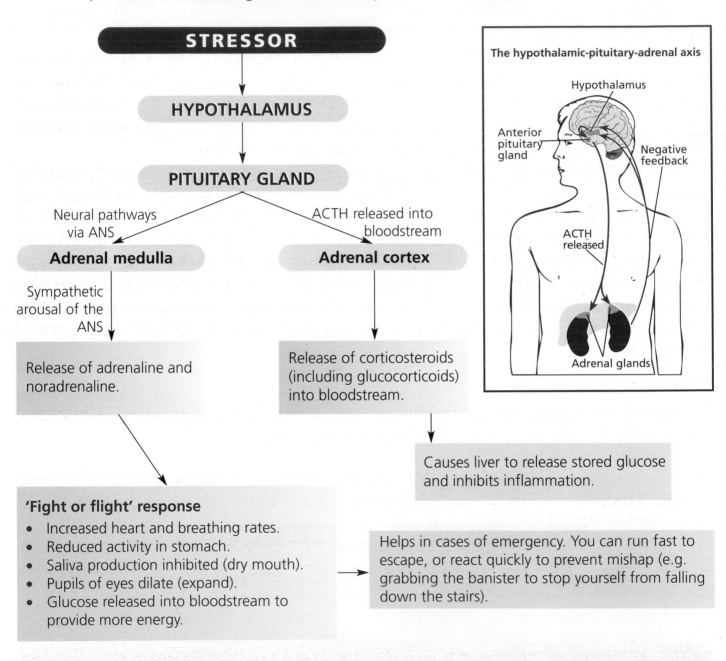

STRESSOR

↓

HYPOTHALAMUS

↓

PITUITARY GLAND

Neural pathways via ANS

ACTH released into bloodstream

Adrenal medulla

Adrenal cortex

Sympathetic arousal of the ANS

Release of adrenaline and noradrenaline.

Release of corticosteroids (including glucocorticoids) into bloodstream.

Causes liver to release stored glucose and inhibits inflammation.

'Fight or flight' response
- Increased heart and breathing rates.
- Reduced activity in stomach.
- Saliva production inhibited (dry mouth).
- Pupils of eyes dilate (expand).
- Glucose released into bloodstream to provide more energy.

Helps in cases of emergency. You can run fast to escape, or react quickly to prevent mishap (e.g. grabbing the banister to stop yourself from falling down the stairs).

The hypothalamic-pituitary-adrenal axis

Hypothalamus

Anterior pituitary gland

Negative feedback

ACTH released

Adrenal glands

OVER TO YOU

Make a list of the sort of situations that might induce a 'fight or flight' response. Do you think you can prepare for such reactions? If so, how?

EVALUATION OF VIEWING STRESS
ONLY IN TERMS OF PHYSIOLOGY

Using *only* physiological means of measuring stress can be both positive and negative. On the positive side of the argument, the amount of 'stress hormones' (e.g. adrenaline, noradrenaline, ACTH, etc.) in the bloodstream provides an *objective* measure of the amount of stress being experienced. However, the negative side of this approach is that it does not take account of how different stressors affect people (e.g. money worries produce a different type of stress than relationship problems do).

Mason (1975, see E&F p.123) found that different stressors produce different relative amounts of adrenaline and noradrenaline in different individuals, depending on the amount of fear, anger, and uncertainty created by the stressor. It would therefore be foolish to assume that measuring levels of hormones in the bloodstream would provide an accurate and reliable account of how much stress that person was feeling.

In addition, different people respond in different ways to stress, and the physiological account fails to account for this as it assumes that people are *passive* in their responses. In fact, people are not simply passive, but *active* in their response to stress. The individual's *interpretation* of how the stress affects them has an effect on their physiological response. For example, Symington et al. (1955, see E&F p.123) compared the physiological responses of two groups of dying patients consisting of those who were conscious and those who were in a coma. There were many more signs of physiological stress in the patients who remained conscious, presumably because they engaged in stressful physiological appraisal of their state.

Supporting Research

There are some studies that provide support for the hypothalamic–pituitary–adrenal axis, and its physiological explanation for the stress response:

- People without adrenal glands cannot produce enough cortisol and need to be given additional quantities of glucocorticoids (such as cortisol) if stressed in order to survive (Tyrell & Baxter, 1981, see E&F p.122).
- Brady's (1958, see E&F p.124) study with 'executive' monkeys provides support, as stress affected the production of digestive hormones causing stomach ulcers that eventually resulted in death.

OVER TO YOU

Use your textbook to consider the relationship between stress and a lie-detector machine (or polygraph, see E&F p.122). Consider ways in which people could 'fool' such a machine. Why does such a machine *not* provide an objective measure of stress?

HOMEOSTASIS

Homeostasis (meaning 'same state') is the steady state that the body tries to maintain, despite large changes in the surrounding environment. Maintaining homeostasis during the stress response is the responsibility of the ANS. Let us consider how this is done.

Carlson (1994) outlined the regulatory mechanisms that govern homeostasis, consisting of four parts:

- A **system variable**, such as temperature, water intake, or breathing rate, that needs to be regulated.
- A **set point**, or baseline value, which is the most ideal and appropriate value of the system variable.
- A **detector**, which is the thing that assesses the current value of the system variable.
- A **correctional mechanism**, which serves to reduce or eliminate the discrepancy between the actual value and the ideal value.

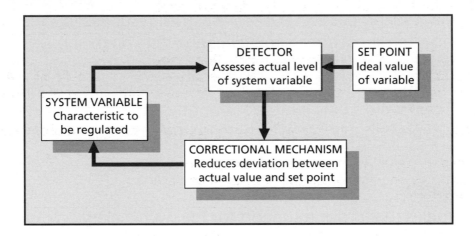

For example, when stressed your breathing rate increases. After stress, it is necessary to bring it back to normal. This is done by the parasympathetic branch of the ANS (the energy-saving branch) that returns the body to the set point.

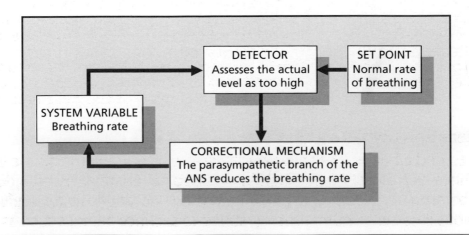

THE GENERAL ADAPTATION SYNDROME

Selye (1936, 1950, see E&F pp.124–126) put rats under enormous stress to assess their responses. He called their overall reaction the *General Adaptation Syndrome* (GAS). There are three stages of GAS, detailed below.

Stage 1: Alarm Reaction Stage

The ANS responds to the stressor:

- Activation of the hypothalamic–pituitary–adrenal axis, with associated release of ACTH.
- Release of glucocorticoids and adrenaline and noradrenaline.
- The individual is ready for 'fight or flight'.

Stage 2: Resistance Stage

All alarm systems are at full capacity, so the parasympathetic nervous system calls for a more cautious use of resources. Coping strategies, such as denial, are used, and the 'fight or flight' response is less effective. When the stress reduces there is a period of adjustment when:

- Adrenaline levels return to normal.
- The body attempts to restore lost energy.
- The body attempts to repair damage.
- Arousal levels are higher than usual but gradually reduce to normal.
- Adrenal glands become enlarged.

Stage 3: Exhaustion Stage

Eventually the physiological systems in the previous stages become ineffective, and the initial ANS symptoms of arousal reappear (increased heart rate, sweating, etc.). In extreme cases, attempts to return to a normal state fail, and the final stage occurs:

- Body resources are diminished due to failure of the parasympathetic system's control of metabolism and energy storage.
- Person becomes depressed, irritable, and unable to concentrate.
- Immune system collapses, and stress-related diseases are more likely.
- The person or animal may die.

EVALUATION OF SELYE'S WORK:

In support

- This work started the study of understanding stress.
- It has been very useful in predicting physiological responses to stress.
- The GAS provides a very useful model of the course of physical injuries and illness in cases where stress is prolonged.

Problems and limitations

- Most (though not all) of Selye's work was based on rats, so it may not apply to all animals, including humans.
- Overemphasis on the physiological responses to stress, without taking account of the effects of human cognitive factors (e.g. personality) in coping.
- Implies a passive response to stressors, despite evidence that people react differently to the same stressor, and the reaction depends on the individual, the situation, and the particular source of stress.

Ethical Considerations of Stress Research

Ethical codes try to find a balance between negative effects (e.g. pain) and the benefits gained from research. Since Selye's rats were literally stressed to death, it is considered unethical. However, it can be argued that since the work has provided the basis for useful research into the causes of serious illnesses in humans it is justified to sacrifice animals such as rats to do this.

STRESS AND PHYSICAL ILLNESS

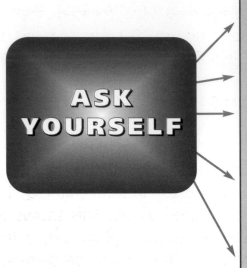

What is the relationship between stress and physical illness?

Does stress cause illness? Can you think of an example of how it might?

Does illness cause stress? Can you think of all the ways in which being ill may increase stress?

Does people's behaviour change when stressed? How does yours change, and could this adversely affect your health?

If a person is stressed, then becomes ill, what happens next with respect to the level of stress and severity of the illness?

The above questions may make you realise that the relationship between stress and health is complex. There are several ways in which stress may be related to illness:

- **Direct effect**. Stress may cause a person to become unwell. The study by Cohen et al. (1991, see E&F p.126) shows that there is a direct effect of stress on health.
- **Vulnerability**. Stress may cause people who are already predisposed to illness to become unwell, as it causes them to be physically vulnerable. The study by Kiecolt-Glaser et al. (1984, see E&F p.128) demonstrates how stress can reduce the efficiency of the immune system.
- **Behavioural effects**. Stress can cause people to behave in ways that may lead to deterioration in health. These can include poor eating habits, smoking, drinking too much alcohol, and experiencing a lack of sleep. Wills (1985, see E&F p.129) found that stressed adolescents are more likely to start smoking; Carey et al. (1993, see E&F p.129) found that stressed adults are more likely to resume smoking. Regarding alcohol, moderate consumption may actually reduce stress (Ogden, 1996, see E&F p.129), but a person who drinks too much is likely to be stressed.
- **Downward spiral of ill health and stress**. Being ill leads to stress, and the further decline in health leads to more stress and more illness. Therefore, a downward spiral is established.

STRESS AND ULCERS

Brady's (1958, see E&F p.124) study of 'executive' monkeys demonstrated the effect of stress on ulcers. Brady showed that the executive monkeys died of perforated ulcers that were caused by stress rather than the shocks themselves. The greatest damage was done during the 'rest' periods, when activity ceased in the SNS and the stomach was flooded with digestive enzymes and acid by the PNS.

Other studies have provided evidence that stress may be a causal factor in stomach ulcers:

- Weiner et al. (1957, see E&F p.124) classified army recruits as 'oversecretors' or 'undersecretors' of digestive enzymes. After four months of stressful training, 14% of the oversecretors and no undersecretors had developed ulcers. This shows that there is a relationship between stress and ulcers in humans. However, a large percentage of oversecretors did *not* develop ulcers, so there must be significant individual differences.
- Pinel (1997, see E&F p.126) showed that stress weakens the defences of the gastrointestinal tract against hydrochloric acid (the acid in the stomach) and this increases vulnerability to developing gastric ulcers.

Evaluation of Research into Stress and Ulcers

The issue of controllability is problematic with studies of stress. Some studies indicate that lack of control causes more stress than having total control. This contradicts Brady's conclusion that stress (rather than another factor) was responsible for the ulcers. In fact, his monkeys were not randomly selected—the executive monkeys were the ones who were quickest to learn to turn off the shock, so they may have been more anxious to start with.

Marshall et al. (1985, see E&F p.124) found strong evidence of another cause for stomach ulcers: the bacterium *Helicobacter pylori*. He claims that the ulcers in Brady's monkeys might have been caused by this bacterium rather than stress, or at least that stress might not have been the *only* cause.

OVER TO YOU

Look at the list of factors concerning the relationship between stress and physical illness presented on the previous page. Use this to explain why a busy executive of a large company may run the risk of eventually developing ulcers.

Describe the procedures and findings of one study into the relationship between stress and the immune system.
(6 marks)

STRESS AND CARDIOVASCULAR DISORDERS

The heart specialists Friedman and Rosenman (1959, see E&F p.141) noted that many of their patients with coronary heart disease (CHD) possessed a particular personality type called Type A personality.

TYPE A PERSONALITY

Behaviour

- Tend to be easily aroused to hostility.
- Have a sense of time urgency.
- Have competitive achievement strivings.
- Show an inability to delegate.
- Are unable to relax properly during rest periods.

Effects on the body

- Behaviours such as shouting, being impatient, intolerant, and worrying about deadlines speeds up arteriosclerosis, the process by which arteries fur up (a natural process) leading to increased likelihood of heart attack at a young age.
- Type A behaviours cause people to secrete high levels of hormones associated with the 'fight or flight' response (e.g. cortisol and adrenaline) and this may damage the heart, increasing the chances of CHD.

Recent Developments

Some researchers believe that only *some* aspects of Type A personality are linked to CHD. In a large-scale review, Booth-Kewley and Friedman (1987) concluded that chronic negative emotional states are important. This implies that it is hostility and feeling 'hard done by' that is related to CHD, rather than impatience and hurriedness.

How might this be? Matthews et al. (1977, see E&F p.141) found that hostility led to increased activity of the sympathetic nervous system and this led to the deterioration of an already vulnerable coronary system in Type A individuals.

Type C personality has also been implicated with illness (but not specifically CHD). Type C individuals are pleasant, hard working, conventional, and sociable. However, they are also repressed and respond to stress with a sense of helplessness. This may lead to vulnerability to cancer; Morris et al. (1981, see E&F p.140) found a link between suppression of anger and the development of malignant tumours, as emotional suppression is associated with increased stress, lowered effectiveness of the immune system, and stress. In addition, Thomas and Duszynski (1974, see E&F p.140) conducted a longitudinal study on medical students over 15 years and found that those who developed cancer also reported less family closeness. This may be due to stress, because people with poor social support systems suffer greater stress.

To give you an idea of the type of question you might be asked:

Describe the procedures and findings of one study into the relationship between stress and physical illness. **(6 marks)**

> **NOTE:** There are several studies you could use; the one we've just covered (Brady 1958, see E&F p.124), or Friedman and Rosenman (1974, see E&F p.141), or Kiecolt-Glaser et al. (1984, see E&F p.128). Remember the advice at the beginning of the book, choose a study and stick to it. Don't do the procedures of one study and then realise half-way through that you don't know the findings; make sure you know both before you start. Also, ensure that you cover only procedures and findings, as you won't get marks for any other information. The sample answer given here is for the Brady (1958) study.

Brady (1958) used pairs of monkeys, both of which were placed in a restraining chair that limited their movement. They were given an electric shock at certain intervals unless a lever was pressed within a short interval to prevent this. Only one monkey—the 'executive monkey'—could press the lever, and both monkeys received exactly the same shocks. Brady carried out a schedule of giving shocks at 20-second intervals for 23 days, on a 6 hours on and 6 hours off basis. He later tested various other schedules, including 18 hours on and 6 hours off, or 30 minutes on and 30 minutes off.

The findings of the study were that on the original schedule (6 hours on, 6 hours off) the executive monkeys died due to a perforated ulcer, but the yoked monkeys survived. No monkeys died from ulcers on the other schedules. When Brady tested the stomach of the executive monkeys on the 6 hours on, 6 hours off schedule, he found that stomach acidity was greatest during the rest period.

Outline two ways in which the body responds to stress. **(3 marks + 3 marks)**

When under stress the sympathetic branch of the nervous system stimulates the adrenal medulla to release the hormones adrenaline and noradrenaline into the bloodstream. These produce the reactions associated with the 'fight or flight' response, such as increased heart rate.

A second reaction is that the hypothalamus stimulates the pituitary gland to secrete the hormone ACTH (adrenocorticotrophic hormone), which in turn stimulates the adrenal cortex to release corticosteroids. These cause several reactions including stimulating the liver to release stored glucose to provide extra energy, inhibiting inflammation in case of injury, and suppressing any allergic reactions, e.g. difficulty with breathing.

OVER TO YOU

Describe the procedures and findings of one study into the relationship between stress and cardiovascular disorders. **(6 marks)**

SOURCES OF STRESS

ASK YOURSELF

What causes you stress?

Can you list and group these causes?

Do some things cause more stress than others?

This shows that there are many sources of stress; we will look at two areas:

LIFE CHANGES

For example:

- Moving house
- Going on holiday
- Losing your job

Can you think of some more?

WORKPLACE STRESSORS

For example:

- Job demands
- Work overload
- Horrid boss

Can you think of some more?

WHAT FACTORS MODERATE THE EFFECTS OF STRESS?

The individual. Some people cope with stress better than others: Type A, hardiness, and optimism (see E&F pp.139–141).

Culture. Stress exists in all cultures and communities but may differ both in the type of stress experienced and the way it is interpreted. For example, people in some cultures may find looking after infirm, elderly relatives easier because it is considered a responsibility rather than a burden.

Gender. Men and women respond differently to stress.

LIFE EVENTS

Holmes and Rahe (1967) constructed the *Social Readjustment Rating Scale* (SRRS, see E&F p.131) on which each life event was given a score and assessed as a 'life change unit' (LCU). For example:

- Death of a spouse   100
- Jail term   63
- Fired at work   47
- Vacation   13

This scale has been revised and used in over a thousand studies. It shows a positive relationship between scores and physical illness, e.g. a person scoring over 300 LCUs in a period of one year has much more chance of becoming mentally or physically ill than a lower scorer.

Do Life Events Cause Stress?

When considering whether life events cause stress, these are the essential points that you need to be aware of:

- The link between LCUs and illness is correlational, but correlation does *not* mean causation.
- Life changes may lead to behaviour that damages health, which is an indirect link.
- Some life changes on the scale are positive, e.g. being promoted at work, or having a busy Christmas with your family. Where the stress response leads to feelings of happiness it is referred to as *eustress*. There is no evidence that eustress is ill health, but the absence of positive life changes might increase stress.
- Personality and the amount of social support can influence the effect of life changes.
- The amount of stress for each life event (e.g. pregnancy) is not the same for everyone. You have to take account of circumstances, and individual differences in coping.

DAILY HASSLES

DeLongis et al. (1982, see E&F pp.133–134) devised a *hassles scale* to measure the effect of problems encountered as part of the routine of life (e.g. getting essays in on time, doing the washing). They compared the SRRS with their hassles scale and found the hassles scale to be a better predictor of ill health than the SRRS, as both the frequency and intensity of hassles were significantly correlated with overall health status and bodily symptoms (see E&F p.134). They also measured uplifts (e.g. good weather, recreation), but these seemed to have little effect on health.

However, the findings of DeLongis et al. may be biased. Their sample consisted of people aged over 45, so the hassles cannot be generalised. Measuring hassles ignores *ambient stressors*—chronic global conditions of the environment such as noise, poor housing, and poverty. Also, they ignored the fact that the same hassle can be experienced in different ways by different people, or by the same person on different occasions.

WORKPLACE STRESSORS

Both pressure of work and the work environment itself are sources of stress. Here are the main factors that affect workplace stress.

Environment

There are a number of environmental factors that affect workplace stress:

- **Overcrowding**. Calhoun (1962, see E&F pp.134–135) studied how the stress of overcrowding limited breeding activity in rats. Also, Freedman et al. (1975, see E&F p.135) correlated the incidence of pathological conditions in humans with overcrowded urban living conditions.
- **Temperature**. Baron and Ransberger (1978, see E&F p.135) demonstrated that incidences of violence could be related to high temperatures.
- **Pollution**. Non-smokers find working in a smoky environment unpleasant, and this leads to problems for smokers who have to go elsewhere to smoke.
- **Noise**. Glass et al. (1969, see E&F p.136) found that unpredictable noise causes the most stress, but even predictable noise creates some stress.
- **Predictability and controllability**. Langer and Rodin (1976, see E&F p.138) found that the less control and the lower the predictability, the more stress experienced.

Interpersonal Factors

Matteson and Ivancevich (1982, see E&F p.138) found that inability to get along with others was the most common source of stress in the workplace. In addition, Karasek et al. (1982, see E&F pp.138–139) showed that job satisfaction was related to the amount of support received from co-workers.

The concept of *burnout* (extreme emotional exhaustion) is liable in jobs that have a high emotional demand such as counselling, nursing, or teaching. Maslach and Jackson (1982, see E&F p.139) identified three psychosocial components to burnout as being emotional exhaustion, depersonalisation, and perceived inadequacy.

Role Conflict

When demands of the organisation conflict with the needs of workers, stress increases. Shirom (1989, see E&F p.137) found a correlation between CHD and perceived role conflict amongst white-collar workers. Margolis and Kroes (1974, see E&F p.137) found that white-collar foremen were seven times more likely to develop gastric ulcers than blue-collar workers, suggesting greater role conflict for those with more responsibility. Also, when the worker has to express one emotion whilst feeling another (e.g. staying cheerful when you are feeling unhappy), this causes role conflict. This is particularly likely in the policing and medical professions. Having too much work to do in too little time also causes role conflict. Sales (1969) reported that stress increases when workers effectively have to choose between quantity and quality of work.

Shift Work

Disrupted body rhythms make people feel unhappy, fatigued, or ill, and can increase the incidence of industrial accidents. Aschoff and Wever (1981) used the term *internal desynchronisation* to describe an imbalance between body rhythms and the sleep/wake cycle. Czeisler et al. (1982, see E&F p.138) found a correlation between shift work among manual labourers and raised accident rates, absenteeism, and ill health. They recommend shifts that go forwards clockwise and last for at least three weeks.

OVER TO YOU

Check out Kobasa's (1979, see E&F pp.140–142) work on hardiness and assess her suggestions for reducing the effect of workplace stress.

INDIVIDUAL DIFFERENCES IN COPING WITH STRESS

Gender

Do men and women differ in their response to stressors? Stoney et al. (1987, see E&F p.142) argued that men respond more strenuously to stressors. Stone et al. (1990, see E&F p.142) found that women showed lower increases in blood pressure when performing stressful tasks. Hastrup et al. (1980, see E&F p.143) found that some female hormones may help women cope. Carroll (1992, see E&F p.143) reported that social support is very important in reducing stress, and women are more likely to have confidantes and close friends. Haynes et al. (1980) found that Type A women are more likely to have CHD than Type B women; just as Friedman and Rosenman (1959, see E&F p.141) found with males.

EVALUATION

- Considerations of why men suffer more CHD than women may have important applications.
- Practical applications are also implicit in social support data.
- There is an emphasis on the importance of friendships for men.

Culture

Do different cultures experience different levels of stress? Anderson (1991) talks of *acculturation stress*, which is caused when minorities try to adopt the majority values, norms, and lifestyle. He found that African-Americans suffer more physical and mental ill health than white Americans. They also experience more life events, hassles, and racism. Black Americans experience higher levels of CHD than white Americans or black Africans. Cooper et al. (1999) stated that this could be explained by genetic factors, social factors (e.g. urban living), or psychosocial factors (e.g. greater prejudice, being poorly paid). Weg (1983) found that the long life expectancy of the Russian population he studied might be related to lower stress levels within the culture. This longevity may not be the direct result of reduced stress though because other factors, such as diet, genetics, and a good social support network were present.

EVALUATION

- Assessing cultural differences in stress is very difficult as other variables may operate.
- Understanding the relative stressors of cultures is essential when investigating health.
- Often only small samples are studied, and therefore generalisations are difficult.
- There may be some bias from researchers. It is very difficult for researchers from one culture to make objective assessments of the stresses experienced by people in another culture.

Personality

Does personality determine how well a person copes with stress? The hostile aspects of Type A personality are associated with CHD (see Friedman & Rosenman, 1959, 1974, E&F pp.140–141). Type C personality is associated with various cancers (see Morris et al., 1981, E&F p.140). The characteristics of hardiness (commitment, challenge, and sense of personal control) seem to prevent stress. Evidence from several large-scale studies (e.g. Kobasa et al., 1982, see E&F p.141) indicates that hardiness and exercise help prevent illness in highly stressed managers. Also, Kobasa et al. (1985, see E&F p.141) found that exercise, social support, and hardiness promote health in stressed executives.

EVALUATION

- Typologies such as A, C, and hardiness are not easy to assess.
- In Kobasa et al.'s work there was bias in sampling, as the research used white, middle-class males, and the validity of the measurements of hardiness was questioned (Funk, 1992, see E&F p.142).
- A practical application is that advice on attitude change may alleviate stress.

To give you an idea of the type of question you might be asked:

Describe how one factor may contribute to stress in the workplace.   (6 marks)

Shift work is now commonplace in the Western world, so it is important to consider the effect that it has on workers. Shift work can cause body rhythms such as body temperature to be out of synchronisation, and this causes stress. Aschoff and Wever (1981) used the term 'internal desynchronisation' to describe these effects that include fatigue, lethargy, and malaise. This can have a detrimental effect on mental health and the effect on work is that there is less productivity and a greater number of industrial accidents (Czeisler et al., 1982). Czeisler et al. investigated shift work patterns in a real factory and recommended that people should work on the same shift pattern for at least three weeks, and that shifts should move forwards in a clockwise manner. When this regime was introduced productivity increased, the number of accidents decreased, and there was a marked increase in job satisfaction, mental health, and better family relationships.

Describe the procedures and findings of one study into life changes as a source of stress.   (6 marks)

Holmes and Rahe (1967) constructed a scale known as the Social Readjustment Rating Scale (SRRS) in order to measure the degree of adjustment required by various life events that were part of everyday life, such as moving house, going on holiday, or starting a new job. The researchers assigned the arbitrary value of 50 'life change units' to getting married, and then rated 43 events according to the degree of readjustment they required. In order to do this they asked people to assign a value to the other events in relation to how much adjustment they required relative to getting married.

   Holmes and Rahe found a positive relationship between the likelihood of physical illness and scores on the SRRS for events of the previous year. For example, a person scoring between 200 and 300 life change units appeared to have a 50% chance of developing an illness. This rose to 80% for those scoring more than 300. The design of this research is correlational, so it does not allow us to be certain about any cause and effect relationship between life events and illness, but it does suggest that life events may at least contribute to some types of illness, although the overall relationship found was quite small.

OVER TO YOU

Describe two ways in which gender may modify the effects of stressors.

(3 marks + 3 marks)

CRITICAL ISSUE: STRESS MANAGEMENT

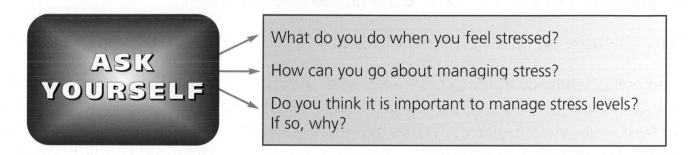

ASK YOURSELF

What do you do when you feel stressed?

How can you go about managing stress?

Do you think it is important to manage stress levels? If so, why?

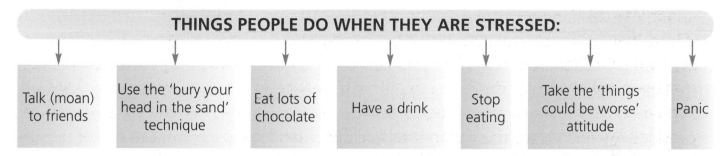

THINGS PEOPLE DO WHEN THEY ARE STRESSED:

Talk (moan) to friends

Use the 'bury your head in the sand' technique

Eat lots of chocolate

Have a drink

Stop eating

Take the 'things could be worse' attitude

Panic

There are many ways of coping with stress. Their effectiveness depends on the type of stressor, the particular individual, and the circumstances. We will look at physiological and psychological methods.

PHYSIOLOGICAL METHODS

- Biofeedback
- Anti-anxiety drugs

Most physiological methods are emotion-focused because they deal with reducing the associated anxiety.

PSYCHOLOGICAL METHODS

- Cognitive therapies
- Increasing control
- Social support

Some, but not all, psychological methods are problem-focused.

Lazarus and Folkman (1984, see E&K p.144) distinguish between emotion-focused and problem-focused strategies of stress management:

- Emotion-focused strategies attempt to directly reduce the stress response in the body.
- Problem-focused strategies reduce the importance of the problem, thus reducing the stress response in the body.
- Often tackling the problem itself (problem-focused) is not possible so a more realistic approach is to reduce the stress response (emotion-focused).

OVER TO YOU

How would you classify the things people do when they are stressed that appear above; problem-focused, emotion-focused, or neither?

BIOFEEDBACK

Biofeedback training is one of the physiological techniques that a person can learn to use to reduce their stress levels.

What Is Biofeedback Training?

- The individual is connected to a machine that gives information on ANS activity, e.g. tension in the neck muscles.
- They learn to relax thereby reducing tension.
- This relaxation is rewarding.
- Hence the individual learns by operant conditioning.
- The training involves three stages (see diagram).

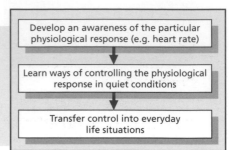

Develop an awareness of the particular physiological response (e.g. heart rate)

Learn ways of controlling the physiological response in quiet conditions

Transfer control into everyday life situations

How Does It Work?

- The individual learns to control involuntary stress responses via operant conditioning.
- The ANS responds to rewards and reinforcement, and is thus influenced by the person seeing the positive effects of relaxation.
- May be the result of restoration of homeostasis through relaxation.
- May be simply the effect of relaxation.

Evidence for Biofeedback

- Miller and DiCara (1967, see E&F p.146) demonstrated operant conditioning of involuntary muscles in rats.
- Dworkin and Dworkin (1988, see E&F p.145) worked with teenagers with spinal curvature who learnt to control spinal muscles and correct their posture.
- Budzynski et al. (1973, see E&F p.145) studied people who successfully reduced the number of tension headaches they suffered from.
- Curtis (2000, see E&F p.145) successfully treated sufferers of migraine headaches and Reynaud's disease.

EVALUATION

In support

- It has produced significant benefits, as evidenced by research studies.
- It is particularly effective with children who may be difficult to treat by other methods.
- Attanasio et al. (1985, see E&F p.147) found that they had more success treating children than adults. Children were less sceptical, and more enthusiastic, so it has a greater chance of working.

Problems and limitations

- Requires specialised equipment.
- Can be more expensive and difficult to use at home than other methods.
- It may not be the biofeedback itself that is important but the person developing a sense of control over their well being, learning simple relaxation techniques, all with a commitment to getting better.
- There is no evidence that it is more effective than simple relaxation with adults.
- Dworkin and Miller (1986, see E&F p.146) were not able to replicate Miller and DiCara's findings with rats, which casts doubt on the response of ANS to operant conditioning.

ANTI-ANXIETY DRUGS

The use of anti-anxiety drugs is another physiological method for dealing with the stress response, and they can be classified into barbiturates, benzodiazepines, and buspirone.

Barbiturates

- Work on the CNS and are very effective in reducing anxiety.
- There are side effects such as problems of concentration, lack of coordination, and slurred speech.
- Tend to be addictive, with withdrawal effects such as delirium and increased sweating.
- Now largely replaced with benzodiazepines due to side effects.

Benzodiazepines

- Act on neurotransmitters, especially GABA (gamma-amino-butyric-acid), e.g. Valium and Librium (see E&F p.147–148).
- GABA is produced when the body wants to relieve anxiety, and benzodiazepines increase it.
- This reduces serotonin activity, which increases arousal.
- When serotonin is acting on centres in the brain that reduce anxiety then decreased serotonin will arouse them and reduce anxiety.
- There are side effects such as drowsiness and memory impairment.
- Can react with alcohol unpredictably (Ashton, 1997, see E&F p.148).
- Can cause dependency and withdrawal symptoms.

Buspirone

- The most recent development in anti-anxiety drug therapy.
- Helps the effects of the neurotransmitter serotonin.
- Does not have sedative effects.
- Has side effects of headaches and depression (Goa & Ward, 1986, see E&F p.148)
- There are no withdrawal symptoms.

EVALUATION

- These drugs are effective at reducing intense feelings of stress and panic, but they do not address the actual causes of stress (but it is not always possible to do this anyway).
- Because of side effects and withdrawal symptoms Ashton (1997, see E&F p.148) recommended that benzodiazepines should be limited to short-term use of no more than four weeks, that all drugs should only be used to treat intense stress and anxiety, only minimum effective doses should be prescribed, and for those already dependant, withdrawal should be gradual.

COGNITIVE THERAPIES

Cognitive therapies offer an especially appropriate psychological method of dealing with stress. The assumptions behind the cognitive approach are that it is not the problem that is the core issue, but whether the way you think about the problem is *maladaptive* or not, and if you can be trained to restructure your thinking and self-beliefs, the problem may simply disappear.

Stress Inoculation Training

WHAT IS IT?

- A method to prevent stress responses occurring in the first place in order to *inoculate* the individual against stress.
- Meichenbaum (1977, 1985, see E&F p.149) developed a programme with three main phases: assessment, stress-reduction techniques, and application and follow-through.
- Assessment involves asking the question "What's the problem?"
- Stress-reduction involves relaxation techniques, and self-instruction (e.g. "If I keep calm, I can cope" and "Stop worrying, it's pointless").
- Application and follow-through involves imagining and role-playing the stress-reduction techniques and then applying them to real-life situations.

EVIDENCE FOR STRESS INOCULATION TRAINING

- Meichenbaum (1977, see E&F p.149) found that stress inoculation training generalises to several situations, so if people are trained in one situation (e.g. to cope with rat phobia) this generalises to another (e.g. a snake phobia). Therefore, it is more useful than specific treatments.

EVALUATON

- Based on well-established techniques such as relaxation and gaining control.
- Good at treating responses to moderately stressful situations.
- Not so good with responses to very intense stressful situations.
- Improves self-confidence and self-efficacy (belief in the ability to cope) in those who are depressed, and provides a sense of control.

Hardiness Training

WHAT IS IT?

- The use of three coping strategies developed by Kobasa (1986, see E&F p.150) to enhance hardiness; focusing, reconstructing stress situations, and compensating through self-improvement.
- Focusing involves being aware of physical signs of stress.
- Reconstructing stress situations by listing how a situation might have turned out better or worse allows the individual to feel more positive because they have to recognise that things *could* have been worse than they were.
- Compensating through self-improvement involves taking on another challenge that can be mastered to prove that you can cope in the face of a stressor that cannot be changed.

EVIDENCE FOR HARDINESS TRAINING

- Fischman (1987) taught a small number of executives these strategies, and they had greater job satisfaction, fewer headaches, and better sleep patterns.
- Sarafino (1990, see E&F p.150) reported that those who have undergone hardiness training score higher on a test of hardiness, report feeling less stressed, and have lower blood pressure than they did before.

EVALUATON

- Fischman's study was done on a small scale, and there was no follow-up, so results may have been down to increased attention and communication only.
- Some studies offer limited support, such as Canellen and Blaney (1984) who found that hardiness training only works in conjunction with social support.
- Some research offers no support, such as Schmied and Lawler (1986) who found no relationship between hardiness and illness in female secretaries.
- The original research was based on a male population and may not generalise to women.

ROLE OF CONTROL IN THE PERCEPTION OF STRESS

Another psychological technique for managing stress is that of increasing a person's sense of control.

Having a sense of control over a situation has been shown to reduce stress. Glass et al. (1969, see E&F p.136) studied the effects of noise on commitment to an insoluble task and found that those who could control the noise were more persistent at attempting to solve the task. Langer and Rodin (1976, see E&F p.138) found that the health of residents in old people's homes tended to deteriorate if they were not given more personal control over their lives. Those who had choices and were allowed to make decisions were happier, more active, and lived longer than those who had no choices available to them.

Evidence for Increased Sense of Control

Personal control is an important element of hardiness, and it also reduces the extent to which a situation may be experienced as stressful. It has been suggested that having a sense of control may boost the immune system:

- Breier et al. (1987, see E&F p.151) found that those who could control noise had lower levels of adrenaline than those who had no control over noise levels.
- Laudenslager et al. (1983, see E&F p.151) found that increasing control had a direct effect on the immune system in rats that were injected with cancer cells, as they were more likely to reject the cancer cells if they were in control of electric shocks.
- Sense of control may reduce the chance of learned helplessness. However, as Brady's study of executive monkeys showed (see E&F p.124) control does help to fight infection, but responsibility over time can lead to serious detrimental effects on health.

Evaluation

Although having a sense of control increases self-esteem and general effectiveness, there are occasions when low control can alleviate stress, as with Brady's monkeys. Being a passenger in an aircraft can be less stressful than being a pilot! This applies particularly in uncontrollable situations.

To give you an idea of the type of question you might be asked:

Explain one physiological approach to stress management. **(6 marks)**

Biofeedback is one physiological approach to stress management. It is a technique in which a person is connected to a machine that provides information (feedback) about the working of a particular activity in the body, such as blood pressure, together with instructions on how to control it. These instructions usually involve relaxation training.

The technique works by operant conditioning. Seeing the effect of reduction in, for example, blood pressure, acts as a reinforcer. Eventually the bodily activity can be controlled without the machine providing feedback.

Miller and DiCara (1967) pioneered research on biofeedback and they believed that even the involuntary muscles that are controlled by the autonomic nervous system could be voluntarily controlled by operant conditioning.

Outline two psychological approaches to managing the effects of stress.
(3 marks + 3 marks)

According to Kobasa, one way to manage stress is to develop or increase hardiness. This involves three stages: firstly, recognising the physical signs of stress; secondly, by considering how a stressful situation can be dealt with (and how much worse it could be); and thirdly, by recognising that some stressors cannot be avoided nor dealt with and it's then a good idea to master another challenge so that you are reassured that you can cope.

Another way of managing the effects of stress involves stress inoculation training (developed by Meichenbaum). This involves three stages: firstly, assessing how you usually cope with stress and abandoning the poor coping mechanisms that you might be employing; secondly, learning stress reduction techniques such as relaxation; and thirdly, role-playing to practise techniques so you are well prepared to cope when stress comes into your life.

OVER TO YOU

Outline one strength and one weakness of one method of stress management.
(3 marks + 3 marks)

Individual Differences
ABNORMALITY

What's it about?

Research into individual differences looks at why people differ along certain dimensions such as intelligence, personality, and mental health. This involves examining the role that both genetics and the environment play in shaping us into the people that we become. Studies of individual differences embrace a range of perspectives. The biological approach explores our differences in terms of our genetics, biochemistry, and neuroanatomy. The psychodynamic approach focuses on our early childhood experiences and unresolved conflicts. The cognitive perspective suggests that differences between us stem from different ways of thinking about the world. The behaviourists explain our differences by looking at different reinforcement histories and conditioning. In addition to these perspectives psychologists also devise classification systems and methods of measuring individual differences, and treatments when differences are considered abnormal.

What's in this unit?

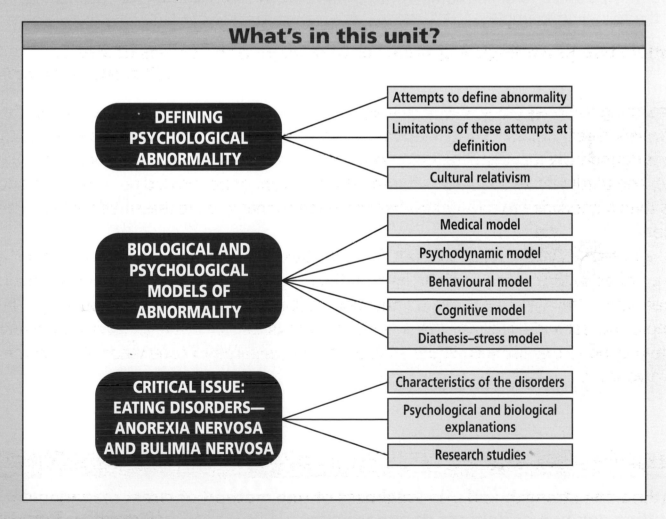

DEFINING KEY TERMS AND CONCEPTS

You need to be able to define and explain the key terms listed in blue below. The other concepts listed in black will aid your understanding of abnormality. Make a list of definitions of the following key terms, and if you get stuck, go to the glossary at the end of the book.

Abnormality	Statistical infrequency/	Enmeshment
Anorexia nervosa	deviation from statistical	Ethnocentrism
Bulimia nervosa	norms	Ideal mental health
Cultural relativism	Aversion therapy	Medical/biological model
Deviation from ideal mental	Behavioural model of	of abnormality
health	abnormality	Modelling
Deviation from social	Cognitive model of	Psychodynamic model of
norms	abnormality	abnormality
Eating disorder	Cognitive restructuring	Systematic desensitisation
Failure to function	Defence mechanisms	Token economy
adequately	DSM-IV	

You may be asked to define some of these key terms in the exam. To give you an idea, look at the following example.

With reference to clinical characteristics, explain what is meant by 'bulimia nervosa'. (6 marks)

Bulimia nervosa involves binge eating—usually in secret—followed by inappropriate behaviour that attempts to compensate for any resulting weight gain. This often involves self-induced vomiting, but may also include taking large numbers of laxatives, misuse of diuretics and enemas, excessive exercise, or fasting.

If the main method of purging is self-induced vomiting, then there are likely to be medical side-effects, such as erosion of tooth enamel and an imbalance of sodium and potassium in the body fluids. In order to be diagnosed as bulimic on DSM-IV criteria, the individual would have to indulge in binging and compensatory behaviour at least twice a week over at least a three-month period.

A typical pattern of behaviour involves an overwhelming urge to eat, accompanied by considerable tension, followed by a loss of control that results in binge eating. The binge eating provides a release of tension. This is, however, followed by feelings of guilt and self-disgust. It is a vicious cycle from which sufferers find it difficult to escape, as the person's self-evaluation depends excessively on their shape.

People suffering from bulimia nervosa tend to be within 10% of the normal weight range, but their weight fluctuates considerably.

OVER TO YOU

Outline any two definitions of abnormality. (3 marks + 3 marks)

DESCRIBING AND EVALUATING KEY STUDIES

One kind of AO1 examination question is described as the 'APFCC' question. In this question you are asked to describe the aims, procedures, findings, conclusions, and give criticisms (APFCC) of a study into a named topic. In any question you will be asked for one or two of these, for example, 'aims and conclusions' or 'findings and conclusions'. There is not a requirement that these are given in balance as the question is marked out of 6 marks (for example, if you provide findings only then you may receive a maximum of 4 marks). You may be asked for the 'findings plus one criticism', in which case the question is marked as '3 marks + 3 marks'.

You may also be asked questions about research more generally, rather than about a specific study. In this case the question will say 'Describe the findings of research into…' (6 marks). You may also be asked about 'conclusions'. In such questions you may describe the findings/conclusions from one study, or from several studies, or even from a theory (which is a form of research).

If the question asks for 'procedures and findings', any other material will not receive credit, such as information relating to aims or conclusions. Make sure you understand the difference, for example, between a finding (the facts) and a conclusion (what the findings show us).

For the module on Individual Differences you need to know the following APFCC studies:

KEY STUDY TOPICS	EXAMPLE	WHERE TO FIND IT	OTHER RELATED RESEARCH
Biological explanations of anorexia	Holland et al. (1988)	Appendix	Strober and Humphrey (1987, see E&F p.186) Park et al. (1995, see E&F p.186) Garfinkel and Garner (1982, see E&F p.188)
Biological explanations of bulimia	Kendler et al. (1991)	Appendix	Strober and Humphrey (1987, see E&F p.186) Barlow and Durand (1995, see E&F p.188)
Psychological explanations of anorexia and bulimia	Behar et al. (2001)	Appendix	Cooper (1994, see E&F p.191) Nasser (1986, see E&F pp.191–192)
Psychological explanations of bulimia	Jaeger et al. (2002)	Appendix	Lee et al. (1992, see E&F p.192)
If asked to give information on a study of biological/psychological explanations of eating disorders, you can use any of the studies listed above.			

OVER TO YOU

You need to be able to write for three minutes on aims, procedures, findings, conclusions, and criticisms. In order to do this well in the examination it might help to identify key words and concepts to recall. You only need a few for each of the APFCCs (in other words a few key concepts for the aims and a few for the procedures—a maximum of five). Do this for each study listed above.

DEFINING PSYCHOLOGICAL ABNORMALITY

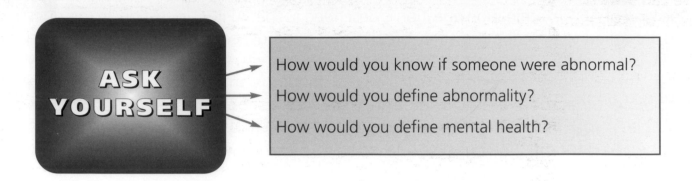

ASK YOURSELF

How would you know if someone were abnormal?

How would you define abnormality?

How would you define mental health?

Several theories have been proposed to aid our understanding of abnormality. The starting point of all these theories is an attempt to define abnormality, but this is harder than most people think.

After reading your textbook you should be familiar with the following ideas:

- Statistical infrequency.
- Deviation from social norms.
- Failure to function adequately.
- Deviation from ideal mental health.

This unit also requires an understanding of different theoretical perspectives including:

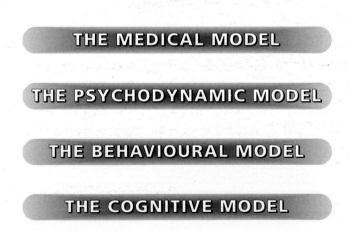

THE MEDICAL MODEL

THE PSYCHODYNAMIC MODEL

THE BEHAVIOURAL MODEL

THE COGNITIVE MODEL

For each, you will need to be able to:

- Describe the model.
- Give examples of how the model is used to explain and treat abnormality.
- Evaluate the model.

We can now consider each of these approaches to defining psychological abnormality in turn.

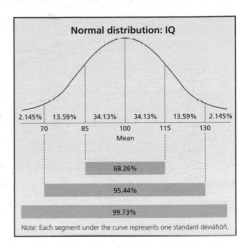

Statistical Infrequency

When considering statistical infrequency (see E&F p.158) the focus here is on rarity. If very few people are deemed to show the behaviour or thinking, it is described as abnormal. Given that some psychologists argue that most human traits are distributed along a normal curve, it could be argued that people who are 2 standard deviations above or below the mean (i.e. in the extreme 2.145% of the population) are abnormal.

There are certain limitations to this approach:

- Where does one draw the line? Why should being in the bottom 2.145% be seen as abnormal, but not being in the bottom 5%?
- The definition fails to distinguish between rare desirable and rare undesirable behaviour, i.e. people in the top 2.145% are viewed differently from people in the bottom 2.145%.
- The definition doesn't take account of cultural variations.
- Some types of mental illness are thought to be increasing, including depression, and therefore they are not particularly rare.

Deviation From Social Norms

To define people's mental health in terms of deviation from social norms (see E&F p.159) suggests that those who behave in a socially deviant or incomprehensible way should be regarded as abnormal because they break with conventions and do not do what is normally expected. This approach has obvious limitations:

- Norms change over time so that what might have been seen as socially deviant 50 years ago may be the norm today, such as living together before getting married.
- Whether behaviour is perceived as deviant is dependent on context. Taking off one's clothes to get in a bath is the norm. However, taking them off in a lesson is not!
- At times, breaking with the dominant culture is something to be applauded rather than criticised as being abnormal. For example, freedom fighters who opposed apartheid in South Africa were not abnormal, but people who believed in racial equality.

Failure To Function Adequately

Underlying this definition (see E&F p.161) is the notion that people who cannot cope with the demands of everyday life, such as getting up, getting dressed, and being able to look after themselves, may in some ways be perceived as abnormal. Rosenhan and Seligman (1989, see E&F p.162) expanded this approach to cover a list of seven abnormal characteristics: suffering, maladaptiveness, vividness and unconventionality of behaviour, unpredictability and loss of control, irrationality and incomprehensibility, observer discomfort, and violation of moral and ideal standards.

The limitations of this approach are as follows:

- It involves making value judgements about others as to what constitutes failure to function adequately, and such judgements will always be open to error and misinterpretation.
- The person themselves may not think they have a problem even though others think they do. It might not worry them that they don't get up or get dressed, so using failure to function adequately as a criterion for abnormality may not be appropriate.
- Suffering is part of human life and it is difficult to decide when suffering is maladaptive after serious life events have occurred.

Deviation From Ideal Mental Health

This definition (see E&F p.163) looks at the problem of defining abnormality by focusing on what we understand by normal/mentally healthy, and working backwards from that. Jahoda (1958, see E&F p.165) suggested that normal mental health includes:

- **Self-attitudes**. Having high self-esteem and a strong sense of identity.
- **Personal growth**. The extent to which an individual grows, develops, and becomes self-actualised affects their mental health.
- **Integration**. How the above two concepts are integrated, which can be assessed by how an individual will cope with a stressful situation.
- **Autonomy**. The degree to which a person is independent of social influences and able to regulate himself or herself.
- **Perception of reality**. Being free from the need to distort one's own perception of reality, and demonstrating empathy and social sensitivity.
- **Environmental mastery**. The extent to which an individual is successful and well adapted.

Abnormality would therefore be an absence of these qualities. On the positive side, this approach considers how people's lives can be improved, but there are also important limitations:

- There is some concern that measuring mental health differs markedly from measuring physical health (e.g. how do we know that someone has a strong sense of identity?).
- After looking at the criteria it might be suggested that few people are in fact mentally healthy.
- The list of attributes has been criticised for being ethnocentric in that it describes individualist cultures (e.g. the United States) rather than collectivist ones (e.g. China).

CULTURAL RELATIVISM

Given that cultures differ in their beliefs, values and norms, it has been argued that we cannot make absolute statements about what is normal and what is abnormal in human behaviour. For example, in the Trobriand Islands it is normal for a son to clean his dead father's bones and give them to relatives to wear, and it would be seen as abnormal if the widow did not wear the bones of her deceased husband. In British culture, such behaviour would be a cause of concern. The concept of *cultural relativism* means that value judgements are relative to individual cultural contexts and we cannot make absolute statements about what is normal or abnormal in human behaviour.

To give you an idea of the type of question you might be asked:

Outline the 'statistical infrequency' and 'deviation from social norms' definitions of abnormality. **(3 marks + 3 marks)**

The statistical infrequency definition of abnormality focuses on rarity and suggests that any behaviour that is particularly rare within a population can be deemed abnormal. This definition is based on the notion that many human traits follow a normal distribution. People who are two standard deviations either above or below the mean (i.e. within 2% of the population) may be perceived as abnormal.

Another definition of abnormality suggests that people who deviate from social norms are abnormal. The underlying suggestion here is that societies develop codes and norms to govern our behaviour. People who act in bizarre ways or break these norms are perceived as abnormal.

Describe some of the limitations associated with each of the definitions identified above. **(6 marks)**

One limitation of the statistical infrequency approach is that the definition fails to distinguish between rare 'desirable' behaviour and rare 'undesirable' behaviour. Another limitation is that the definition fails to take into account cultural and historical variations in that, whilst single mothers in Britain were relatively rare at the turn of the nineteenth century, they are now much more frequent. Also, where does one decide to draw the line in terms of rarity—2% or 5%?

One major concern with the deviation from social norms definition of abnormality is that what may be seen as deviant in one century may not be seen as deviant in another. In addition, whether behaviour is seen as deviant is often dependent on context in that, whilst taking off one's clothes to get into a bath is normal, the same behaviour in a classroom is not. Finally, people who deviate from social norms may be opinion leaders, who are challenging the status quo in order to improve society, as was the case with the leaders of the civil rights movements in the United States. It would not be reasonable to label such people as abnormal.

OVER TO YOU

Explain the terms 'abnormality' and 'cultural relativism'. **(3 marks + 3 marks)**

BIOLOGICAL AND PSYCHOLOGICAL MODELS OF ABNORMALITY

ASK YOURSELF

Why do people become mentally ill?

How does our biology influence our mental health?

Do our early childhood experiences make some of us more vulnerable to mental illness?

Do people who are mentally ill think about their experiences differently from other people?

What models have been proposed to aid our understanding of mental illness?

THE MAIN MODELS OF ABNORMALITY INCLUDE:

MEDICAL MODEL

PSYCHODYNAMIC MODEL

BEHAVIOURAL MODEL

COGNITIVE MODEL

The medical approach

The psychodynamic approach

The behavioural approach

The cognitive approach

MEDICAL MODEL

Assumptions of the Medical Model

The medical model (see E&F pp.168–172) assumes that abnormal behaviours result from physical problems and should be treated medically. Key areas of interest focus on genetics, biochemistry, infections, and neuroanatomy. The implication of this model for treatment is that it is possible to cure the patient by changing their biological processes, and the following treatments are seen to be suitable:

- Electroconvulsive therapy (ECT).
- Drugs.
- Psychosurgery.

SUPPORTING STUDIES

There have been a number of studies that have revealed a link between biology and mental illness:

- Masterson and Davis (1985, see E&F p.168) found that relatives of schizophrenics were 18 times more likely to be diagnosed with schizophrenia than randomly selected members of the population.
- Sherrington et al. (1988, see E&F p.169) conducted a gene-mapping study that found evidence of a link between schizophrenia and a gene located on chromosome 5 (although subsequent research has been unable to confirm this).
- In the late nineteenth century the neurologist von Krafft-Ebing (see E&F p.169) studied sufferers of the mental illness 'general paresis', which was believed to be caused by the syphilis bacterium. He argued that if this was the case then it should not be possible to re-infect someone who had general paresis with syphilis, because they would have immunity. This was found to be true, and he proved that the paretics he tried to re-infect must have had syphilis before. Once this causal relationship had been established a cure could be found and general paresis was eradicated.
- Barr et al. (1990, see E&F p.168) found increased incidence of schizophrenia in mothers who had flu when they were pregnant, thereby suggesting that the cause of the disorder might be a disease.
- The condition phenylketonuria (PKU, see E&F p.171)—a form of mental retardation caused by an inability to process the amino acid phenylalanine—can be simply and effectively treated by physical means.

EVALUATION

In support

- The medical model does explain some disorders, e.g. PKU.
- The model is based on well-established sciences.
- It does help provide some treatments for some disorders, e.g. depression, but treatments do not help all sufferers, e.g. some schizophrenics.
- A positive ethical issue is that it removes the 'blame' culture from the patient.

Problems and limitations

- It raises the question of whether mental illness is the same as physical illness.
- By focusing on the symptoms, less attention is given to the patients' feelings, experiences, and life events as possible causes.
- A negative ethical issue is that genetic explanations of mental illness may result in relatives becoming anxious, and such explanations also raise questions and concerns about the use of sterilisation to prevent the continuation of such disorders.

PSYCHODYNAMIC MODEL

Assumptions of the Psychodynamic Model

The psychodynamic model (see E&F pp.172–176) contrasts sharply with the medical model by suggesting that mental illness 'arises out of unresolved unconscious conflicts in early childhood'. The model is based on the Freudian understanding that much of our behaviour is driven by unconscious motives and that childhood is a critical period of development. Key areas of interest focus on:

- The mind—the conflicts between the id, ego, and superego.
- The stages of psychosexual development.
- Defence mechanisms.

Conflicts occur most often between the id's desire for immediate gratification and the superego's desire to maintain moral standards and ideals. When considering Freud's stages of psychosexual development (oral, anal, phallic, latency, and genital), the psychodynamic viewpoint states that at times of great personal stress a person may regress to an earlier stage of development or fixation. Conflicts cause anxiety, and the ego defends itself against anxiety by using defence mechanisms such as *repression, projection,* and *displacement*. The implication of this model for treatment is to attempt to bring the repressed material into consciousness to gain insight. This is achieved by psychoanalysis, including *dream analysis* and *free association*.

SUPPORTING STUDIES

Psychodynamic theories tend to gain support from case studies rather than experimental data:

- Freud (1910, see E&F p.174) and his colleague Breuer studied the case of Anna O. This case study explains Anna's inability to drink, despite her tormenting thirst, being traced back to her witnessing her governess' dog drinking from her glass. Also, Anna's disturbed eye movements were traced back to caring for her sick father and needing to hide her anxiety and tears.

EVALUATION

In support

- The model changed people's perspectives about mental illness by looking at psychological factors.
- It identifies traumatic childhood experiences as having a role in adult disorders.
- A positive ethical point is that the person is not responsible for their disorder or behaviour, since it is hidden from them in their unconscious.

Problems and limitations

- There is an overemphasis on the patient's past, rather than their current problems.
- There is an overemphasis on sexual experiences, rather than exploring other interpersonal and social factors.
- Freud has been accused of sexism since the theory stresses that biology is destiny, rather than seeing inequality in terms of social or cultural factors.
- The model is non-scientific since it cannot be falsified (it is not possible to disprove these theories).
- Ethically speaking, the emphasis on early childhood may result in parental blame.
- There are also problems surrounding false memory syndrome, as it has been found that patients undergoing psychoanalysis have made untrue allegations about childhood abuse that have no basis in fact.

BEHAVIOURAL MODEL

Assumptions of the Behavioural Model

The behavioural model (see E&F pp.176–180) suggests that most human behaviour is learned and that mental disorders arise from maladaptive learning. Key areas of interest focus on:

- Classical conditioning.
- Operant conditioning.
- Observational learning and modelling.

The implication of this model for treatment is that if the abnormal behaviour is the result of maladaptive learning, then the behaviour can be 'unlearned' using one of the following techniques:

- Aversion therapy and systematic desensitisation (based on classical conditioning).
- Token economy and modelling (based on operant conditioning).

SUPPORTING STUDIES

The nature of the behaviourist approach means that it lends itself well to research:

- Watson and Rayner's (1920, see E&F p.178) well-known study of Little Albert demonstrated classical conditioning of the fear response by frightening him with a loud noise every time he saw a white furry object. Eventually any neutral white fluffy stimulus produced the same fear response as the frightening stimulus.
- Menzies and Clarke (1993, see E&F p.178) found that only 2% of children who suffered from a water phobia had had a traumatic experience with water, suggesting that phobias are not always conditioned.
- Ayllon and Azrin (1968, see E&F p.179) studied the use of a token economy in an institutional setting whereby female patients who had been hospitalised for 16 years were put on a token economy regime and rewarded for making beds and combing their hair. They found that the number of chores they voluntarily performed each day rose from 5 to 40.
- Bandura et al. (1969, see E&F p.179) studied the use of modelling to treat phobias, where the patient models the response of the therapist to the feared object. They found that using live examples (such as real snakes) worked better than using symbolic representations of the feared object (such as models of snakes).

EVALUATION

In support

- It is successful in treating specific phobias.
- Some psychologists suggest that the behaviourist model is sensitive to environmental cues and social or cultural factors. However, others argue that the model supports the dominant culture by getting patients to conform to what is expected by society (Allyon and Azrin's study has been used to argue this).
- A positive ethical point is that this model gives the patient the power to change, since they can unlearn what has been learned.
- The patient is not seen as a victim of an illness.

Problems and limitations

- The focus is on the symptoms rather than the cause of the symptoms and this, according to the psychoanalysts, will lead to symptom substitution (the idea that another disorder will develop since the cause of the initial disorder has not been dealt with).
- By exaggerating the importance of the environment it minimises the role of biological factors such as genetics.
- It is oversimplistic.
- The treatments used have been criticised for being unethical, e.g. aversion therapy and token economies.
- The emphasis on behaviour tends to devalue the person's feelings and experiences.
- There is some concern that the treatments are for the benefit of society rather than to benefit the patient.

COGNITIVE MODEL

Assumptions of the Cognitive Model

The cognitive model (see E&F pp.181–183) states that maladaptive behaviour is caused by faulty and irrational cognitive processes. Key areas of interest focus on:

- Making incorrect inferences.
- Being dominated by the 'shoulds', 'oughts', and 'musts' of life.
- The cognitive triad, involving negative thoughts about oneself, the world, and the future.

The implication of this model for treatment is that if the problem is caused by distorted thinking then the therapist has to help the patient replace the irrational and distorted thoughts with ones that are rational. This is achieved by the process of *cognitive restructuring*, which intends to make the patient's thoughts and beliefs more positive and rational.

SUPPORTING STUDIES

Research has tended to explore links between disorders and the way people think, as well as seeing if changing patients' thought patterns improves their condition:

- Beck and Clark (1988, see E&F p.182) found that distorted and irrational beliefs are common among patients with mental disorders, most notably anxiety disorders and depression. However, the link has not been shown for most other disorders.
- Meichenbaum's (1977, 1985, see E&F p.149) stress inoculation training uses the cognitive restructuring technique successfully.

EVALUATION

In support

- This model focuses on people's experiences, feelings, and interpretations.
- It gives people power to change and increases their self-belief.
- A positive ethical point is that it allows the person to take responsibility for changing their undesirable behaviour.

Problems and limitations

- The model is limited in its application in that it works better with anxiety disorders than schizophrenia.
- It tends to ignore other possible causes such as genetics or faulty biochemistry.
- It is unclear whether the negative thinking is the cause of the depression or actually the result of the depression.
- It raises the ethical question of whether people have the right to say that someone's belief system is faulty, especially if that person's life experiences support their negative world view.
- It could be argued that this model implies that the person is responsible for their unhappiness.

THE MULTI-DIMENSIONAL APPROACH

Which Model Is the Best?

Asking the question "Which model is the best?" is not particularly helpful, as it takes the wrong approach. Rather, it is more sensible to ask how the models can be used to explain a range of disorders or offer treatments at different levels or stages of the disorder.

Some models are more useful to explain schizophrenia (e.g. biological model), whilst other models are more useful at explaining phobias (e.g. behavioural model).

Most psychologists adopt a multi-dimensional approach to abnormality. One way to express this is in terms of the *diathesis–stress model*.

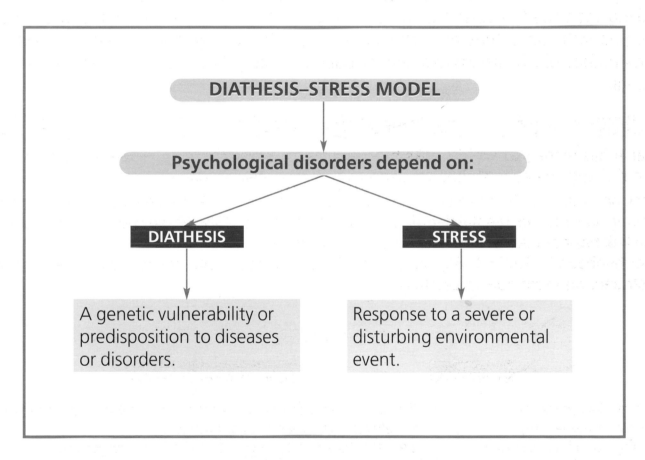

The key notion in the diathesis–stress model is that both diatheses *and* stress are necessary for a psychological disorder to occur. This approach explains the following:

- When one identical twin develops a disorder, their twin does not always go on to develop the disorder—because an *environmental trigger* is required.
- When an individual has a disorder but their sibling who has had similar childhood experiences does not develop the disorder—because they are genetically different, so only one sibling had the *genetic vulnerability* in the first place.

To give you an idea of the type of question you might be asked:

Outline assumptions of the psychodynamic model in relation to its views on the treatment of abnormality.
(6 marks)

Underlying the psychodynamic model of abnormality is the idea that mental illness is the result of unconscious unresolved conflicts, which the Freudians usually trace back to early childhood experiences.

Treatment involves getting the repressed material back into the patient's consciousness so that they can gain some insight into their condition and confront their fears or desires. To do this, Freudians undertake dream analysis, since they believe that dreams are 'the royal road to consciousness'. In addition, patients are also asked to use free association, which involves them saying whatever comes into their mind.

The analyst then interprets the patient's dreams and thoughts, revealing their hidden fears and desires. Once these are revealed, it is believed that the patient is better able to cope with life.

Interestingly, even if the patient vehemently disagrees with the interpretation given, it does not necessarily convince the therapist that he or she is wrong, as this is seen as resistance of the patient's mind to their unacceptable impulses.

Give two criticisms of the behavioural model in relation to its views on the causes of abnormality.
(3 marks + 3 marks)

One problem with the behavioural model is that it is largely based on research with non-human animals. The principles of classical and operant conditioning may be appropriate explanations for simple behaviours but conditioning ignores the influence of emotion and thinking. Such influences are not part of non-human animal behaviour.

A second criticism is a positive one. Explanations derived from the behavioural model have been successful in terms of producing therapies that are effective for certain disorders such as phobias. This means that the explanation is correct, at least for these disorders. It is also a good explanation because it is very testable—psychologists can conduct experiments to demonstrate how conditioning results in behaviours like phobias.

OVER TO YOU

Outline assumptions of the cognitive model in relation to its views on the treatment of abnormality.
(6 marks)

CRITICAL ISSUE: EATING DISORDERS—ANOREXIA NERVOSA AND BULIMIA NERVOSA

What characterises eating disorders?

How do the models of mental illness help us understand eating disorders?

Are women more likely to suffer from eating disorders than men? If so, how can we explain the gender differences?

CHARACTERISTICS OF THE DISORDERS

ANOREXIA NERVOSA

- Intense fear of becoming fat despite being underweight.
- Distorted thinking about body image and weight.
- Body weight is less than 85% of expected weight.
- Amenorrhoea (absence of menstruation) for 3 or more cycles.
- 90% of cases diagnosed are female.
- Onset is usually in adolescence.
- Potentially very serious as 5% die of the disorder.
- Most common in middle-class individuals.

BULIMIA NERVOSA

- Numerous episodes of binge eating resulting in huge amounts of food being eaten in a 2-hour period.
- Lack of control over eating behaviour when bingeing.
- Body weight is usually within 10% of normal weight, but fluctuates.
- Bingeing occurs on average at a rate of twice a week for a 3-month period.
- Self-evaluation depends excessively on their shape.
- Age of onset is usually around 20.
- 50% more common in females than in males.

Can be of purging type, in which self-induced vomiting, misuse of laxatives, diuretics, enemas, or other medications are used to prevent weight gain.

Can be of non-purging type, in which fasting or excessive exercise is used to prevent weight gain.

EXPLANATIONS OF EATING DISORDERS

Explanations of eating disorders vary depending on the model being used. One major difficulty in explaining eating disorders is that although there are differences between anorexia nervosa and bulimia nervosa, people may move between the two disorders in their quest for a sub-optimal bodyweight. For this reason they have been described as 'variations on a theme' and explanations for anorexia nervosa are often relevant for bulimia nervosa. Where the approach is more relevant to one eating disorder than another it will be highlighted.

The Biological Approach

This approach explores the causes of eating disorders in terms of genetics, biochemistry, neuroanatomy, and infection. Each of these will be considered in turn.

EVIDENCE FOR THE INFLUENCE OF GENETICS

Research with twins suggests that anorexia seems to be more likely than bulimia to be influenced by genetic factors. In a study of anorexia in twins and triplets, Holland et al. (1988, see E&F p.187) found that there were the following concordance rates: MZ—56% and DZ—5%. In a study of bulimia in twins, Kendler et al. (1991, see E&F p.187) found that there were the following concordance rates: MZ—23% and DZ—9%.

EVALUATION OF GENETICS RESEARCH

- If the cause were purely genetic there would be a concordance rate of 100%.
- Observational learning could play a key role with identical twins, rather than genetics.
- Perhaps being an identical twin is a contributing factor, since they may be treated more similarly than non-identical twins.
- These results do not explain why there has been a large increase in the number of cases in recent years.
- Males with anorexic twin brothers do not seem to develop anorexia.

EVIDENCE FOR THE INFLUENCE OF BIOCHEMISTRY

Research suggests that neurotransmitters such as serotonin and noradrenaline may be implicated in explanations of both anorexia and bulimia. Fava et al. (1989, see p.188) found links between anorexic behaviour and changes in levels of serotonin and noradrenaline in the brain. Eating large amounts of starchy foods containing carbohydrates is thought to increase serotonin levels and this may improve mood. Bulimics often display low levels of serotonin, yet have increased levels of plasma endorphins, so there is the possibility that there is an underlying neurotransmitter dysfunction.

EVALUATION OF BIOCHEMISTRY RESEARCH

- People with eating disorders have been helped by drugs that act on serotonin.
- It is difficult to establish cause and effect, in that biochemical imbalance could be the result of the eating disorder rather than the cause.
- Despite the link between starchy foods and increased serotonin levels, people with bulimia don't focus on eating only starchy foods.

EVIDENCE FOR THE INFLUENCE OF NEUROANATOMY

Garfinkel and Garner (1982, see E&F p.188) have suggested that it is possible that anorexics have disturbed functioning of the hypothalamus, as the hypothalamus is very important in regulating food intake.

EVALUATION OF NEUROANATOMY RESEARCH

* Post mortems of patients with eating disorders have not revealed lesions in this part of the brain.
* The question is whether the eating disorder leads to changes in the neuroanatomy of the brain rather than vice versa.

EVIDENCE FOR THE INFLUENCE OF INFECTION

Park et al. (1995, see E&F p.186) studied four females who suffered from anorexia who had a bout of glandular fever shortly before onset of the disorder. This may have influenced function of the hypothalamus.

EVALUATION OF INFECTION RESEARCH

* They used a small sample size.
* Other people who have had glandular fever do not go on to develop anorexia.
* Correlations do not establish causes.

The Psychodynamic Approach

This approach links eating disorders to sexual development, family systems theory, and the struggle for autonomy. Let's consider each one in turn.

INFLUENCE OF SEXUAL DEVELOPMENT

Fear of sexual desires or pregnancy result in not wanting to take anything in, to avoid pregnancy, and a wish to remain pre-pubescent. It has also been suggested that anorexics and bulimics dislike their body because of childhood abuse. This results in them wanting to reject or destroy their body.

EVALUATION OF THE INFLUENCE OF SEXUAL DEVELOPMENT

* One main problem with these ideas is that it is extremely difficult to disprove them.
* In addition, some people who have been sexually abused do not go on to develop an eating disorder.

INFLUENCE OF FAMILY SYSTEMS THEORY

Minuchin et al. (1978, see E&F p.189) stated that the family plays a key role in the development of anorexia by enmeshing the individual child (so the family does everything together), preventing the child from becoming independent, and finding it difficult to resolve conflicts. The child rebels against the family constraints by refusing to eat. This allows the family to displace their own anxieties onto caring for the 'ill' child. One study in support comes from Kalucy et al. (1977, see E&F p.189) who found high levels of parental conflict in families of anorexics.

EVALUATION OF THE INFLUENCE OF FAMILY SYSTEMS THEORY

- Conflict could be the result of living with someone who suffers from anorexia, rather than the cause.
- It does not explain why it affects girls more than boys.
- It does not explain why there has been a sudden increase in cases.

INFLUENCE OF THE STRUGGLE FOR AUTONOMY

Bruch (1971, see E&F p.190) found that food can become symbolic within the family dynamic, and can be used as a currency of affection. The mother gives food to the child to comfort him/her, but chooses when to give the food. This may mean that the mother's needs take precedence over the child in that the mother would feed the child when she herself was hungry. In this environment, the anorexic is engaged in a struggle for autonomy and control to establish his or her own identity. In addition, the affected child is unable to distinguish between his or her own internal needs (whether hungry or satiated) and his or her own emotions. One study in support comes from Halmi (1995) who found that bulimics had trouble distinguishing hunger from other bodily needs and emotions. So when they are anxious or upset they mistakenly believe that they are also hungry.

EVALUATION OF THE INFLUENCE OF THE STRUGGLE FOR AUTONOMY

- Whilst this is an interesting interpretation, it is extremely difficult to test.
- The anorexic may agree with the therapist because they want to be liked, rather than because they believe the interpretation to be true.

The Behavioural Approach

This approach focuses on conditioning theory, and social learning theory and modelling. Let us consider both of these.

INFLUENCE OF CONDITIONING THEORY

Leitenberg et al. (1968, see E&F p.190) suggest that both classical and operant conditioning are involved with eating disorders. Initially the anorexic associates eating with anxiety. Their anxiety arises from their fear that eating will lead to weight gain, which will make them unattractive. By losing weight the person reduces their anxiety. Having begun to lose weight, the 'not eating' behaviour is maintained by reinforcement from others admiring their slim figure.

EVALUATION OF CONDITIONING THEORY

- It does not totally explain why the onset tends to be during adolescence.
- It does not explain why there are marked individual differences, in that many women diet, but not all go on to develop anorexia.
- It fails to explain why the person with anorexia continues to diet when they are no longer receiving compliments for their weight loss.

SOCIAL LEARNING THEORIES AND MODELLING

These theories suggest that the mass media and role models contribute to the development of anorexia. Cooper (1994, see E&F p.191) pointed out that in Western societies women are admired for being slim and losing weight, and actresses who put on weight are castigated in the press. Cross-cultural research supports this idea. Nasser (1986, see E&F p.191) studied Egyptian women who were studying either in London or in Cairo. Whilst no cases of anorexia were reported in Cairo, 12% of the sample studying in London had developed anorexia. Lee et al. (1992, see E&F p.192) noted that bulimia was rare in the Chinese populations of Singapore, Malaysia, and Hong Kong and suggested that this could be explained by socio-cultural differences. Obesity is rare among the Chinese and isn't seen as a weakness or loss of control; the Chinese diet is low in fat and high in fibre and means that people do not have to be restrained with what they eat; and Chinese women's success is linked to their success within the family rather than their physical appearance.

EVALUATION OF SOCIAL LEARNING THEORY AND MODELLING

- Given that most women in Western societies are exposed to slim attractive women as role models, it doesn't explain why some women develop anorexia and others do not.
- Cross-cultural research may reflect different diagnostic processes rather than different disorders.
- It does help us understand why there may have been an increase in recent years, and why women sufferers outnumber men.

The Cognitive Approach

This focuses on cognitive biases and suggests that people with eating disorders have distorted beliefs about their own image and food, often describing food as the 'enemy'.

EVIDENCE FOR COGNITIVE BIAS

There is clear evidence to show that people with eating disorders think differently about their body weight and food, and this influences how they feel about their body size and self. Garfinkel and Garner (1982, see E&F p.193) found that anorexics typically overestimate their body size. Cooper and Taylor (1988, see E&F p.193) found that bulimics show a substantial discrepancy between their desired body size and the estimation of their own body size. In addition, Fallon and Rozin (1985, see E&F p.194) found that females rate their ideal body weight as significantly lower than the weight males thought most attractive. All these things place extra pressure on females to be thin.

EVALUATION OF COGNITIVE BIAS

- It is not clear whether the distorted thinking is the cause of the eating disorder, or the result.
- If the cognitive biases exist before the onset of the disorder, they may play a part in its development.
- If the cognitive biases develop after the onset of the disorder, they cannot be a causal factor.

To give you an idea of the type of question you might be asked:

Outline one psychological explanation for anorexia nervosa. **(6 marks)**

The psychodynamic model of abnormality explains anorexia nervosa by looking at family life (family systems theory) and the young person's struggle for autonomy.

Minuchin et al. suggested that anorexia is the result of the adolescent rebelling against family constraints. In particular, the adolescent is usually in a family where they do everything together (enmeshing the individual), where the child is prevented from becoming independent, and the family has difficulties in resolving any conflicts. By refusing to eat, the child is making a stand for independence. A similar idea is expressed by Bruch who argued that food is often used by the mother as a currency of affection, and so by refusing food, the child gains some autonomy.

Another strand of the psychodynamic explanation focuses on sexual development, suggesting that the anorexic wants to remain prepubescent and that their fears of sexual desire and pregnancy result in their not wanting to ingest food (take anything in). Others link anorexia with sexual abuse, arguing that the child wants in some way to destroy or reject their body.

Give two criticisms of the explanation you gave above. **(3 marks + 3 marks)**

One of the main difficulties with psychodynamic explanations of anorexia nervosa is that they are difficult to disprove and they have been accused of lacking objectivity. In addition, by being based on case studies it is difficult to generalise the findings. Kalucy et al. (1977) did find that there was some evidence of higher parental conflict in families of anorexics, but it is difficult to ascertain whether the conflict occurred as a result of having a person who refuses to eat living in the family, rather than being the cause of the eating disorder.

This raises another problem in that the research often takes place after the patient has developed the eating disorder, and hence is dependent on memories of earlier experiences, which may not be accurate.

OVER TO YOU

Describe three ways in which anorexia nervosa differs from bulimia nervosa.
(2 marks + 2 marks + 2 marks)

Social Psychology
SOCIAL INFLUENCE

What's it about?

Social psychology focuses on our interaction with each other and argues that humans are social creatures who are born into families and cultures. It is our interaction with others that influences the way we perceive and understand our world.

Particular areas of interest for social psychologists include studies on conformity and obedience, as well as looking at how a minority group can persuade the majority to change their minds or behaviour. This area of psychology also explores group behaviour, interpersonal attraction, leadership, and explanations of aggression and altruism.

Underlying much of social psychology is the view that humans construct their social worlds and that situational variables have a key role in explaining why people behave as they do.

What's in this unit?

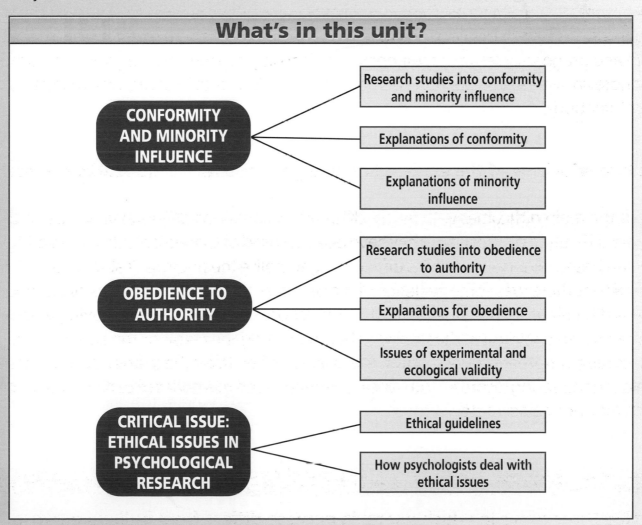

CONFORMITY AND MINORITY INFLUENCE
- Research studies into conformity and minority influence
- Explanations of conformity
- Explanations of minority influence

OBEDIENCE TO AUTHORITY
- Research studies into obedience to authority
- Explanations for obedience
- Issues of experimental and ecological validity

CRITICAL ISSUE: ETHICAL ISSUES IN PSYCHOLOGICAL RESEARCH
- Ethical guidelines
- How psychologists deal with ethical issues

DEFINING KEY TERMS AND CONCEPTS

You need to be able to define and explain the key terms listed in blue below. The other concepts listed in black will aid your understanding of social influence. Make a list of definitions of the following key terms, and if you get stuck, go to the glossary at the end of the book.

Conformity/majority influence
Deception
Ecological validity
Ethical guidelines
Ethical issues
Experimental validity
Informed consent
Minority influence
Obedience to authority
Protection of participants from psychological harm

Social influence
Agentic state
Buffers
Compliance
Debriefing
Demand characteristics
Dispositional explanation
Dissociation
Groupthink
Identification
Informational social influence

Internalisation
Legitimate authority
Maltreatment
Mundane realism
Normative social influence
Norms
Right to withdraw
Situational explanation
Social contract

You may be asked to define some of these key terms in the exam. To give you an idea, look at the following example.

Explain what is meant by 'social influence', 'minority influence', and 'majority influence'.   **(2 marks + 2 marks + 2 marks)**

Social influence describes the way in which a person or group of people affect the attitudes and behaviour of an individual. Normative social influence occurs when people conform to the majority view in order to be liked or avoid ridicule.

Minority influence refers to the process by which a consistent firm minority may change the beliefs and/or behaviours of the majority. Consistency is thought to be important for the minority to influence the majority, since it not only exposes the majority to an alternative view, it also demonstrates a degree of certainty.

Majority influence refers to the process by which the majority alters the attitudes and behaviours of the minority. This may be due to normative social influence, but it can also be due to informational social influence, where the minority yields to group pressure because they perceive the majority as having more knowledge or information.

OVER TO YOU

Explain what is meant by 'obedience' and 'conformity'.   **(3 marks + 3 marks)**

DESCRIBING AND EVALUATING KEY STUDIES

One kind of AO1 examination question is described as the 'APFCC' question. In this question you are asked to describe the aims, procedures, findings, conclusions, and give criticisms (APFCC) of a study into a named topic. In any question you will be asked for one or two of these, for example, 'aims and conclusions' or 'findings and conclusions'. There is not a requirement that these are given in balance as the question is marked out of 6 marks (for example, if you provide findings only then you may receive a maximum of 4 marks). You may be asked for the 'findings plus one criticism', in which case the question is marked as '3 marks + 3 marks'.

You may also be asked questions about research more generally, rather than about a specific study. In this case the question will say 'Describe the findings of research into…' (6 marks). You may also be asked about 'conclusions'. In such questions you may describe the findings/conclusions from one study, or from several studies, or even from a theory (which is a form of research).

If the question asks for 'procedures and findings', any other material will not receive credit, such as information relating to aims or conclusions. Make sure you understand the difference, for example, between a finding (the facts) and a conclusion (what the findings show us).

For the module on Social Psychology you need to know the following APFCC studies:

KEY STUDY TOPICS	EXAMPLE	WHERE TO FIND IT	OTHER RELATED RESEARCH
Conformity/majority influence	Zimbardo et al. (1973)	Appendix	Asch (1951, 1956, see E&F p.202) Perrin and Spencer (1980, see E&F pp.208–209) Smith and Bond (1993, see E&F p.209)
Minority influence	Moscovici et al. (1969)	Page 116 and Appendix	Nemeth et al. (1974, see E&F p.207)
Obedience	Milgram (1963)	Appendix	Hofling et al. (1966, see E&F p.216) Bickman (1974, see E&F p.216)

OVER TO YOU

You need to be able to write for three minutes on aims, procedures, findings, conclusions, and criticisms. In order to do this well in the examination it might help to identify key words and concepts to recall. You only need a few for each of the APFCCs (in other words a few key concepts for the aims and a few for the procedures—a maximum of five). Do this for each study listed above.

SOCIAL INFLUENCE RESEARCH

Research into social influence focuses on some classic studies on conformity, minority influence, and obedience to authority. You need to have a good understanding of these studies and be able to describe and criticise them, especially considering ethical and cross-cultural issues. Most of these studies have important implications for society, so try to think of how they relate to the real world, and what the implications of the findings are.

You can ask yourself the following questions:

- Do Milgram's studies on obedience to authority shed any light on what happened during the 1930s and 1940s in Nazi Germany?
- Can you think of any examples where a minority viewpoint has influenced a majority viewpoint?
- Are there individual differences in conformity, or do people tend to follow a set pattern?
- What do these studies tell us about basic human nature?
- Before we generalise findings to other cultures, what needs to be done to reduce the likelihood of introducing problems of ethnocentrism?
- Can we test these concepts in the same way in other cultures?
- How could you develop the social influence research in an ethically acceptable way?
- With social influence research that has raised important ethical issues, do you think that the end justifies the means?

STUDIES ON CONFORMITY
Sherif (1935, see E&F p.201)
Asch (1951, see E&F p.202)
Zimbardo (1973, see E&F p.204)

STUDIES ON MINORITY INFLUENCE
Moscovici (1969, see E&F p.207)

STUDIES ON OBEDIENCE TO AUTHORITY
Milgram (1974, see E&F p.213–p.215)
Hofling et al. (1966, see E&F p.216)
Bickman (1974, see E&F p.216)

CONFORMITY AND MINORITY INFLUENCE

Although we may not be aware of it, most days we are influenced by others and conform to group norms and social expectations. Majority influence has been described as yielding to group pressure. Failure to conform can result in our being ridiculed or rejected.

ASK YOURSELF

Is conformity desirable?

What has research into conformity revealed to us?

Why do people conform?

What factors increase the likelihood of conformity?

What theories have been proposed to aid our understanding of conformity?

EXPLANATIONS OF CONFORMITY

There are three theories of conformity that need to be considered:

- Informational social influence.
- Normative social influence.
- Conforming to social roles and expectations.

These theories have all arisen out of research studies on conformity and it is important to know how they came about and the evaluative points (both positive and negative) that have been raised. Let us look at the theories of conformity one at a time.

INFORMATIONAL SOCIAL INFLUENCE
This often occurs when there is no correct or obvious answer to a question posed. In these circumstances we often turn to others for information, since we don't know what else to do.

Supporting study
Sherif's (1935, see E&F p.201) study of conformity using the autokinetic effect. Participants estimating the distance a non-moving light had appeared to move changed their personal estimates when placed in a group so that a group norm emerged.

Evaluation—in support
- Clearly shows that group norms emerge when people are in an ambiguous situation and are uncertain about their response.

Evaluation—problems
In terms of methodology:
- The study was artificial.
- He used a situation in which there was no obvious answer.

In terms of ethics:
- Unethical in that participants were deceived.

NORMATIVE SOCIAL INFLUENCE

This occurs when we want to be liked by a group or want to avoid embarrassment. Hence, we go along with the consensus even though we might not change our private opinions.

Supporting study

Asch's (1951, 1956, see E&F p.202) study of conformity in unambiguous situations. Unlike Sherif (1935), he used a task that was not ambiguous. Participants were asked to state which line was the same as the target. The naïve participant was placed in a group with six others, who were confederates of the experimenter. On critical trials, the confederates gave the wrong answer, and on 37% of these trials, participants conformed and gave the wrong answer. The variables manipulated included seating position, size of the group, and unanimity.

Evaluation—in support

- The study was very influential in showing the power of group pressure.
- It provided a paradigm for future studies on conformity.

Evaluation—problems:

In terms of methodology:

- The task was trivial and not important to participants' belief systems.
- There are problems with generalisation in that the findings may be the result of the study being conducted at a particular historical time.
- More recent studies failed to replicate Asch's results, e.g. Perrin and Spencer (1980, see E&F p.208).
- It was an all-male student sample.

In terms of ethics:

- Unethical in that participants were deceived.
- Asch did not obtain informed consent.
- The study caused stress to participants.

CONFORMING TO SOCIAL ROLES AND EXPECTATIONS

This theory suggests that we internalise what is expected of us when we take on certain roles and conform to these expectations.

Supporting study

Zimbardo's (1973, see E&F p.204) Stanford prison study. Participants agreed to take part in a mock prison set up, which involved their being assigned to either the role of prisoner or guard. After a short while the prisoners became subdued, submissive, slouched, and looked at the ground. The guards seemed to enjoy the power given and some became very aggressive. The study was stopped early.

Evaluation—in support

- It was an interesting study revealing the power that roles play in influencing our behaviour.
- Zimbardo did get consent from the participants, however there is some debate about how informed the consent was.

Evaluation—problems

In terms of methodology:

- There is some concern that the participants may have been play-acting.

In terms of ethics:

- The study caused stress to participants.

COMPLIANCE, IDENTIFICATION, AND INTERNALISATION

Kelman (1958, see E&F p.203) suggested that conformity can result in our changing our private opinions as well as our public opinions. He suggested that there are three different types of conformity, that serve three different purposes:

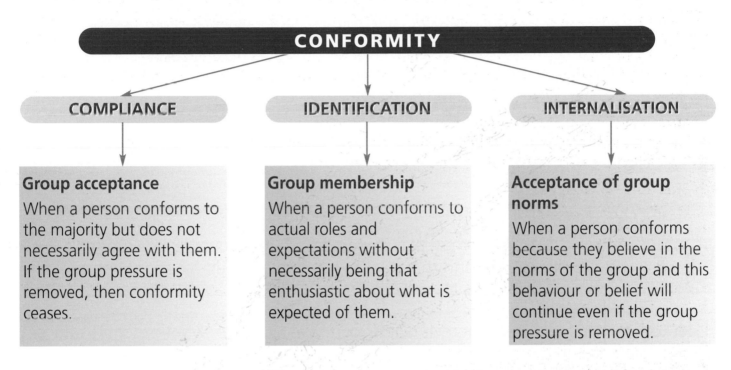

CONFORMITY

COMPLIANCE

Group acceptance

When a person conforms to the majority but does not necessarily agree with them. If the group pressure is removed, then conformity ceases.

IDENTIFICATION

Group membership

When a person conforms to actual roles and expectations without necessarily being that enthusiastic about what is expected of them.

INTERNALISATION

Acceptance of group norms

When a person conforms because they believe in the norms of the group and this behaviour or belief will continue even if the group pressure is removed.

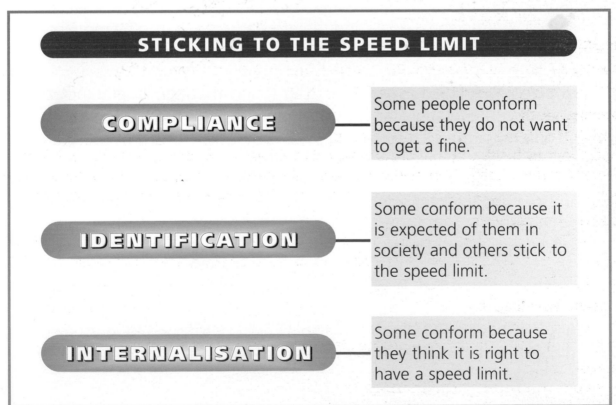

STICKING TO THE SPEED LIMIT

COMPLIANCE — Some people conform because they do not want to get a fine.

IDENTIFICATION — Some conform because it is expected of them in society and others stick to the speed limit.

INTERNALISATION — Some conform because they think it is right to have a speed limit.

FACTORS THAT MIGHT INFLUENCE WHETHER PEOPLE CONFORM

There are a number of factors that influence whether or not a person will conform, and you can use the mnemonic CHIGGUT to help you remember them:

C **ultural factors**. Smith and Bond 1993 (see E&F p.209) suggested that there might be a difference between individualist cultures and collectivist cultures. The former are less likely to conform as shown by research that showed that 14% of Belgian students conformed to giving a wrong answer in comparison with 58% of Indian teachers in Fiji.

H **istorical factors** may influence conformity in that it has been argued that America in the 1950s was more conformist than in the 1960s and 1970s. Replications of Asch's study in later decades have found lower levels of conformity (Perrin & Spencer, 1980, see E&F p.208).

I **ndividual differences** may play a part in whether people are more likely to conform. It has been found that people with a high need for social approval and low self-esteem are more likely to conform.

G **ender differences**. There is some controversy as to whether there are sex differences in the likelihood of conforming to a group. Eagly (1978, see E&F p.211) has suggested that any differences may be explained by women being more oriented towards interpersonal goals and therefore they appear to be more conformist in experimental situations.

G **roup size**. Asch (1951, see E&F p.202) found that conformity increased as the number of confederates rose from 1–3, but after this the group size did not make much difference except if the answer was obviously wrong and a very large number of people gave the wrong answer. In these cases the participants became suspicious.

U **nanimity**. This is a key variable in determining the likelihood of conformity. Asch (1951, see E&F p.202) found that if the naïve participant had one supporter they were less likely to conform.

T **ype of task**. If the task is difficult or the participant isn't quite sure what to do, then conformity is more likely. However if the task is familiar, conformity is less likely, as was demonstrated in Perrin and Spencer's (1980, see E&F p.208) study where engineers did not conform so readily as participants did in the Asch study.

To give you an idea of the type of question you might be asked:

Give two explanations for why people conform to majority influence.
(3 marks + 3 marks)

Two main ways of explaining why people conform to majority influence are informational social influence and normative social influence. The first was demonstrated in Sherif's study, where he found that when people were in an ambiguous situation they would often conform to a group norm simply because they did not have enough information or were uncertain about what to do. They therefore defer their decision to others, thinking that the group majority has more information or knowledge than they have.

Normative social influence suggests that people conform to the majority to be liked and accepted, or to avoid ridicule. This was demonstrated in Asch's study where, despite being aware that their answer was wrong, the majority of participants still went along with the group norm at least once.

Outline findings of research into conformity.
(6 marks)

Research into conformity has shown that people can be persuaded to yield to group pressure. For example, Asch found in his study that in 37% of the critical trials where confederates gave the wrong answer the naïve participant would also give the wrong answer, despite the right answer being obvious. Sherif found that when participants were placed in a situation where the answer was ambiguous there was a tendency for a group norm to emerge when participants were tested in groups rather than individually.

Research by Perrin and Spencer in the 1970s suggested that perhaps Asch's results were the effect of the dominant culture in 1950's America. They tested engineering students and found much lower rates of conformity. Studies by Smith and Bond found that individualistic cultures were less likely than collectivist cultures to be swayed by the group decision.

OVER TO YOU

Describe the aims and findings of one study on conformity.
(3 marks + 3 marks)

CONFORMITY AND MINORITY INFLUENCE

MINORITY INFLUENCE

Can you think of any examples from history where the minority changed the majority view?

What factors do you think would make people switch to a minority viewpoint?

Is there a difference in the way a minority influences a group, and the way a majority influences a group?

Minorities can and do influence majorities, as social and scientific innovations clearly demonstrate. Research has explored how the behaviour of the minority can influence the majority.

Example

Study:	**Moscovici et al.'s (1969, see E&F p.207) study of the influence of a consistent minority on the responses of a majority in a colour perception task**
Aims:	To demonstrate that a minority can influence the majority view.
Procedure:	Groups of six participants were presented with blue slides that varied in intensity. Participants were asked to name aloud the colour of the slide. There were two confederates of the experimenter in the group, who were instructed to say that the slides were green either on every trial or on two thirds of the trials.
Findings:	When the confederates said green on every trial the percentage of green responses from the other participants was 8%. When the confederates said green for two thirds of the trials, the participants said the slide was green in only 1% of the trials.
Conclusions:	When members of a minority are consistent in their opinions, they can on some occasions influence the majority.
Criticisms:	The study does show that minorities can persuade the majority to change their opinion, but it could be argued that discussing the colour of slides is not of major importance to a person's belief systems, and therefore the task was a bit trivial to prove the case for switching to minority opinions.

EXPLANATIONS OF MINORITY INFLUENCE

There are a number of theories that try to explain how a minority will influence a majority, so let us consider each of these in turn.

Dissociation Model of Minority Influence

This theory was developed by Mugny (1991) and Perez (1995). It states that minority ideas are taken up, but are often dissociated from the people from whom the ideas originated, especially if they are disliked. By dissociating themselves from the minority group, the majority avoids any identification with them.

Self-categorisation Theory

David and Turner (1996) suggested the self-categorisation theory in which minority ideas are unlikely to be taken up if they are seen as originating from an 'out group'. Out groups describe groups against which we define ourselves. Out groups are perceived as having different values and beliefs from us. However, if the minority views stem from an 'in group' they are more likely to be taken up. In groups describe groups we share our values and beliefs with.

Social Impact Theory

This theory, introduced by Latané and Wolf (1981, see E&F p.206), suggests that all social influence, whether minority influence or majority influence, is dependent on three factors:

Strength
This describes the number of people present and the consistency with which the message is expressed.

Status and knowledge
The higher the person's status and expertise, the greater the influence.

Immediacy
The closer the person is both physically and emotionally, the greater will be their effect.

Dual Process Theory

Moscovici (1976, 1980, see E&F p.205) suggested that majority and minority influence work in different ways and made a distinction between compliance and conversion. Majority influence arises from compliance with the emphasis being placed on social factors, such as the person wanting to belong to the group and to be liked. Minority influence is thought to cause conversion in that the emphasis is focused on cognitive factors and changing private opinions. Moscovici (1985, see E&F p.206) argued that conversion is most likely to occur under certain conditions:

Consistency
The minority must be consistent in their opinion.

Flexibility
The minority must not appear to be rigid and dogmatic.

Relevance
The minority will be more successful if their views are in line with social trends.

Commitment
A committed minority will lead people to rethink their position on an issue, and this is conversion not compliance. Majority influence involves the reverse: compliance but not conversion.

The research of Moscovici and others has also explored whether the *behaviour* of the minority can influence the likelihood of others taking up their viewpoints. Moscovici (1985) suggested some behavioural styles that minorities should have if they want to exert an influence.

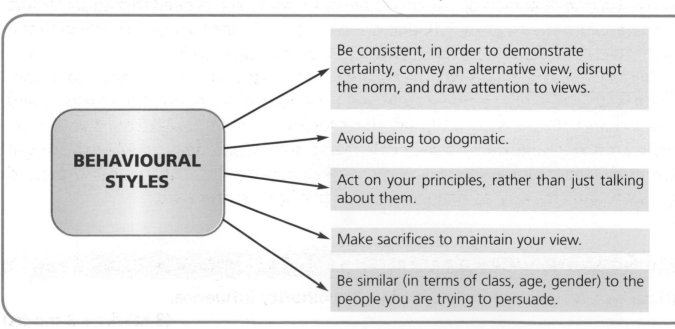

BEHAVIOURAL STYLES

- Be consistent, in order to demonstrate certainty, convey an alternative view, disrupt the norm, and draw attention to views.
- Avoid being too dogmatic.
- Act on your principles, rather than just talking about them.
- Make sacrifices to maintain your view.
- Be similar (in terms of class, age, gender) to the people you are trying to persuade.

To give you an idea of the type of question you might be asked:

Outline findings of research into minority influence. (6 marks)

Research into minority influence has shown that certain characteristics are more likely to enable the minority to influence the majority. These include being consistent. Moscovici found that when his confederates were consistent in saying that a blue slide was green, the percentage of participants who agreed that the blue slide was in fact green was higher (8%) than when the confederates said that the slide was green on two thirds of the trials (1%).

Similarity between the minority and majority is also thought to aid the influence of the minority since David and Turner found that people were unlikely to change their views to those of an out group.

Research by Perez found that people often seem to forget where the views they may later adopt originated from, if they want to dissociate themselves from the minority group.

Explain the difference between majority influence and minority influence. (6 marks)

Majority influence—sometimes referred to as conformity—is a form of social influence whereby an individual will change their behaviour or beliefs in accordance with a larger group's behaviour or views. It occurs when a person changes their views or behaviour in order to yield to imagined or real group pressure. Moscovici argued that social factors dominate when the majority influences the minority, in that people comply with the majority view in order to be liked and accepted, or to avoid ridicule.

Minority influence occurs when a majority is influenced, in respect of their behaviour or beliefs, by a minority, so that people reject the established norm of the majority and move towards the views of the minority. Moscovici suggests that cognitive factors dominate minority influence in that people change their private opinions when they begin to explore the minority viewpoint. This is more likely to occur if the minority view expressed is consistent and shows a commitment to the specific view expressed.

OVER TO YOU

Outline two reasons why people yield to minority influence.
(3 marks + 3 marks)

OBEDIENCE TO AUTHORITY

Why do people obey authority figures?

What difficulties arise when doing research into obedience?

What variables might contribute to people's willingness to obey others?

DIFFERENCES BETWEEN OBEDIENCE AND CONFORMITY

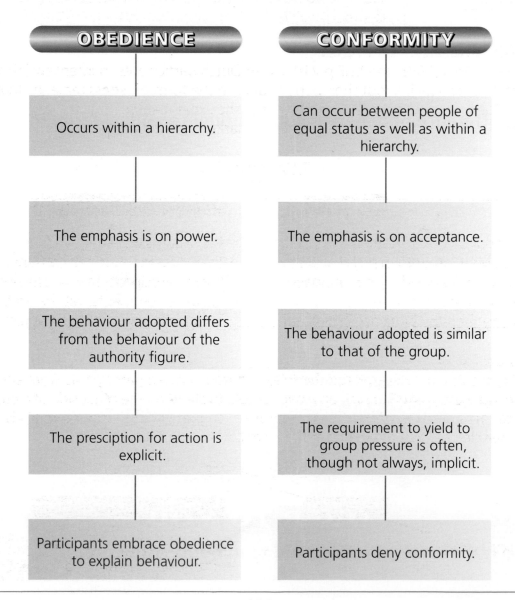

OBEDIENCE	CONFORMITY
Occurs within a hierarchy.	Can occur between people of equal status as well as within a hierarchy.
The emphasis is on power.	The emphasis is on acceptance.
The behaviour adopted differs from the behaviour of the authority figure.	The behaviour adopted is similar to that of the group.
The presciption for action is explicit.	The requirement to yield to group pressure is often, though not always, implicit.
Participants embrace obedience to explain behaviour.	Participants deny conformity.

STUDIES OF OBEDIENCE

Nurses Obeying Doctors

Hofling et al. (1966, see E&F p.216) conducted a study in which nurses were instructed by a 'Dr Smith' to give a patient 20mg of the drug Astroten. This instruction broke several rules as it was above the maximum dose, no written authority was given, and the nurses did not know if Dr Smith was a genuine doctor.

21 of the 22 nurses in the study obeyed Dr Smith and were willing to give the 20mg dose of Astroten.

EVALUATION

In support

- Raises important questions about hospital practices.
- Has ecological validity.

Problems and limitations

- Does not follow ethical guidelines.
- Nurses were deceived.
- There was no informed consent.
- Nurses did not have the right to withdraw.
- Attempts to replicate Hofling's research have failed (e.g. Rank & Jacobsen, 1977).

Obedience With Interview Techniques

Meeus and Raaijmakers (1995, see E&F p.218) asked Dutch participants to interview job applicants and give them negative feedback about their performance in the form of 'stress remarks' that ranged from mild to severe. The interviewees were confederates of the experimenter.

88% of the participants delivered all 15 stress remarks to the interviewee.

EVALUATION

In support

- Interesting variation on Milgram's work, dealing with psychological rather than physical stress.
- Has greater ecological validity and mundane realism than Milgram's work.
- Provides an insight into obedience in Holland.

Problems and limitations

- Participants were deceived.
- There was no informed consent.
- Some participants may not have minded giving negative comments, yet the experimental design assumed that they would.

The Effect of Uniforms

Bickman (1974, see E&F p.216) explored the role of uniforms when participants were either asked for a dime for a parking meter, asked to pick up a bag, or told to stand on the other side of a bus stop.

Obedience rates differed with different uniforms, so participants were more likely to obey if the experimenter was dressed as a guard rather than a milkman or civilian.

EVALUATION

In support

- Has ecological validity.

Problems and limitations

- Participants were deceived.
- There was no informed consent.

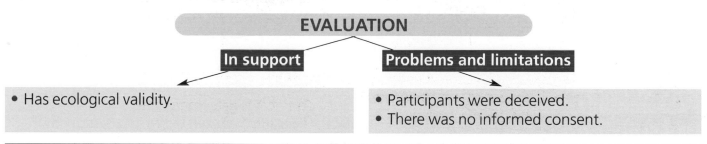

Electric Shocks and Learning

Milgram (1974, see E&F p.213) conducted a study that was designed to see whether participants would obey an experimenter when instructed to give another person potentially dangerous electric shocks. They were instructed to give the learner an electric shock (ranging from 15–450 volts) every time they made a mistake. No shocks were actually given and the learner was a confederate of the experimenter.

Obedience rates showed that 65% of the participants gave a potentially lethal shock to the learner. Milgram (1974, see E&F p.215) carried out several variations on his basic experiment, to increase the obviousness of the learner's plight, or to reduce the authority or influence of the experimenter. The obedience rates for these different conditions are shown in brackets:

- **Increasing the distance between experimenter and participant**. The orders were given by telephone rather than face-to-face (20.5%).
- **Remote feedback**. Where the victim was not seen or heard (66%).
- **Voice feedback**. Where the victim could be heard but not seen (62%).
- **Proximity**. Where the victim was only 1 metre away from the participant (40%).
- **Touch proximity**. Where the victim was only 1 metre away from the participant and the participant had to force their hand onto the shockplate (30%).
- **Reducing the authority of the experimenter**. Where the experimenter was not a scientist, but a member of the public (20%).
- **Making the location less credible**. Where the experiment was conducted in a seedy office rather than a prestigious university (48%).
- **Refusal to conform**. Where another confederate refused to give shocks (10%).

Cross-cultural research by Smith and Bond (1993, see E&F p.217) in Europe yielded a total obedience rate of 80% or more in Italy, Austria, Spain, Germany, and Holland. However, there were slight variations in the key aspects of the procedure used in each of these countries, so it is difficult to interpret these findings. Ancona et al. (1968) replicated the study in Italy, to find a total obedience rate of 80%, and Schurz (1985) studied Austrians and found the obedience rate to be 85%. Kilham and Mann (1974, see E&F p.223) found that Australian males only conformed 40% and Australian females only conformed 16%.

EVALUATION

In support

- Helped people review their value systems and become aware of destructive obedience.
- 74% of participants were glad to have taken part.
- It "made visible the invisible, and showed how social forces direct and control us".
- A creative and inventive way of studying obedience.
- Participants did believe they were giving actual shocks.
- Exposed the power relationship between experimenter and participant.

Problems and limitations

- Caused psychological stress and embarrassment.
- Deceived participants.
- There was no informed consent.
- Pressure was placed on participants who wanted to withdraw.
- May have lowered participants' self-esteem during debriefing.
- Biased sample since all were volunteers.
- Unrealistic experimental set up.
- Possibly lacks ecological validity.
- With some cross-cultural studies, the person being shocked was a student and this opens discussion of the effect of similarity between victim and participant.

EXPLANATIONS FOR OBEDIENCE

Psychologists have used studies of obedience to try and establish why people obey others. Such studies demonstrate the power of authority and the willingness of participants to obey authority figures. Their explanations can be divided between *situational* and *dispositional* explanations. Situational explanations can be summed up by Milgram's comment that it is "not so much the kind of person a man is as the kind of situation he finds himself in that determines how he will act", whereas dispositional explanations look at the person's personality.

Let us now consider each of these explanations for obedience in turn.

Situational Explanations for Obedience

The following are features of the situation that are conducive to obedience.

LEGITIMATE AUTHORITY

We assume that the people in authority have some knowledge or expertise, and therefore think they know more than us. For this reason we have a tendency to defer responsibility for our actions to their authority.

FOR EXAMPLE: In Milgram's study the assumption was that the experimenter knew what he was doing— after all, he was a psychologist!

GRADUATED COMMITMENT

This is sometimes called the foot-in-the-door technique. It works because once we agree to a fairly reasonable small request we then tend to feel obliged to agree to greater requests, even if they are unreasonable.

FOR EXAMPLE: In Milgram's study having agreed to give 15 volt shocks, it was difficult to then refuse to give 45 volts.

THE AGENTIC STATE

People argue that they are not responsible for their own actions, and are merely carrying out the orders of the authority figure. The alternative to the agentic state is the autonomous state, in which we are aware of the consequences of our actions and therefore voluntarily direct our behaviour.

FOR EXAMPLE: In Milgram's study the participants argued that the university had sanctioned the study.

BUFFERS

A buffer is anything that prevents the person seeing the consequences of their actions.

FOR EXAMPLE: In Milgram's study this occurred when the participants could not see the victim.

Dispositional Explanations for Obedience

Adorno et al. (1950, see E&F pp.220–221) felt that there are certain dispositional factors that contribute to whether or not a person will obey orders.

PERSONALITY

Adorno et al. suggested that childhood experiences played a key role in the development of personality and this results in some people developing an authoritarian personality. People with authoritarian personalities have rigid beliefs in conventional values, are hostile to out groups, are intolerant of ambiguity, and have a submissive attitude to authority figures.

PASSIVITY

Some people dislike confrontation so much that they will do anything to avoid it. Thus, rather than challenge authority, they will prefer to do what they are told to avoid a scene or embarrassment.

MORAL DEVELOPMENT

Kohlberg suggested that different people reached different levels of moral development, and that very few reach level 6 where universal ethical principles govern the person's behaviour. Some people remain at level one or level two where the fear of punishment or the promise of reward dominate their decisions.

RESISTING OBEDIENCE

It has been suggested that by understanding obedience, people will be more able to resist obeying others when their instructions are a cause of concern. Based on knowledge of situational factors it has been suggested that the following methods might work:

- Educate people about the problems of 'blind obedience'.
- Remind people that they are responsible for their own actions.
- Provide role models who refuse to obey.
- Question the motives of authority figures when you think they are giving unreasonable orders.

In terms of dispositional factors, there is a greater likelihood of resisting obedience if the person:

- Wants to maintain control.
- Is confident enough to be independent.
- Has a high level of moral development.
- Has a need to maintain their individuality.

THE QUESTION OF EXPERIMENTAL VALIDITY AND ECOLOGICAL VALIDITY

Research into social influence raises questions about *experimental validity* and *ecological validity*. You need to know the differences between these two types of validity, so let us consider each in turn.

Experimental Validity

This measures whether the experimental design actually did the job it set out to do. If the experimental set up was not believable then the participants probably would not behave as they would normally do in such situations. For example, did the participants in Milgram's research really believe they were giving the 'learner' electric shocks, or was the situation such that the participants were not behaving how they would usually behave? Orne and Holland (1968, see E&F p.214) argued that the study lacked experimental realism because the participants didn't really believe that they were giving the person an electric shock. However, replications of Milgram's research have shown that 70% of the participants reported that they had believed the whole set up. In addition, Orne and Holland argued that the obedience of the participants was due more to the result of demand characteristics and the participants doing what was expected of them rather than real obedience. This too has been challenged, since surely the lab environment is a real-life social setting where power relationships still occur. Finally, Orne and Holland pointed out that by paying the participants, Milgram may have made participants feel obliged to continue, since they had entered into a social contract. Again, Milgram replied that this is a reflection of real-life situations where people feel obliged to do as others tell them because they have agreed to do what is required of them.

Experimental validity is the extent to which research has *internal validity* and *external validity* because it concerns what goes on *inside* and *outside* the experiment.

Ecological Validity

This describes the extent to which we can *generalise* the findings of a study to other situations, other individuals and to everyday life. If the research set up is like real life, i.e. it appears real, it is said to have *mundane realism*. Milgram argued that his study, by exploring the demands of an authority figure, did have mundane realism. Although the authority figure was a psychologist in a laboratory it does not diminish the fact the he was still an authority figure, and was viewed as such by the participants. Indeed, the taking part in an experiment is a social situation, and Milgram's initial findings have been given support by other research such as that of Hofling et al. (1966, see E&F p.216) and Bickman (1974, see E&F p.216).

One aspect of ecological validity is also referred to as *external validity* because it concerns issues *outside* the study.

To give you an idea of the type of question you might be asked:

Describe the aims and conclusions of one research study of obedience to authority. **(6 marks)**

Milgram's famous study on obedience was designed to see whether participants, taking the role of a teacher, would obey an experimenter who asked them to give another participant, the 'learner', a series of electric shocks every time he or she made a mistake. His aim was to see whether ordinary Americans displayed the same kind of mindless obedience as observed in Nazi officers during the Second World War.

Milgram was attempting to test the hypothesis that 'Germans are different', in that they had a character defect that meant they would blindly obey an authority figure regardless of what harm they were required to inflict. This hypothesis had, until then, been used to explain why they had engaged in the genocide of millions of Jews and others in the 1930s and 1940s.

From his research, Milgram concluded that this hypothesis was incorrect, since the findings indicated that the majority of normal people would obey a malevolent authority figure, even to the point when they may be responsible for killing an innocent party. He also concluded there are several situational factors that can affect an individual's willingness to obey an authority figure. The location of where the study took place, along with who gave the orders, influenced obedience rates.

Milgram believed that it was essential to make people aware of the dangers of blind obedience. He concluded that it is "not so much the kind of person a man is as the kind of situation he finds himself in that determines how he will act".

Give two criticisms of the research study outlined in the above question. **(3 marks + 3 marks)**

Firstly, one major criticism of Milgram's research was that he deceived the participants, and this raises ethical issues because it prevents participants from being able to give informed consent. Milgram deceived the participants by telling them the study was about the effect of punishment on learning, when it was about obedience. He also deceived them by letting them think that they were really giving the learner electric shocks. Baumrind also criticised the study by arguing that it put the participants under great stress and again raises ethical concerns.

Secondly, it has been argued that the study lacked ecological validity, as it took place in an experimental laboratory. Whilst this is undoubtedly true, it clearly did expose the power relationship between the experimenter and participant, and in this sense it could be argued that it demonstrated the power of the scientific establishment.

OVER TO YOU

Give two explanations as to why people obey authority. **(3 marks + 3 marks)**

CRITICAL ISSUE:
ETHICAL ISSUES IN PSYCHOLOGICAL RESEARCH

What limits would you place on the ways psychologists go about their quest for knowledge?

Which studies of social influence would you dislike taking part in, and why?

Does the outcome of research justify the means taken to obtain it?

Given the controversy surrounding the nature of experimental research, both the American Psychological Association (APA) and the British Psychological Society (BPS) developed ethical guidelines (see E&F p.231). These are standards of conduct adopted by psychologists and are designed to preserve 'the well-being and dignity of research participants'.

ETHICAL GUIDELINES

Here is a summary of the BPS ethical guidelines for research with human participants:

- Investigations should be considered from the standpoint of the participant where possible.
- Participants should not be deceived.
- Participants should give informed consent.
- Participants should be debriefed after the research.
- Participants should be informed of their right to withdraw from the research.
- Information about the participant should be kept confidential.
- Participants should be protected from physical and mental harm.
- Observations should respect the privacy and well being of the participant.
- Observations should only take place where the observed would expect to be observed by strangers.
- Psychologists have an obligation to inform the participant if they feel the future well-being of the participants may be endangered.

Given the above ethical guidelines, it is clear that these raise issues when doing research in the area of social influence.

What would have happened if Milgram's participants hadn't been deceived, or if Asch's participants were told that the study was on conformity rather than the judgement of line lengths? How would Milgram's participants react after being debriefed, and had they been allowed to withdraw from the study? Did Zimbardo's study cause participants undue stress?

One major critic of Milgram was Baumrind (1964, see E&F p.217), and we have prepared a summary of the key issues in the Milgram–Baumrind debate.

PARTICIPANTS SHOULD NOT BE DECEIVED:

Baumrind's concerns
Participants were deceived on two counts. First, they were told that the study was about the effects of punishment, and then they believed that they were giving someone real electric shocks and that the confederate was another participant.

Milgram's reply
Without the deception the study couldn't have taken place, and it did reveal truly surprising results. Participants were debriefed and 74% said they were glad that they had taken part in the study.

PARTICIPANTS SHOULD GIVE INFORMED CONSENT:

Baumrind's concerns
Participants hadn't given their consent to take part in a study on obedience.

Milgram's reply
Whilst this was the case, other writers such as Rosnow argued that the study helped people review their value systems and made them aware of the destructiveness of obedience.

PARTICIPANTS SHOULD BE PROTECTED FROM PSYCHOLOGICAL HARM:

Baumrind's concerns
Participants experienced a loss of self-esteem, dignity, and trust in authority, and it was a stressful experience for some.

Milgram's reply
Milgram argued that the participants were fully debriefed, and psychiatric examination one year after the study revealed no sign of psychological damage. In addition, stress was not anticipated.

PARTICIPANTS SHOULD BE ALLOWED TO WITHDRAW FROM THE STUDY:

Baumrind's concerns
Participants who wanted to withdraw were informed that they had no choice but to go on.

Milgram's reply
By persuading participants to remain, Milgram was demonstrating the power of the scientific establishment and authority figures, and he argued that they were not physically detained.

In addition to Baumrind's points, there was some concern over confidentiality in that the names of the participants were published in the press and they were also interviewed.

OVER TO YOU

In what ways could it be argued that Asch, Hofling et al., Zimbardo, and Meeus and Raaijmakers did not consider ethical guidelines to the extent they should have done?

DO THE ENDS JUSTIFY THE MEANS?

Social psychologists face a dilemma when investigating social influence. On the one hand they want to use their research skills to advance our knowledge and understanding of humanity, but on the other hand they have a responsibility to the people who are willing to take part in their research. The participants are not objects of study, but human beings.

One major concern revolves around whether deception should take place. Without deception, it is argued that participants' behaviour would not be an accurate portrayal of how they behave. Attempts to get round this difficulty by using role play exercises has led psychologists to argue that role plays simply result in participants guessing how they should behave, rather than behaving how they would normally. Preventing psychologists from undertaking any research that might involve stress or conflict would necessarily result in a somewhat 'lopsided' view of psychology. However, if psychologists do undertake such research they can be accused of abusing their power and being disrespectful of fellow human beings.

It has been suggested that psychologists should do a *cost–benefit analysis* of the research, with the benefits focusing on the gains for both psychology and in some cases the participants, whilst the costs focus on the perceived harm to the participants or the profession. Diener and Crandall (1978, see E&F p.233) suggested the following drawbacks to the cost–benefit approach:

- It is almost impossible to predict both costs and benefits prior to conducting a study.
- Even after the study, it is hard to quantify costs and benefits, partly because it can depend on who is making the judgements. For example, a participant may judge the costs differently from the researcher, and benefits may be judged differently in years to come.
- It tends to ignore the substantive rights of individuals in favour of practical, utilitarian considerations.

Baumrind felt very strongly that Milgram's study should not be judged on a cost–benefit analysis, since this directed emphasis away from human suffering. Milgram argued that his study had revealed important findings, summarised in the following quotes:

"It is not so much the kind of person a man is as the kind of situation he finds himself in that determines how he will act."

"Participants who refused to obey showed a powerful affirmation of human ideals."

"My body of work makes visible the invisible to show us the subtle and not so subtle forces at play around us, how they direct us and even control us. We are so immersed in these networks of power and rituals of communication that we no longer see them...just as the fish is the last to notice it is surrounded by water."

COST–BENEFIT ANALYSIS

Ethics are determined by a balance between ends and means, or a cost–benefit analysis. Some things may be less acceptable than others, but if the ultimate end is for the good of humankind then psychological researchers may feel that an undesirable behaviour, such as causing stress to an animal or deceiving participants as to the nature of the study, is acceptable.

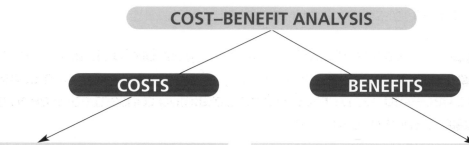

COST–BENEFIT ANALYSIS

COSTS

- Participants may be distressed at finding out something about themselves that they would have preferred not to know.
- Participants may feel that they have been 'tricked' or lied to.
- Participants may have lowered self-esteem as a result of taking part in the study.
- Participants are not given the opportunity to give informed consent.
- Participants may say that they are pleased that they took part in the study because they feel obliged to, rather than because they did (*demand characteristics*).
- May bring the psychological profession into disrepute as an 'institutionalised candid camera'.

BENEFITS

- The results may make us more aware of our own and others' behaviour and raise consciousness about important issues.
- Milgram's study may result in people taking more responsibility for their own actions and not blindly obeying others.
- Asch's research may make us challenge group norms and stand up for our own beliefs, and the rights of others.
- Zimbardo's research may help us understand why some of the atrocities that take place in prisons occur, and how being given power can change people in a negative way.
- Hofling et al.'s research may encourage people working in institutional settings like hospitals to check whether the orders given are in the best interest of the patient.
- Such obedience research can also benefit the participants by giving them insight into their own behaviour.

OVER TO YOU

What do you think about Milgram's viewpoint? Is he justified in his research?

Go through the above lists of costs and benefits and add any more 'cost' and 'benefit' points that you can think of.

INFORMED CONSENT

It is considered the right of participants to provide *voluntary informed consent*. This means several things:

- Being informed about the purpose of the research.
- Being informed about what will be required.
- Being informed about your rights as a participant, e.g. the right to confidentiality, and the right to withdraw.
- To give your full consent to take part in the study.

However, there are many situations where this is just not possible to obtain prior to the study commencing. In an attempt to resolve the difficulty of obtaining informed consent when participants are being deceived, other methods of obtaining consent have been proposed, and we will now consider each one in turn.

Presumptive Consent

This involves asking members of the population, who are similar to the participants, whether they would consider the research to be acceptable.

Prior General Consent

This involves asking people who volunteer to take part in research general questions before they are chosen.

FOR EXAMPLE: *"Would you mind taking part in a study that involved your being misinformed about its true nature?"*

"Would you mind being involved in a study that might cause you stress?"

Participants who agree may later be chosen, since it is assumed that they have agreed in principle to take part. This consent is sometimes referred to as *partially informed consent* for obvious reasons.

Retrospective Consent

Some psychologists suggest that by fully debriefing the participants and giving them the opportunity to withdraw their data, the participants have provided retrospective consent. The assumption is that giving them the right to withdraw their data gives them the same power as if they had refused to take part in the first place.

However consent is obtained you need to remember that people sometimes agree to take part in a study without really thinking through exactly what it involves. In other cases, the consent is given by another person, such as a parent or other authority figure.

CRITICAL ISSUE: ETHICAL ISSUES IN PSYCHOLOGICAL RESEARCH (continued)

To give you an idea of the type of question you might be asked:

Outline two ethical issues that arose in one study into conformity.

(3 marks + 3 marks)

Asch's study of conformity has been criticised mainly on the grounds of deception. The participants were not told the true purpose of the study but instead were led to believe that they were taking part in a study of perception of line length. This means that they did not give fully informed consent. Although they could not realistically be told the whole truth at the outset, there are some solutions—such as presumptive consent or prior general consent—and these methods were not used.

Another criticism is that the participants were put in an extremely embarrassing and difficult situation. Evidence that they experienced great stress was provided by Bogdonoff et al., who conducted a similar study and showed that it caused the participants to have considerably raised levels of arousal (increased heart rate, and so on). Interviews with Asch's participants after the study indicated that they had found the experience very stressful because of the conflict involved in having to choose between agreeing with the majority and giving their true opinion.

Describe the ways in which psychologists deal with ethical issues in their research.

(6 marks)

Undertaking research in psychology, especially in social psychology, often raises the ethical issue as to whether participants can be fully informed. If this is not possible, then participants cannot give fully informed consent. To help psychologists resolve such issues, a set of guidelines has been published, both by the BPS and APA, which suggests that where possible psychologists should not deceive their participants. One way around deception is to use role-play in which participants simply play a role but are informed about the purpose of the study. This, however, is often not practical since participants do not behave as they normally would.

If deception is deemed necessary, there are other ways to deal with the problem. Psychologists often attempt to gain presumptive consent, whereby they ask people from a similar population as the sample whether or not they think that the study is acceptable. If they do, then it can go ahead. Another strategy is to debrief the participants after the study. This is known as retrospective consent

OVER TO YOU

Explain what is meant by deception and protection from psychological harm in the context of psychological research.

(3 marks + 3 marks)

Research Methods

What's it about?

Everyone has theories about what causes behaviour. The difference between these 'common-sense' ideas and theories in psychology is that psychological theories are tested to see if they are true. In order to systematically test theories, psychologists conduct research. As behaviour is so variable, psychologists need to use a wide variety of methods. The research methods available include experiments, questionnaires and surveys, interviews, observations, and methods using correlations.

What's in this unit?

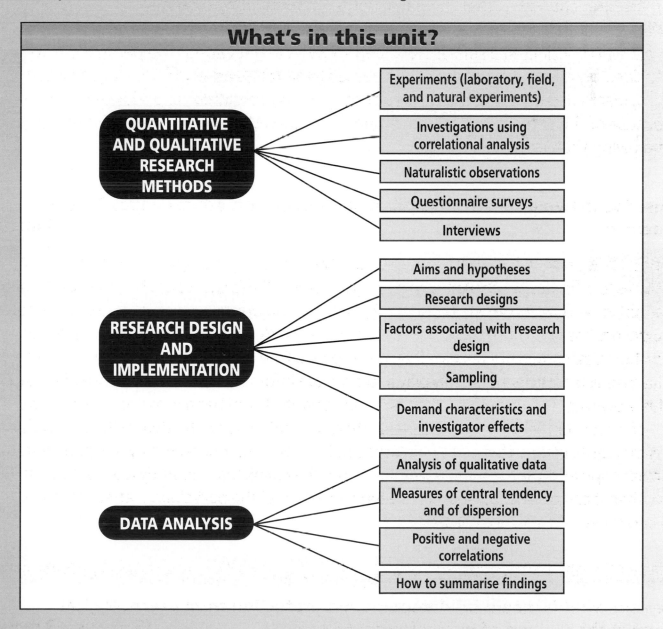

QUANTITATIVE AND QUALITATIVE RESEARCH METHODS
- Experiments (laboratory, field, and natural experiments)
- Investigations using correlational analysis
- Naturalistic observations
- Questionnaire surveys
- Interviews

RESEARCH DESIGN AND IMPLEMENTATION
- Aims and hypotheses
- Research designs
- Factors associated with research design
- Sampling
- Demand characteristics and investigator effects

DATA ANALYSIS
- Analysis of qualitative data
- Measures of central tendency and of dispersion
- Positive and negative correlations
- How to summarise findings

DEFINING KEY TERMS AND CONCEPTS

In this part of the specification questions may be asked about specialist terms, but you are not expected to be able to provide a '3 marks-worth' answer. Most questions will require you to understand the meaning of terms in the context of a piece of research.

Bar chart	Investigator effects	Pilot study
Confounding variables	IV (independent variable)	Positive correlation
Correlational analysis	Laboratory experiment	Qualitative data
Demand characteristics	Matched pairs (matched	Quantitative data
Directional (one-tailed)	participants) design	Quasi-experiment
hypothesis	Mean	Questionnaire survey
DV (dependent variable)	Median	Random sampling
Experiment	Mode	Range
Experimental/alternative	Mundane realism	Reliability
hypothesis	Natural experiment	Repeated measures
Field experiment	Naturalistic observation	design
Frequency polygon	Negative correlation	Research
Histogram	Non-directional (two-tailed)	Scattergraph/scattergram
Independent groups	hypothesis	Standard deviation
design	Null hypothesis	Validity
Interview	Opportunity sampling	

You may be asked for a brief explanation and then required to explain this in the context of a described study. For example, 'Explain what is meant by a pilot study and give one reason why it might be appropriate to use a pilot study as part of this investigation' (1 mark + 2 marks). Or you may simply be expected to describe the concept in the context of the study. For example, 'Describe one way that demand characteristics might influence your findings' (2 marks). To give you an idea, look at the following example.

Identify one ethical issue that you would have to consider when conducting this study and explain how you would deal with this. **(1 mark + 2 marks)**

One issue would be deception. I would deal with this by debriefing participants afterwards and telling them everything they should have known in order to provide informed consent. I would then give them the opportunity to withhold their data. They would also have the right to withdraw during the study.

OVER TO YOU

Explain one way in which participant reactivity might have influenced the results obtained in this study.

[Answer this with reference to any study you know.] **(2 marks)**

QUANTITATIVE AND QUALITATIVE RESEARCH METHODS

THE DIFFERENCE BETWEEN QUANTITATIVE AND QUALITATIVE METHODS

Quantitative Methods

Some research methods allow us to collect information that can be expressed as numbers.

FOR EXAMPLE: 4 boys and 2 girls were playing hop-scotch. John's reaction time with no alcohol averaged 0.21 seconds; with one litre of alcohol it was 0.28 seconds.

Such methods are known as *quantitative* because the results produce numerical data. They typically use a lot of people or animals and produce a little data from each of them. Using such methods enables us to generalise the findings to a larger population. The aim of such methods is to derive 'laws' of behaviour. Such methods include experiments and surveys.

Qualitative Methods

Qualitative methods use fewer people or animals (sometimes only one) but study them in greater depth, focusing on detailed, descriptive data.

FOR EXAMPLE: You may ask Jenny to give a detailed account of her relationship with each of her children or interview Lewis to try and ascertain the type of experiences he finds stressful and how he tries to cope with them.

In this case no numerical data is collected. Such methods are more likely than the quantitative ones to be based in the 'real world'. They include case studies and some observations (although observations can produce quantitative data as well).

NOTE: The essential difference between the two methods is that quantitative methods generate information in numerical form, while qualitative methods generate information that uses language (verbal and written descriptions).

OVER TO YOU

Methods such as interviews and questionnaires can produce either quantitative or qualitative data. Think of the way in which a questionnaire may be written so that it provides quantitative data. Now think of the type of interview that may produce qualitative data (for guidance, see E&F pp.253–254).

Then make a list of the differences between qualitative and quantitative research methods.

THE EXPERIMENTAL METHOD

The experimental method is the only method that allows us to draw conclusions about cause and effect. In order to illustrate how an experiment would be designed, we will use the example used in the textbook (see E&F pp.240–241).

The hypothesis
Loud continuous noise reduces performance on a memory test.

The independent and dependent variables (IV and DV)
Another way of expressing this is to say that memory *affects* performance, or performance *depends on* memory. The variable that we believe has an effect (noise) is called the IV, the one that is affected is called the DV because, if our hypothesis is correct, it *depends on* the IV. The DV is therefore the amount of material that is remembered.

The IV is manipulated while all other variables (the room, the material to be memorised, the time of day, and so on) are kept the same. These variables must be kept the same for both groups or they may affect the result. They are known as *confounding variables* and they must be controlled.

Experimental group
A group of people perform a memory task against a background of loud noise.

Control group
A similar group of people do the same task in peace and quiet.

The same test of memory is given to both groups and the results are compared.

EXPERIMENTAL CONTROL

The most important principle of the experimental method is control; the IV is manipulated, the DV is free to vary, but all other variables must be controlled.

Controlling Confounding Variables

This is the most important element of the experimental method. The IV is manipulated and the DV is measured, but the only way we can be certain that any changes in the DV are caused by the IV is to keep everything else constant. This is really basic common sense and if you were setting up an experiment you would control certain things as a matter of course. For example, in the experiment on the effect of noise on memory, every participant should be given the same time to learn the material to be memorised; they should be tested in a similar room; they should be tested at the same time of day, and so on. These variables that need to be controlled are known as *confounding (or extraneous) variables* because they have the potential to confound the results of the study.

Matching the Participants

When experiments are conducted it is also essential to ensure that, if two different groups of participants are used, they are *matched* on any important variables. What variables are important? Well, think of what we are measuring (the DV) and start with any factors that might influence this. In our example, the DV is amount of material remembered, so we need to try and match on ability to remember things. It would be wise, for example, to match them on intelligence.

   Other variables on which it is common to match are age and sex. However, if you are asked what factors you should match on in an exam question, don't just automatically say "age and sex". Think about what is being measured (the DV) and match on that.

Randomisation

Often the matching of participants can be a problem, so you are more likely to use randomisation. It's easy to match on sex and not too difficult on age, but as for intelligence and other traits, it's not so straightforward. One way around this is to split the whole group of participants randomly into two (or three or four) groups. In this way, the groups should hopefully be fairly similar. Alternatively, you can simply take participants in the order of their arrival. The process of randomly splitting the groups is called *randomisation*. Randomisation is fundamental to any controlled experiment.

OVER TO YOU

In our example of the effect of noise on memory, can you think of any other confounding variables that might need to be controlled? (See E&F p.242 where another one is mentioned.)

If you were designing a study to see if watching violent television affected the amount of aggression that children displayed, what confounding variables would you need the control during the study? What is the most essential trait on which to match the two groups of child participants? (Think about what you are measuring; about what the DV is.)

When planning an experiment, what would be the easiest way to randomly split participants into two groups?

ADVANTAGES AND DISADVANTAGES
OF THE EXPERIMENTAL METHOD

There are a number of advantages and disadvantages of the experimental method that you need to be aware of as they will help you to evaluate experimental studies.

Advantages of the experimental method include:

- **Cause and effect**. The experimental method is the only method that establishes cause and effect. However, although in the example of the effect of noise on memory this is the case, the example of the investigation into catching malaria (see E&F p.243) demonstrates that it is not always possible to be absolutely certain of cause and effect; sleeping with a window open does not actually cause malaria, but it increases the likelihood of being bitten by infected mosquitoes, which is the true cause. Nevertheless, information from experiments provides a starting point for further research.
- **Replication**. Because everything is carefully controlled, it's possible for other researchers to repeat the study. Replication is important because if it confirms the original findings, then there is greater confidence in the validity of the theory being tested.
- **Objectivity**. This is a more objective method than others. However, total objectivity is impossible since the experimenter's interests, values, and judgements will always have some influence, and the control of all confounding variables is impossible. Nevertheless, the experimental method offers the best chance of objectivity.

Disadvantages of the experimental method include:

- **Artificiality**. The major criticism of experiments is that they are artificial and do not measure 'real life' behaviour. In other words they lack *ecological validity*. This is a particular problem with social behaviour. However, there may be times when artificiality is required in order to isolate the behaviour in which the researcher is interested. There is a distinction between *mundane realism* (where situation is made to resemble everyday life) and *experimental realism* (where situation is artificial but still interesting enough to produce full involvement from participants), and it seems that experimental realism may be more important than mundane realism in producing findings that generalise to real-life situations.
- **Demand characteristics**. Orne (1962, see E&F p.244) found that there are features of the experiment that give clues as to what is being studied, and people try to guess what the study is about and will then act accordingly. They often try to act in a way that supports the hypothesis.
- **Evaluation apprehension**. When people are watched and/or they know their behaviour is being recorded they may not act as they normally would. Sigall et al. (1970, see E&F p.244) used a test of copying numbers out of a telephone book and found that participants did not comply with their request to repeat the task taking more time, thus showing that they would avoid any behaviour that might cause them to be evaluated negatively by the researcher.

TYPES OF EXPERIMENTAL INVESTIGATION

All experiments investigate the effect of an IV on a DV, but there are a number of different ways in which this can be done, depending mainly on how rigorous the controls are.

Laboratory Experiments

WHAT IS A LABORATORY EXPERIMENT?

Laboratory experiments are conducted in a laboratory or other contrived setting that is not the participants' natural environment.

Advantages of laboratory experiments:

- The researcher can precisely manipulate the IV and carefully measure the DV, using measuring instruments if necessary. Considerable control can be exercised over any potential confounding variables.
- They are replicable—a laboratory study can be repeated and therefore the reliability can be checked.
- Of all the experimental methods, this is the one that gives most confidence that the IV has caused changes in the DV.

Disadvantages of laboratory experiments:

- They lack ecological validity.
- There may be problems of *evaluation apprehension* and *demand characteristics* (see page 153).

Field Experiments

WHAT IS A FIELD EXPERIMENT?

Field experiments are experiments in which the IV is manipulated in a natural setting. They are conducted anywhere where people live and work, such as schools, factories, hospitals, or on a train.

Advantages of field experiments:

- Since they use an experimental design, cause and effect can occasionally be established to some extent, but note the limitations listed in the disadvantages section.
- As the study is in a natural setting it has high *ecological validity.*
- There is control over the IV.
- Studies can, within reason, be replicated.

Disadvantages of field experiments:

- Random allocation of participants to experimental and control conditions is difficult, if not impossible, and this threatens the ability to establish cause and effect relationships.
- There is less control over extraneous variables, so cause and effect is less certain.
- When considering ethics, most field experiments cannot involve *informed consent,* cannot offer the *right to withdraw,* nor can involve a *debriefing.*

Quasi-experiments

> The local school is about to introduce a completely new reading scheme into one of its two Year 1 classes while the other Year 1 class keeps the old scheme. How could a psychologist investigate whether the new scheme is better or worse than the old one? The head teacher is quite happy to release data on reading ability but on no account can the psychologist influence any organisational aspects of the school. What problems might there be in drawing conclusions from the data provided?
>
> In one maternity ward of the local hospital, newborn babies stay with their mothers all the time and are never removed by nurses for feeding, even at night. In another ward, babies stay with their mothers in the day but are put in the nursery from midnight until 8 o'clock the next morning, during which time they are cared for by nurses. The choice of which ward to go in is largely the choice of the mothers, so long as room permits. How could a psychologist investigate whether this affects mother–child bonding? What problems might there be in drawing conclusions from any data?

WHAT IS A QUASI-EXPERIMENT?

True experiments based on the experimental method provide the best way of being able to draw causal inferences. However, it is often the case that there are practical or ethical reasons why it is not possible to carry out a true experiment, and in such situations, investigators often carry out what is known as a quasi-experiment ('quasi-' means 'almost but not really').

Quasi-experimental designs resemble experiments, but are weak on some of the characteristics. The essence of a true experiment is that the IV is manipulated and everything else is controlled. Two essential features of a true experiment are:

- Direct manipulation of the IV by the experimenter.
- Random allocation of participants to the different groups.

Often this is impractical with psychological research in the real world and instead the psychologist will look at naturally occurring variables by using a quasi-experimental design. Quasi-experiments tend to fall short of being true experiments in the following ways:

- The manipulation of the IV is often not under the control of the experimenter.
- It is usually not possible to allocate the participants randomly to groups.

Both the examples at the top of the page involve independent variables that occur naturally. When investigating these variables, neither of the two essential elements of a true experiment can be met, so a quasi-experiment can be used instead. In the case of the school, the classes are not necessarily the same. In the case of the hospital wards, the new mothers are definitely not matched as they have, for the most part, chosen to be in a particular ward. This means that there are already differences in the two groups even before the effect of the IV is investigated.

The type of quasi-experiment that would be used to investigate a naturally occurring independent variable is known as a natural experiment, and these are discussed on the next page.

Natural Experiments

WHAT IS A NATURAL EXPERIMENT?

Natural experiments are a type of quasi-experiment. They are studies in which a naturally occurring IV is investigated, and the IV is not deliberately manipulated by the researcher.

Advantages of natural experiments:

- People behave fairly naturally as they are usually unaware that they are taking part in an experiment, even if they know they are being observed.
- It allows us to study the effects on behaviour of IVs that would be impractical or unethical to manipulate.

Disadvantages of natural experiments:

- Findings can be difficult to interpret.
- Observed differences in behaviour between groups may be due to individual differences rather than to the effect of the IV, as participants are not assigned randomly to groups.
- Cause and effect is more difficult to establish, as it is difficult to ascertain which aspects of the IV are having an effect.
- Raises the ethical issue of *voluntary informed consent*, and requires ethical sensitivity.

TYPES OF NON-EXPERIMENTAL INVESTIGATON

There are different types of investigative methods that are not experimental, and these include naturalistic observation studies, studies using correlational analysis, and interviews and questionnaire surveys.

Naturalistic Observation

WHAT IS A NATURALISTIC OBSERVATION STUDY?

Naturalistic observation involves looking at behaviour without interfering with it in any way. A crucial element is that the observer should not influence behaviour but remain inconspicuous.

Advantages of naturalistic observations:

- They have high ecological validity.
- There are no problems of demand characteristics or evaluation apprehension.
- A richness of behaviour can be observed.
- They are particularly useful when researching children or animals.

Disadvantages of naturalistic observations:

- They only provide descriptions of behaviour rather than explanations for it.
- There may be problems of reliability due to observer bias or imprecise recording of data.
- Such studies are difficult to replicate.

Investigations Using Correlational Analysis

WHAT IS A CORRELATION?

Studies using a correlational design investigate whether there is an association or relationship between two variables. For example, whether there is a relationship between aggression and amount of violent television watched, or whether people in the same family have similar IQs.

You have seen how to use the experimental method to investigate whether, for example, exposure to intense noise levels *causes* a drop in performance (see E&F p.242). In a correlational study no causal relationship can be determined. As an example, to investigate the relationship between violent behaviour and watching violent television, we would simply measure the amount of violent television a particular person watches and how aggressive they are, and then compare the two. If there is a relationship, we cannot say that one causes the other as there are other possible explanations. As well as the possibility that watching violent television causes aggression, it is possible that aggressive people like watching violent television, or that children from disadvantaged homes watch lots of television and are violent.

Advantages of using correlational analysis:

- The greatest use of correlation is in *prediction*. If two variables are correlated, you can predict one from the other.
- It is a useful method when manipulation of variables is impossible.
- Establishing *no* relationship between variables is useful in eliminating cause and effect.
- It is often possible to obtain large amounts of data on a number of variables more rapidly and efficiently than with experimental designs.

Disadvantages of correlational analysis:

- Cause and effect is impossible to establish.
- Interpretation of the results is difficult.
- A third, unknown, variable may be involved.
- Direction of causality is uncertain.

POSITIVE AND NEGATIVE CORRELATIONS

A *positive correlation* is one in which one variable increases as the other variable increases. If we are told that there is a positive correlation between health and optimism, it means that in general people high in optimism are also healthy, whilst those low in optimism are less healthy.

A *negative correlation* is one in which one variable increases as the other decreases. A negative correlation between work productivity and stress means that the *more* stressed a person is, the *less* work they produce; conversely, the *less* stressed they are the *more* work they do.

A *correlation coefficient* is a number that expresses the degree to which two things are related, and ranges from +1 to −1. If two variables are very closely related, the coefficient will be close to 1, say 0.9; if they are weakly related it will be low, say 0.13. A positive correlation is expressed as a positive number (+0.7) and a negative correlation is expressed as a negative number (−0.6).

Interviews and Questionnaire Surveys

Psychologists often want to talk to people, to find out about their experiences and opinions. There are many types of ways in which interviews can be conducted, and these have been detailed below. The advantages and limitations are mentioned in the 'comments' column.

TYPES OF INTERVIEWS AND QUESTIONNAIRE SURVEYS

Name	Description	Comments
Non-directive interview	The person is free to discuss anything.	Provides rich in-depth information. Not replicable, but not intended for that. Particularly useful in a case study.
Informal interview	General topics explored in depth.	Provides detailed information on general areas of interest. Not replicable.
Informal guided interview	The interviewer identifies issues to be raised and decides during the interview when and how to raise these issues.	Provides detailed information on specific topics. Difficult, but not impossible, to replicate.
Structured open-ended interview	All interviewees are asked the same question in the same order. Uses open-ended questions (no fixed answers).	Replicable. Permits good comparison between people.
Clinical interview	All interviewees are asked the same question initially, then their answers determine subsequent questions.	The name comes from its original use in a clinical setting. Very useful in talking to people about mental health problems. Used by Piaget when talking to children.
Fully structured interview	A standard set of questions in a fixed order. There is a restricted number of answers (e.g. yes/no; agree/disagree).	Allows replication and comparison between people. Quick and easy to collect data.
Questionnaire surveys (written interviews)	Written questionnaires are completed by participants with no spoken interview.	Replicable. Provides a lot of data quickly and cheaply.

NOTE: In all interviews, especially unstructured ones, there may be problems of *interviewer bias*. It is also possible that people may not tell the truth in order to give a good impression, which is known as *social desirability*.

ETHICAL CONSIDERATIONS OF DIFFERENT METHODS

It is of paramount importance that studies are conducted in an ethical manner. Listed below are some of the ethical issues raised by the different types of research methods.

Experiments:

- Participants may feel that they should do things they would not do normally. Milgram's research demonstrates this.
- Participants should be given the *right to withdraw* but they may feel reluctant to do so.

Field experiments:

- Most do not lend themselves to obtaining *informed consent* from participants.
- It is difficult for participants to know that they have the *right to withdraw*.
- It is also difficult to offer *debriefing*.

Natural experiments:

- There are problems of *informed consent* since this cannot be obtained.
- Researchers need to be sensitive if investigating the effects of an unpleasant event, such as a natural disaster.

Naturalistic observations:

- If participants do not know they are being observed—a situation called an *undisclosed observation*—then there are issues of *invasion of privacy* and *intrusion*. This would apply if, for example, one-way mirrors were used or if people were observed in public places.
- There may be issues of *confidentiality* if the place in which the psychologists made their observations (such as a hospital or school) can be easily identified, or if it was known they were visiting it.
- If the observer participates in a group (*participant observation*), he or she may influence the group behaviour without prior consent.

Correlational analysis:

- There can be problems with the way in which the public interpret the results of correlations, where they might think that correlation equals causation. This is especially true with *socially sensitive issues* such as the relationship between race and IQ.

Interviews:

- *Confidentiality* should always be respected, especially where personal issues are involved. It may not be sufficient to simply withhold someone's name since they may still be identifiable. Interviewers should take great care to avoid material getting into the wrong hands.
- Interviewees should not feel obliged to answer questions that they find embarrassing, and should be reassured that they do not have to answer any questions they do not want to answer.

AIMS AND HYPOTHESES

An aim is a general statement of *why* the study is being carried out. To illustrate this, we will use levels of processing theory (see E&F p.46).

FOR EXAMPLE: To investigate levels of processing theory.

An hypothesis states precisely *what* you expect to show. You need two of these; an experimental (alternative) hypothesis and a null hypothesis. The experimental (alternative) hypothesis states that some difference or effect will occur.

FOR EXAMPLE: "Free recall from LTM is higher when there is semantic processing at the time of learning than when there is non-semantic processing."

The null hypothesis states that the IV has no effect on the DV.

FOR EXAMPLE: "Semantic processing will have no effect on the amount of free recall from LTM."

NOTE: The term 'experimental hypothesis' only applies when using the experimental method. Otherwise, you should use the term 'alternative hypothesis'.

The experimental (alternative) hypothesis can directional or non-directional:

DIRECTIONAL
One-tailed
States the *direction* in which the results are to go. A one-tailed hypothesis is used in the example above because the whole essence of levels of processing theory is that one type of processing leads to better recall.

NON-DIRECTIONAL
Two-tailed
Sometimes we think the IV will affect the DV but we are not sure how, so we do not state the direction. For example, if we say that "arousal affects performance", it may make it worse or better.

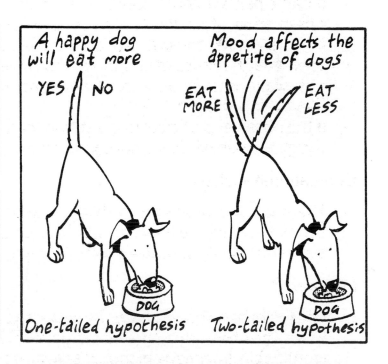

OVER TO YOU

Try the activity that asks you to identify IVs and DVs in a number of experimental set ups (see E&F p.258); the answers are provided.

RESEARCH DESIGNS

When conducting experiments, there are three research designs that are available to use. We will carry on using the levels of processing example (see E&F p.46) to explain the features of each one.

Independent Groups Design

Different participants are used in each of the conditions. One group of participants processes words semantically (e.g. by thinking of another word that means the same). The other group processes words physically (e.g. by counting the number of letters in each word).

Matched Pairs (Matched Participants) Design

This design uses two separate groups of people who are matched on a one-to-one basis on important variables, such as age or sex. This controls for some individual differences.

Repeated Measures Design

The same group of people is used in each of the two conditions. Each participant is tested on free recall after semantically processing some words and then tested on free recall after physically processing some words. This controls for all individual differences.

ADVANTAGES AND LIMITATIONS OF DIFFERENT RESEARCH DESIGNS

You need to be familiar with the various advantages and limitations of the different research designs that can be used.

Independent Groups Design

Advantages of the independent groups design include the following:

- There are no problems of *order effects* (see page 148).
- No participants are lost between trials.
- It can be used when a repeated measures design is inappropriate (e.g. when looking at gender differences).

Limitations of the independent groups design include the following:

- There may be important *individual differences* between participants to start with. To minimise this there should be *randomisation* (for explanation see page 137).
- You need more participants than you do with a repeated measures design.

Matched Pairs (Matched Participants) Design

Advantages of the matched pairs design include the following:

- It controls for some individual differences between participants.
- Can be used when a repeated measures design is inappropriate.

Limitations of the matched pairs design include the following:

- It is quite difficult to match participants in pairs. You need a large pool of participants from which to select.
- You need more participants than you do with a repeated measures design.

Repeated Measures Design

Advantages of the repeated measures design include the following:

- It controls for all individual differences.
- It requires fewer participants.

Limitations of the repeated measures design include the following:

- It cannot be used in studies in which participation in one condition affects responses in the other.
- Participants are likely to guess the purpose of the study, thus introducing problems with demand characteristics.
- There are problems of *order effects* (see page 148).

ORDER EFFECTS AND COUNTERBALANCING

When a repeated measures design is used there may be problems that result from participants doing the same task twice. The second time they carry out the task they may be:

- Better than the first time because they have had practice.
- Worse than the first time because they are tired or bored.

The problems are known as *order effects* because they arise due to the order of the conditions, but we cannot tell whether differences are genuinely due to the IV or the to order effects.

Solution

Use a technique called *counterbalancing,* where the group is split into two:

- Half the participants do Condition A (e.g. semantic processing) followed by Condition B (e.g. physical processing).
- Half the participants do Condition B followed by Condition A.

So, any order effects are balanced out. Counterbalancing can only be used when the total number of participants in the study is known. If this is not known, you will have to allocate participants to either Condition A followed by Condition B, or Condition B followed by Condition A, on a random basis (known as *randomisation* of order presentation).

FACTORS ASSOCIATED WITH RESEARCH DESIGN

In order for research to be properly conducted, there are certain guidelines that should be followed, and these are listed below:

- **Standardised instructions**. All participants are to be given identical instructions.
- **Standardised procedures**. All participants are to be treated in exactly the same way.
- **Control of variables**. As far as possible, confounding variables must be controlled, as they mask the effect of the IV. Any variables that change between conditions, such as participants becoming more tired, or being more motivated in one condition than another, are difficult to control. Such confounding variables are known as a *constant error.* It is important to control, or keep constant, certain variables such as time of day and location. These are known as *controlled variables.*
- **Operationalisation**. Some variables such as 'performance' are very general so we need to decide on a precise way to measure them. For example, we could measure 'performance in LTM' by the number of words remembered. This is known as *operationalising* the variable because it is defined in terms of the operations taken to measure it.
  Advantage: • Generally provides a clear and objective definition of even complex variables.
  Disadvantages: • Use of operational definitions are entirely circular.
                          • Often covers only part of the meaning of the variable or concept (e.g. operationalising verbal ability by solving anagrams when verbal ability cannot *only* be accessed in this way).
                          • Everyone is not always agreed on the accuracy of the operationalisation.
- **Pilot study**. This is a small-scale study carried out before the main one in order to check procedures, design, and so on. It helps sort out problems and allows for adjustments, thereby saving time and money.

RELIABILITY

One of the most important aspects of measurements is that they should be reliable. If measures are taken on more than one occasion they should be *consistent* or they are meaningless. If a speedometer gave different readings at the same speed it would be useless. The same applies to measuring behaviour. We can consider reliability in terms of *internal reliability* and *external reliability.*

Internal Reliability

This refers to how consistently a method measures *within itself*. For example, a ruler should measure the same distance between 0cm and 5cm as it does between 5cm and 10cm.

SPLIT-HALF TECHNIQUE

- Used for establishing the internal reliability of psychological tests; i.e. whether it gives consistent results across the tests.
- Take half of the scores (e.g. even-numbered questions) and compare them with the other half (e.g odd-numbered questions) to see how similar they are.
- The same participant does both halves at the same time.

INTER-RATER RELIABILITY (OR INTER-JUDGE RELIABILITY)

- Used when determining the reliability of observations, i.e. making sure that when several observers are coding complex behaviour of participants they agree with each other.
- To improve reliability in observations more than one observer must be used.
- All observers must have precise, clear categories of behaviour.
- All observers must be trained in the use of this system.
- Inter-rater reliability can be measured using a correlational analysis.

External Reliability

This refers to how consistently a method measures over time when repeated. Results from an IQ or personality test should not differ markedly from one occasion to another. This can be measured by using *test–retest method*, where the same test is given to participants on two separate occasions to see if their scores remain relatively similar. The interval between testings must be long enough to prevent a *practice effect* from occurring, but not so long that the measures may have changed anyway (e.g. reading ability may change over a period of six months).

NOTE: For *reliability* read *consistency*. When exam questions ask about 'reliability', substitute the word 'consistency' and you will be on the right track.

VALIDITY

Validity refers to whether a technique can achieve the purpose for which it was designed. 'Valid' means 'true', and measures are valid if they measure what they are supposed to measure. We will look at the validity of research studies, especially experiments, and ask whether the measurements taken will be a true reflection of what they are supposed to be measuring. For example, did the technique used by Milgram *really* measure obedience? One of the major problems with establishing validity in psychological research is that the more precisely and carefully you control conditions (by using a laboratory-type set up), the less valid the measures are likely to be in terms of how they generalise to the real world.

We need to distinguish between two types of validity; *internal validity* and *external validity*.

Internal Validity

Internal validity refers to the validity of an experiment within the confines in which it is carried out. It is the extent to which the measurements are accurate and the extent to which they measure what they are supposed to measure; thus it refers to the extent to which it is possible to establish *causality*. Internal validity establishes whether the IV really caused the results. Experiments may lack internal validity because of experimenter effects (see E&F pp.273–274), demand characteristics (see E&F pp.271–272), and participant reactivity (see E&F pp.270–171). In order to be valid, it is necessary to have standardised instructions (see E&F p.263) and randomisation (see E&F p.242).

External Validity

External validity refers to the validity of a study outside the research situation itself. Thus, it provides some idea of the extent to which the findings can be *generalised*. It can be referred to as *ecological* or *population validity*. When considering the issue of external validity and generalisability, it is necessary to consider four main aspects:

- **Populations**. Is the sample representative? Do the findings obtained from a given sample of individuals generalise to a larger population from which the sample was selected?
- **Locations**. Does the setting and/or situation created in the study generalise to a real-life setting and/or situation?
- **Measures or constructs**. Do the measures used generalise to other measures? For example, does a measure of long-term memory based on remembering word lists generalise to everyday memory?
- **Times**. Do the findings generalise to the past and future? For example, are people as obedient today as they were 30 years ago?

NOTE: Laboratory experiments have high internal validity, but fairly low ecological validity. Field experiments have high external validity, but fairly low internal validity.

SELECTION OF PARTICIPANTS

The *target population* is the whole group to which a researcher wishes to generalise the findings. Obviously the whole target population cannot be used so it is necessary to select just some of them. The *sample* of participants is the actual group of participants that take part in a study. A *representative sample* is a sample that is typical (representative) of the target population. There are several ways in which to select a sample:

- **Random sampling** involves having the names of the target population and giving each one an equal chance of being selected. This can be done by using a computer or drawing names from a hat.
- **Systematic sampling** is a modified version of random sampling that involves selecting, say, every one-hundredth name from a phone book.
- **Opportunity sampling** involves using whoever is available and willing. It is not representative because it is likely to comprise friends of the researcher, students, or people in a particular workplace.

Problems with Random and Systematic Sampling

It is almost impossible to obtain a truly random sample because obtaining a total list of the target population is difficult, not all of the target population may be available, and some people may refuse to take part, thus giving a *volunteer bias*.

Problems with Opportunity Sampling

Opportunity sampling can be an ad-hoc affair, and the sample really depends on who is available at the time. This type of group almost certainly constitutes a *biased sample*.

Random sampling

Opportunity sampling

NOTE: Only if we have a representative sample can we generalise to the target population but such a sample is difficult to obtain. The best we can do is to try and reduce *sampling bias*.

THE SAMPLE SIZE

When considering the ideal number of participants for each condition, there is no definite answer. Each study needs to be designed in such a way as to reduce *sampling bias*, and the following factors need to be taken into consideration:

- The sample should be large enough to be representative.
- The sample must not be so large that the study becomes very costly or time consuming.
- If the target population is large then it is probably going to have quite a lot of variation, so a fairly large sample will be required in order to be representative.
- If the target population is very small, it may be wise to use the *whole* population. This may apply to some very unusual disorders, or to people over the age of 105.
- If the research has important implications and will be used in policy making (e.g. testing a new biological therapy) then the sample size should be larger than a less important study such as an undergraduate research project.

If there is a general rule of thumb that applies to deciding on sample size, it is the following:

"The smaller the likely effect being studied, the larger the sample size needed to demonstrate it."

NOTE: Remember that not all the participants who volunteer to take part in a study are eligible. This adds to the number who need to be approached by the researcher. More importantly, not all participants who start a study will finish it (particularly with longitudinal studies) and this may leave you with a *biased sample.* This was true of Tizard and Hodges (1978, see E&F p.105) study of privation.

OVER TO YOU

Many famous psychological studies have used a biased sample. For example, Asch used students for his conformity studies (see E&F p.202), as did Zimbardo in his prison study (see E&F p.204). Can you think of any other examples where a biased sample was used? Try to think of examples that did not deal with students.

One of the reasons why students are not representative of the general population is that their mean age is low. Suggest *two* other ways in which students are not representative of the general population.

Would you need to use more participants in an independent measures design than a repeated measures design? If so, why?

THE RELATIONSHIP BETWEEN RESEARCHERS AND PARTICIPANTS

Interaction between researchers and participants can cause certain problems. These can be due to the behaviour of the participants or the behaviour of the researcher.

Participant Reactivity

Knowing you are being studied affects behaviour, and this is known as participant reactivity, or the Hawthorne effect. People's behaviour changes when an interest is shown in it, regardless of any other variables being manipulated. Two examples of participant reactivity are demand characteristics and evaluation apprehension:

- **Demand characteristics**. Orne (1962, see E&F p.271) found:
  - Most people do their best to comply with what they perceive to be the demands of the experimental situation, so they try to guess what is expected of them.
  - Others may look out for 'tricks' so they can avoid being caught out.
  - Some may try to do the opposite of what they think is expected.
  - Their interpretation of the situation affects their behaviour in some way.

  Demand characteristics can be reduced by using a *single blind* procedure, where participants do not know which condition they have been allocated to. Instead they are given a false account of the experiment so they will not discover clues as to the nature of the research. This can be problematic ethically as fully informed consent cannot be obtained.
- **Evaluation apprehension**. Concern by participants that they are being judged can alter their behaviour.

Investigator Effects

The researcher can inadvertently affect the results of an experiment. The main problem is *experimenter expectancy*, whereby the investigator's expectations can affect the behaviour of participants being tested. This was shown by Rosenthal's (1966, see E&F p.274) research with flatworms and rats. He demonstrated an expectancy effect when students were training rats to perform tricks, and found that those students who were told their rats had been bred for intelligence managed to teach their rats more tricks than those who had been told that their rats had been bred for dullness.

Investigator effects can be reduced by using a *double blind* procedure, where neither the investigator nor the participants know what the research hypothesis being tested is. However, this is often either impractical or too expensive.

DATA ANALYSIS

DESCRIPTIVE STATISTICS

Descriptive statistics are so named because they *describe* the results obtained from a particular study. For example, if a researcher measured the reading age of a whole class, of particular interest would be the average reading age and the top and bottom scores. We will look at summarising, in terms of central tendency, findings in terms of dispersion, and by drawing graphs and charts.

MEASURES OF CENTRAL TENDENCY

The Mean

The mean is obtained by adding the scores and dividing by the total number.

FOR EXAMPLE: The mean of the scores 2, 6, 8, 5, 7, 6, 3, 3 = *5* (40 ÷ 8).

ADVANTAGE

It is the only measure of central tendency that takes account of *all* scores.

DISADVANTAGE

It can give a distorted impression if there are any very unusual scores.

Example of a misleading mean
Scores
25
27
28
29
34
39
42
288
512 ÷ 8 = **64**

The Median

The median is the halfway point that separates the lower 50% of scores and the upper 50% of scores. If there is an odd number of scores, this the middle value. If there is an even number, it's halfway between the two middle scores.

FOR EXAMPLE: The median of 2, 4, 6, 7, 8, 9, 26 = *7* (the middle score),
and the median of 2, 4, 6, 10, 12, 13 = *8* (halfway between 6 and 10).

ADVANTAGE

It is unaffected by extreme scores. Here 26 is an extreme score, but it does not distort the measure.

DISADVANTAGES

It does not take account of most of the scores. It can be especially misleading if there are only a few scores.

The Mode

The mode is the most frequently occurring score (remember this by thinking of the mode as 'the fashionable one'!).

FOR EXAMPLE: The mode of 2, 5, 7, 8, 5, 4, 2, 7, 8, 7 = *7* (as 7 occurs most frequently).

Sometimes there is more than one mode. When there are two, it is called a *bimodal* distribution.

ADVANTAGES

It is unaffected by extreme scores, and it is useful when we want to know how *most* participants behaved. For example, in Milgram's study we want to know the *modal value* of where on the voltage scale most people went up to. Likewise, we may want to know the most frequent grade that students attained in an exam, or what most people's opinion is of a proposition.

DISADVANTAGES

Limitations of using the mode (the least-used measure of central tendency) are that it tells us nothing about all the other scores; it is often not very 'central'; and it tends to fluctuate from one sample to another.

MEASURES OF DISPERSION

Suppose you measured the reading ages of a class of children. In addition to wanting some indication of the average reading age, you would also want to know the dispersion of scores—the range of them. It would be possible to have two classes in which the mean reading age was 7 years, with one ranging from 6.5 years to 7.4 years and the other ranging from 5 years to 10.5 years. The classes are therefore quite different and would require different teaching methods. There are two principal measures that can be used (the *range* and *standard deviation*), and these have different levels of sophistication.

The Range

The range is the top value minus the bottom value plus 1. When using whole numbers, we add 1 to the value because they have probably been rounded up and down from fractional values, so this makes it more accurate. When the numbers are not whole, simply take the lowest from the highest.

FOR EXAMPLE: The range of 2, 5, 8, 6, 9, 3, 7, 4, 2, 7 = 8 (9–2 + 1).
The range of 2.3, 3.4, 5.5, 6.7, 7.2, 8.9, 9.9 = 7.6 (= 9.9 – 2.3).

ADVANTAGES

It is easy to calculate and see at a glance, and it takes full account of extreme values.

DISADVANTAGES

There are limitations, as it can be distorted by only one extreme score. If there had been one value of 25 in the first list above, the range becomes 24, three times what it was without that single score. Also, it only takes account of two scores (the highest and lowest) so it provides no indication of the *overall* spread of scores.

Standard Deviation

The standard deviation is a measure of dispersion of scores around the mean. It is a very useful measure especially when scores are normally distributed (i.e. fit a normal distribution curve, such as IQ or height, see E&F p.284) because about two-thirds of scores will lie within one standard deviation of the mean. If you don't have a good head for numbers, DON'T GIVE UP as this really is quite simple. Suppose the mean reading age of a group is 7 years and the standard deviation is one year. This means that two-thirds of all children will have reading ages between 6 years and 8 years (one year either side of the mean of 7).

ADVANTAGE

It takes account of all scores, so it provides a very accurate measure of the spread of scores. It is especially useful with normal distributions because it gives a very precise measure of variation.

DISADVANTAGES

There are no disadvantages or limitations as such, except that it is more difficult to calculate than other measures of dispersion.

GRAPHS AND CHARTS

It is helpful to use visual displays to summarise information and to get a feel for what it means. Information presented in a graph or chart makes it easier to understand what has been found, compared to simply presenting information about central tendency and dispersion.

The different types of graphs and charts include frequency polygons, histograms, bar charts, and scattergraphs, each of which will be considered in turn.

Frequency Polygon

This is a simple chart showing how *frequently* scores occur. The x axis (the horizontal one) shows the scores that have been obtained and the y axis (the vertical one) shows the frequency of the occurrence of the participants' scores. Below is a frequency polygon (or *line graph*) showing the scores that 25 male athletes obtained when asked to run 400 metres as quickly as possible.

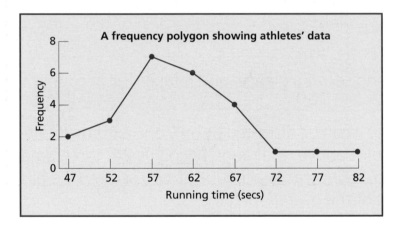

Histogram

Histograms provide another way of showing *frequencies,* but this time by using columns. The data from the athletes could be recorded in the following way:

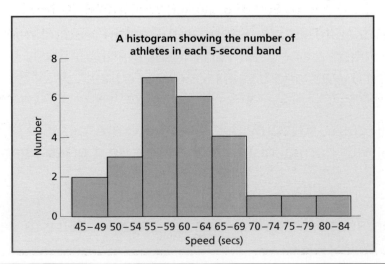

Bar Chart

Bar charts are used when scores are in *categories*, such as how many people are categorised as Type A, Type B, or Type C personality, or, as in the bar chart below, what people's favourite leisure activities are.

In a bar chart the categories are shown along the horizontal axis, and the frequencies are indicated on the vertical axis, as in a histogram. However, in contrast to the data contained in histograms, the categories in bar charts cannot be ordered numerically in a meaningful way. Instead, they are arranged in ascending or descending order of popularity. Another difference from histograms is that the rectangles (bars) do not usually touch each other.

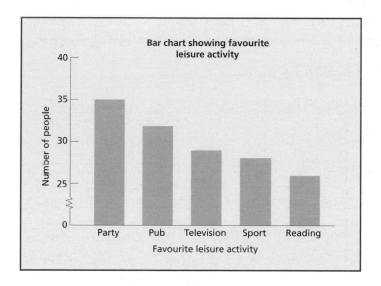

Scattergraphs

Scattergraphs (also known as scattergrams) are used to express *correlations*. To draw such a chart, one variable is put on the horizontal axis, and the other is put on the vertical axis. Then each pair of scores is placed as a dot or cross where the two scores meet.

Scattergraphs enable you to see at a glance whether a correlation is positive, negative, or if there is no relationship. The different graphs are shown below.

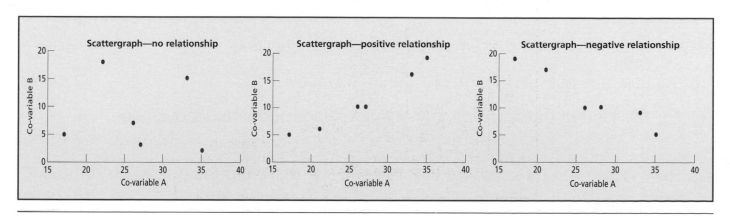

THE RESEARCH METHODS QUESTION

Here is a question you may be asked on this material: a suggested answer is included for the first three parts (but remember that there is not necessarily only one correct answer to some of these questions).

The Research Methods question differs in format from the other questions and is designed to test the AO3 component of the syllabus, which deals with conducting investigations and requires you to design, conduct, and report psychological studies (see page 5 for more details).

Example

Imagine that you have been asked to carry out a questionnaire study to assess whether stress has a negative effect on physical and psychological health.

Explain how you would carry out such a study.

(a) Suggest a suitable directional hypothesis for this study.   (2 marks)

ANSWER: There is a negative relationship between the amount of stress experienced and both physical and psychological health.

(b) How would you select respondents to take part in your study?   (2 marks)

ANSWER: By using an opportunity sample. This could be done by asking people that the investigator knows or has access to, trying to obtain as wide a range of people as possible.

(c) Why would you choose this particular method of selecting respondents?   (2 marks)

ANSWER: This is a convenient and practical way of obtaining a sample and, as long as care is taken, it can provide people from a variety of walks of life.

OVER TO YOU

Have a go at answering the remaining parts to this question:

(d) Suggest one question you might use in this study.   (2 marks)

(e) For this kind of question, identify one advantage and one disadvantage.
                                                                    (2 marks + 2 marks)

(f) How would you try to ensure that respondents answered the questions truthfully?
                                                                    (3 marks)

Sample Questions and Answers

What's it about?

In the previous chapters, after each topic we used examples of parts of questions (mainly the ones that test AO1 for 6 marks each) to show you what type of questions you are likely to have in the exam and how to answer them. In this chapter, you are shown whole questions and answers from every part of the AQA–A AS Level Psychology Specification. After each question, you are offered attempts to answer it by two hypothetical students, Sam and Chris, together with comments from the Senior Examiner about the marks that would be obtained and how the answers provided by Sam and Chris could be improved.

Revision should always be an *active* process; never just a matter of reading. As you work your way through this chapter, first try to plan an answer yourself and think very carefully about what is required. Go back over previous chapters in this guide if you need to. Then consider the answers offered by Sam and Chris and see what you think of them (and whether there are glaring omissions and inaccuracies) *before* reading the examiner's comments. If you think carefully about how an answer could be improved, you are much more likely to remember how to answer questions competently in the exam. Use the examiner's comments to check on what you thought would be an appropriate answer, and see how well you did.

Make sure you understand the *rubric* of the examinations, i.e. how many questions you must answer, how much choice you will be given, and so on. In the main textbook, Section 3 of Chapter 1 (see E&F pp.20–25) provides good advice on studying and taking examinations. Read this before you start working through this chapter; and in particular the marking scheme (see E&F p.24).

Finally, remember the advice in the first chapter of this guide—especially the bit about not panicking. Remember that you *can* do it, so GOOD LUCK!!!

What's in this section?

UNIT 1

COGNITIVE PSYCHOLOGY:
Human Memory

DEVELOPMENTAL PSYCHOLOGY:
Attachments in Development

1-hour exam: Answer one question on Human Memory and one on Attachments in Development. 30 minutes per question.

UNIT 2

PHYSIOLOGICAL PSYCHOLOGY:
Stress

INDIVIDUAL DIFFERENCES:
Abnormality

1-hour exam: Answer one question on Stress and one on Abnormality. 30 minutes per question.

UNIT 3

SOCIAL PSYCHOLOGY:
Social Influence

RESEARCH METHODS

1-hour exam: Answer one question on Social Influence and one on Research Methods. 30 minutes per question.

COGNITIVE PSYCHOLOGY   HUMAN MEMORY

(a) Outline **two** explanations of forgetting in long-term memory. (3 marks + 3 marks)
(b) Describe the procedures and findings of **one** study of capacity in short-term memory. (6 marks)
(c) Outline and evaluate the working memory model. (18 marks)

(a) Outline **two** explanations of forgetting in long-term memory. (3 marks + 3 marks)

WATCH OUT FOR: *Two explanations are required, and both must be relevant to LTM, not STM. This is an AO1 response that should take about 5 minutes to write.*

SAM'S ANSWER: One explanation of forgetting is the decay theory. It is said that the memory trace physically disappears. The second possibility is interference. In this case a new memory replaces an old memory.

CHRIS' ANSWER: The most likely explanation of forgetting in long-term memory is cue-dependent forgetting (retrieval failure). Most of the time memories are available but not accessible because we do not have the right cues. Cues can be provided in the form of words, or the context of initial storage (such as the room, or a smell, or the mood you were in). A second explanation would be interference. This may be proactive—something previously remembered interferes with a more recent memory to prevent recall. Or it can be retroactive—a new memory interferes with past memories to make them less accurate. In fact some research shows that interference does not cause forgetting. It happens when two sets of data are similar, which is not common in the real world.

> **EXAMINER'S COMMENT:** Sam has described two accounts of forgetting and both are appropriate for long-term memory. Both are lacking detail but are not muddled or flawed. Sam's credit would be a generous **2 marks + 2 marks** for this part of the question. Chris' answers are accurate and very detailed for both explanations. He would gain **3 marks + 3 marks**.

(b) Describe the procedures and findings of **one** study of capacity in short-term memory. (6 marks)

WATCH OUT FOR: *The question requires only procedures and findings (no aims or conclusions will be credited). The study must concern capacity in STM—not duration and not LTM. This is an AO1 response that should take about 5 minutes to write.*

SAM'S ANSWER: One study looked at capacity by giving participants a digit span task. Participants listen to a list of numbers and have to recall them. Usually they recall about 7 numbers accurately showing that the span of memory is about 7 items.

CHRIS' ANSWER: One of the earliest experiments in psychology (Jacobs, 1887) introduced the serial digit span task. In this task a participant is presented with a sequence of items, letters, and digits, and required to repeat them back immediately in the same order as they were presented. The participant is progressively given more items to recall on each trial. When accuracy of recall drops to 50% this is identified as the capacity of their STM. Jacobs found that the average span for digits was 9.3 items, whereas for letters it was 7.3.

> **EXAMINER'S COMMENT:** There are a number of things wrong with Sam's answer. It is not clear whether a specific study is being described, or a general summary of studies in this area. The question asks for one study. Giving the researcher's name would help. The last part of Sam's answer ("showing that the span of memory is about 7 items") is not creditworthy as it concerns conclusions rather than findings. The answer is basic, and lacks detail for both procedures and findings, so **2 marks**. Chris has identified a classic study and provided excellent detail on procedures but minimal, though exact, information for findings. There is no requirement to provide a balance in terms of procedures and findings but, for full marks, there would need to be more information on findings, so **5 marks**.

(c) Outline and evaluate the working memory model.   (18 marks)

> **WATCH OUT FOR:** Stick to a brief outline of the working memory model (only 6 marks available for AO1) and use any other material to evaluate the model—do not describe any research evidence or other theories you might use as a means of evaluation. This is an AO1/AO2 response that should take about 15 minutes to write.

SAM'S ANSWER: Baddeley and Hitch wrote the working memory model. This model has three components: the central executive, the phonological loop, and the visuo-spatial sketch pad. The central executive co-ordinates the activities of the other components. The phonological loop deals with sounds and the visuo-spatial sketch pad deals with visual things.

The model was a good idea because it showed that short-term memory was not just a single store, as claimed by the multi-store model, but was actually divided into several components. The reason for this was that Baddeley and Hitch noticed that people could quite often do two tasks at the same time if they were visual and acoustic, but not if they were both visual, or both acoustic. This led them to invent the working memory model.

The alternative was the multi-store model, which just had short-term memory and then long-term memory and also the sensory store. It is short-term memory that is equivalent to the working memory model.

Another model of memory is the levels of processing approach, which doesn't have anything specific to say about short-term or long-term memory, but just claims that we remember things because of how we process them.

The working memory model has also been supported by the word-length effect. This is the observation that people can remember short words better than long ones. This can be explained in terms of the phonological loop because it has a limited capacity and can only allow you 2 seconds. If a word takes longer than 2 seconds to pronounce then it can't be recalled from memory.

CHRIS' ANSWER: The working memory model was developed as an alternative to the short-term memory store, to explain the findings from various studies. Most important was the observation that people can perform two tasks simultaneously with little detriment to either task if both tasks involve different components: visual or acoustic. This led Baddeley and Hitch (1974) to propose

161

that the memory we use when working on a task (thus working memory) is divided into two areas: a visuo-spatial sketch pad that deals with visual material and a phonological loop that deals with auditory material. The activity of both of these modules is co-ordinated by a central executive. The central executive has a limited capacity and functions like attention—its task is to select what to attend to in the environment and then pass this data to one of the components or 'slave systems' in its control.

This model is an advance over the earlier multi-store model because it can better explain the way we process words and do things like mental arithmetic. For example, the phonological loop has been shown to be used in reading. Baddeley and Lewis did a study where people had to read a sentence where words were swapped round. If they had to say something meaningless at the same time (tying up the phonological loop) this reduced their ability to detect mistakes in the sentence. This is evidence of the role of the phonological loop in reading.

The phonological loop is also demonstrated in the word length effect. Baddeley et al. gave word lists to participants and asked them to recall the words immediately in the right order. They were able to recall short words better than long ones. It is argued that this is because the phonological loop can cope with words that take 2 seconds to say. That is the limit of the loop.

These findings can't be explained by the multi-store model. The working memory model is also superior because it explains memory as an active process and one that does not just rely on rehearsal. However, there have been negative criticisms. For example, many feel that the role of the central executive is not clear.

EXAMINER'S COMMENT: Sam's outline of the working memory model is comprehensive and accurate, but lacks detail. The names have been recalled but there is little evidence of understanding of the model. The AO1 credit for this answer would be **3 marks**. The rest of the answer contains some possibly relevant material and there are attempts to use this effectively as evaluation. The other two models of memory are mentioned and some comparisons are made, though they do not tell us much about the *value* of the working memory model. There is also mention of research that has supported the model, although it could have been clearer about how this does support the model. Overall, the material has been used in a reasonably effective manner, the commentary is fairly basic, and there is limited analysis, giving **6 marks** for AO2, a total of **9 marks**. The answer written by Chris reads much better and though it perhaps contains a fairly similar amount of material (only two studies and reference to the multi-store model) everything has been covered in more detail and the material has been used more effectively to provide an evaluation of the model. The outline of the working memory model is accurate and detailed, providing **6 marks** for AO1. It would be hard to suggest what else might be included given the time available. The evaluation is reasonably thorough and material has been used effectively. The only negative criticism is that the commentary is unbalanced—only one negative point is mentioned and this lacks elaboration. As recognition of this small limitation (slightly limited analysis), we would give **9 marks** for AO2, a total of **15 marks**.

Sam's total mark for this question would be 15, probably equivalent to a Grade C, or possibly a Grade B. Chris' total mark for this question would be 26, equivalent to a Grade A.

DEVELOPMENTAL PSYCHOLOGY
ATTACHMENTS IN DEVELOPMENT

(a) Explain what is meant by the terms 'deprivation' and 'privation'. (3 marks + 3 marks)
(b) Outline **one** psychological explanation of attachment. (6 marks)
(c) "Some mothers choose to stay at home to look after their children while other mothers have little choice in the matter and may feel quite worried about the effects of day care." To what extent does day care affect the social and/or cognitive development of children? (18 marks)

(a) Explain what is meant by the terms 'deprivation' and 'privation'. (3 marks + 3 marks)

WATCH OUT FOR: *You must explain rather than define, and make sure you do both terms. This is an AO1 response that should take about 5 minutes to write.*

SAM'S ANSWER: Sometimes young children get separated from their mothers, such as if they have to go to hospital, and this causes them considerable distress. This is deprivation. Privation is when a child has no chance to bond with anyone at all and may grow up to be affectionless.

CHRIS' ANSWER: Deprivation occurs when a child has formed an attachment but loses their primary attachment figure in early childhood. Privation occurs when a child has no opportunity to form an attachment bond in early life. This may occur due to an institutional upbringing. Both deprivation and privation are believed to have long-lasting detrimental effects, but privation is considered to be more harmful.

EXAMINER'S COMMENT: Sam has attempted to provide an explanation for both terms, but the explanation of deprivation is at best muddled. It is not clear what this has to do with deprivation but presumably the mention of distress was a link to deprivation. The second explanation is clearer but lacking detail. Sam would receive **1 mark + 2 marks**. Chris has defined both terms in reasonable detail. The last sentence is of questionable relevance in terms of explaining the terms. It would have been better to provide examples, like the mention of institutional care. This could have been further elaborated. Chris would receive **2(–) and 2(+) marks**; the second answer is not quite good enough for 3 marks and the first explanation isn't as weak as 1 mark. Jointly the answers are 4 marks-worth.

(b) Outline **one** psychological explanation of attachment. (6 marks)

WATCH OUT FOR: *This is an AO1 response that should take about 5 minutes to write. No credit for any evaluation or mention of more than one explanation.*

SAM'S ANSWER: Bowlby used the theory of evolution to explain attachment. He believed that babies innately form a bond with their mother because this keeps them safe from danger by staying close to her. It also teaches them about later relationships. Bowlby believed that babies only form one relationship—this is called monotropy. If no attachment is formed, then they may have problems in later life. Bowlby has been criticised because other people say that children can recover from early bad experiences.

CHRIS' ANSWER: Bowlby believed that children are innately programmed to form one major attachment in early life and that this attachment bond is crucial to satisfactory later social and emotional development. Based on the work of ethologists, Bowlby proposed that there was a critical or sensitive period between the ages of about 7 months to 3 years during which the child is biologically predisposed to form an attachment because this ensures their physical safety. If this does not occur then the consequences in later life can be very serious and include depression, an affectionless uncaring personality, and low intelligence. Bowlby also suggested that this first main emotional relationship acts as an internal working model (or template) for later relationships. If the child feels insecure in this first relationship then they are liable to feel insecure in all subsequent relationships.

> **EXAMINER'S COMMENT:** Sam offers several good points about Bowlby's theory of attachment. The response is generally accurate and contains some detail (e.g. mention of the theory of evolution and use of the term 'monotropy'), but not enough for 5 marks. The criticism that is given is not creditworthy but marks are not deducted for this, so **4 marks**. Chris' answer demonstrates the kind of detail that is required for the full **6 marks**. In fact, there is probably more than 6 marks-worth here.

(c) "Some mothers choose to stay at home to look after their children while other mothers have little choice in the matter and may feel quite worried about the effects of day care." To what extent does day care affect the social and/or cognitive development of children? (18 marks)

> **WATCH OUT FOR:** *Get the right balance between AO1 (6 marks) and AO2 (12 marks). Cut down on description and concentrate on using material effectively to answer the question. Use the quotation to guide you. Social and/or cognitive development is acceptable. This is an AO1/AO2 response that should take about 15 minutes to write.*

SAM'S ANSWER: Some studies show that day care is good for children but others indicate that it is bad. A study in Sweden carried out over a number of years showed that children who had been in day care from an early age were better at school than those who had stayed at home. But a study in Texas showed that children who went to nursery school from a young age were behind the other children in schoolwork and did not mix as well with other children.

The day care provided in Sweden is probably better than in Texas because the Swedish government is in favour of mothers working and puts a lot of money into day care. In Texas most of the children came from poor homes and the nurseries were not very good either.

There are other things to consider when assessing whether day care is good or bad. One thing is that children from very bad homes will do better in day care than if they stayed at home with their mums. On the other hand, if children go into poor quality day care, like that provided by some childminders, they will not do well at all and they will be miserable.

In conclusion, day care is good if it improves the child's circumstances but it can be harmful if it is of poor quality.

CHRIS' ANSWER: Day care refers to the care of children by someone other than the people with whom they are brought up. Early research tended to focus on whether day care was harmful or beneficial, but this is probably too simplistic a view as the effects are complex and may be different for different children.

Andersson (1992) conducted a longitudinal study of day care in Sweden and found that at age 13, children who had entered day care before the age of 1 year were performing better in schoolwork and were socially more mature than those who had entered later or not at all. This implies that cognitive and social development is improved by day care. It is important to note, however, that the children who went into day care came from homes of a higher socioeconomic status than the 'home' children with whom they were compared. Another consideration was that staff–child ratios in Sweden are very low so children get a lot of attention.

A study in Texas by Vandell et al. (1990) yielded rather different results. This showed that children who had spent a great deal of time in day care got on worse with their peers, felt less secure, and did less well academically than other children when they went to school.

The reason for these different findings may be due to differences in quality of the care but could also be due to differences in socioeconomic groups. In Texas the quality of care is generally poorer than in Sweden, due perhaps to the greater funding provided by the State in Sweden. We have already said that the Swedish children were from high socioeconomic groups, whereas this was not true of the Texan children. When assessing the effects of day care, it is therefore necessary to take careful account of the quality of care and of the home background of the children.

It is also necessary to consider individual differences. Some children seem to benefit more from day care than do others. Egeland and Hiester (1995) believe that day care is of little benefit to secure children but has a positive effect on insecure ones. The latter seem to benefit considerably from a more stimulating environment than the ones at home, with possibly more warmth shown by the staff.

Overall, the evidence suggests that good quality day care can be of benefit to children. To be of good quality, it needs to have low child–staff ratios, consistency of care (low staff turnover), a warm atmosphere, and plenty of variety in the activities available. If these conditions are met, there is no reason to believe that day care is anything but beneficial.

EXAMINER'S COMMENT: Sam's answer is somewhat brief but it does answer the question, using psychological research to defend the points made. Descriptions of studies are kept brief and the focus is on effective use of material. Analysis is reasonable insofar as the response does have a good structure. In terms of AO1 the material is generally accurate but limited and lacking detail, a generous **3 marks**. The AO2 content is again limited though reasonably effective and with a reasonable commentary, giving **6 marks** for a total **9 marks** for this part of the question. Chris' answer covers much of the same material as Sam's but provides more detail of the research studies and more evaluative comments on what the research means and the possible limitations of the studies. Chris also provides additional commentary at the start about the difficulty of providing a simple answer, and commentary at the end about quality being the issue and how that can be provided. Full marks for this response, given the time limit set, so **18 marks**.

Sam's total mark for this question would be 16, probably equivalent to a Grade B/C. Chris' total mark for this question would be 28, equivalent to a Grade A.

PHYSIOLOGICAL PSYCHOLOGY STRESS

(a) Outline the main features of Selye's General Adaptation Syndrome. (6 marks)
(b) Describe the findings and conclusions of **one** study into the relationship between stress and physical illness. (6 marks)
(c) Consider the extent to which individual differences modify the effects of stressors. (18 marks)

(a) Outline the main features of Selye's General Adaptation Syndrome. (6 marks)

WATCH OUT FOR: *You need to provide more than a list of the stages. This is an AO1 response that should take about 5 minutes to write.*

SAM'S ANSWER: Selye said there were three stages in his GAS—alarm, resistance, and exhaustion. In the first stage the body tries to cope with the stress and your heart rate may get faster. Then you adapt to the stress, provided it's not too great, and the body settles down but remains 'on alert'. But if this does not work and the stress is too great you get exhausted and ill.

CHRIS' ANSWER: Selye identified three stages that rats passed through when undergoing severe stress. The first was the alarm response, referred to as 'fight or flight', in which adrenaline is pumped into the bloodstream causing increase in heart rate and breathing. Once stress was reduced, the second stage of resistance was reached during which there was a period of adjustment. Adrenaline levels returned to normal, the body attempted to repair any damage, and arousal remained high. If these attempts failed because the stress did not decrease, then the third stage of exhaustion was reached, during which the rats collapsed and died.

> **EXAMINER'S COMMENT:** Sam has identified all three stages and provided some information about each, though in each there are details that are lacking. Overall this response is limited, generally accurate but not very detailed, so **4 marks**. Chris' answer provides more detail and includes use of some technical terms (e.g. 'adrenaline'). It is enough for **6 marks**.

(b) Describe the findings and conclusions of **one** study into the relationship between stress and physical illness. (6 marks)

WATCH OUT FOR: *Only findings and conclusions are creditworthy. Select one identifiable and appropriate study. This is an AO1 response that should take about 5 minutes to write.*

SAM'S ANSWER: One study that showed a relationship between stress and physical illness looked at men who had a kind of personality called Type A. They were very competitive, unpleasant people who got impatient with their fellow workers and other people. When they were followed up over a period of time they were much more likely to have had a heart attack than people who were more relaxed and friendly. This shows that this personality type can cause you to have a heart attack.

CHRIS' ANSWER: In a study of the relationship between coronary heart disease (CHD) and personality, Friedman and Rosenman studied a group of initially healthy men, who, in 1960, were suffering from no heart disease. After 8½ years, however, 70% of those who subsequently developed CHD were found to be Type A personality. This particular personality is characteristic of people who are impatient, hostile, and achievement-orientated. They concluded that Type A behaviours were all attributes that contribute to a stressful life and that this personality type with its associated behaviours was strongly linked to increased chances of heart disease. This was supported by the fact that the relationship still remained when account was taken of various other factors, such as blood pressure, smoking, and obesity.

EXAMINER'S COMMENT: Sam has not named the study, but it is fairly clear that it is the one by Friedman and Rosenman. This is essentially a study of personality and stress but can also be used to demonstrate the link with illness because personality type predisposes some people (Type A) to cope less well with stress. Only the final two sentences are creditworthy, though the rest of the answer is important for identifying the study. The details are fairly basic and the conclusion is not entirely correct because the study only demonstrated a link between stress (personality) and heart attacks, not a cause. Sam would receive **2 marks**. Chris has made the Friedman and Rosenman study more explicitly relevant by stating in the conclusions that the study links stress to illness via personality. The answer reads well but really there is only a limited amount of information provided for both findings and conclusions. The last sentence is more of a (positive) criticism than a conclusion. Chris would receive **4 marks**.

(c) Consider the extent to which individual differences modify the effects
     of stressors.   (18 marks)

WATCH OUT FOR: For AO1 credit you might describe relevant studies, and for AO2 credit evaluate the studies and/or consider what they tell us about individual differences (i.e. look at the conclusions). This is an AO1/AO2 response that should take about 15 minutes to write.

SAM'S ANSWER: Men and women respond differently to stress and this may make a difference to their health. In one study in which people did stressful tasks, the men's blood pressure was higher than the women's. This could be because men get more worked up by doing something like that as they do not like to be seen to fail, so their blood pressure rises.

Personality may also make a difference to how people respond to stress. People who show a personality trait called 'hardiness' are likely to experience less stress than people who are not like that (Kobasa). People who are hardy are committed to their work (but that could sometimes increase stress), see problems as challenges, so that decreases stress, and like to be in control. If you are in control, then you are less stressed. This was shown in a study of older people in a nursing home. It does not always work like that though because Brady's executive monkeys were in control and they died of stress.

Culture can also make stress worse. This would be if people were not from the country they are living in so they had to suffer prejudice. They are also likely to be quite poor and this increases stress. In America, the black people who have lived there for many generations suffer a lot of stress and have high blood pressure. This could be because they are genetically predisposed to heart disease, or because their diets are unhealthy due to poverty and poor education. But the last two factors also contribute to stress.

CHRIS' ANSWER: There are several factors that can mediate the effects of stress. In this answer the effects of gender, personality, and culture will be considered.

With respect to gender, Stone et al. (1990) found that, compared with men, women showed lower increases in blood pressure when performing stressful tasks. This may be due to physiological differences (such as hormones) between men and women but could also be due to differences in attitude. Traditionally men are more competitive than women and this may increase the stress they experience in such conditions.

Another factor that might help women cope better with stress than men is that women are more inclined to seek social support during times of stress, especially if the source of stress is relationships. Several studies indicate that social support can help alleviate stress.

Kobasa (1979) believes that a set of personality traits she calls 'hardiness' can help people cope well with stress. Hardiness involves commitment, challenge, and control. It may be the third characteristic—that of control—that is particularly relevant here. Many studies indicate that when people feel in control of their lives they are much better able to cope with stress. For example, Langer and Rodin (1976) showed that when elderly residents in a nursing home were able to make decisions about the arrangement of their rooms and what films to watch, they lived longer than residents not offered this choice. However, Funk (1992) considers that the concept of hardiness is rather vague and difficult to assess.

Culture is another individual difference that may modify the effects of stress. Again we return to the issue of social support. Weg (1983) looked at a group of people in Georgia who have very long life expectancy. Although there might be physical reasons for this—such as genes and a healthy diet—he noted that these people provide a great deal of social support for each other, which reduces stress.

One aspect of culture that has attracted attention is what Anderson (1991) calls acculturation stress: the problems experienced by minority groups in adapting to majority values, norms, and lifestyles. These groups also experience stress in the form of prejudice and discrimination.

Overall, assessing the effect of individual differences in modifying the effects of stress is problematic because it is impossible to isolate 'stress' from other social, psychosocial, and biological factors. Any one of a number of factors, such as genes, social class, level of education, and lifestyle may interact to increase or modify the impact of potentially stressful events.

EXAMINER'S COMMENT: Sam's response is a reasonable attempt to answer the question. It examines information about all three sources of individual differences, describing some studies and offering reasonable commentary and limited analysis of these. There is a good balance between description and evaluation—providing more of the latter, as is required, though the descriptive material is limited (lacks precise details, no studies mentioned for culture), so **3 marks**. The evaluation is reasonably effective, worth possibly as much as **7 marks**, since the commentary is better than basic, giving a total of **10 marks**. Chris' answer provides more descriptive details and also a more informed and careful analysis. The final paragraph is excellent in actually attempting to offer a conclusion by considering some wider issues. It is a coherent and effective response and should receive the maximum of **18 marks**.

Sam's total mark for this question would be 16, probably equivalent to a Grade B/C. Chris' total mark for this question would be 28, equivalent to a Grade A.

INDIVIDUAL DIFFERENCES ABNORMALITY

(a) Describe **three** characteristics of anorexia nervosa.　(2 marks + 2 marks + 2 marks)
(b) Outline assumptions of the biological (medical) model
　　of abnormality in terms of its view on causes of abnormality　(6 marks)
(c) "Individuals who are described as abnormal are not that
　　different from the rest of us." Outline and evaluate attempts
　　to define psychological abnormality.　(18 marks)

(a) Describe **three** characteristics of anorexia nervosa.　(2 marks + 2 marks + 2 marks)

WATCH OUT FOR: *Record three characteristics, each in enough detail for 2 marks. This is an AO1 response that should take about 5 minutes to write.*

SAM'S ANSWER: Three characteristics of anorexia nervosa are low weight (85% of normal weight), distorted body image, and loss of menstrual periods.

CHRIS' ANSWER: The first characteristic of anorexia nervosa is fear of weight gain. Anorexics think about food all the time and find strange ways to restrict their food intake and/or exercise excessively. Second, anorexics have low body weight. A weight below 85% of normal weight for height and age is considered abnormal. Third, anorexics have a distorted body image. They often think they are still fat when they are severely underweight and deny the seriousness of their low weight.

> **EXAMINER'S COMMENT:** Sam has recorded three characteristics, but virtually nothing else. Each is correct but lacking detail, therefore 1 mark for each, so **3 marks**. In contrast, Chris has offered some detail for each of the three characteristics and would receive the full 2 marks for each, so **6 marks**.

(b) Outline assumptions of the biological (medical) model of abnormality in
　　terms of its view on causes of abnormality.　(6 marks)

WATCH OUT FOR: *The focus is on the biological (medical) model and assumptions (in the plural) related to causes not treatment. This is an AO1 response that should take about 5 minutes to write.*

SAM'S ANSWER: The basic assumption of the biological model is that abnormality is an illness with a physical cause. Mental illness may be caused by something you inherit, or some disease, or it may be due to abnormal hormone levels. Whatever it is, these causes are physical. Mental illness is just like physical illness, and it should be treated like physical illness by using drugs or other somatic therapies.

CHRIS' ANSWER: The main assumption of the biological (medical) is that mental illness is the same as physical illness, i.e. it is caused by physical factors. There are various possible physical factors. First, it may be caused by genetic material so that mental illness is inherited. Second, mental illness may be due to abnormal levels of neurotransmitters (such as serotonin) or hormones. Third, it may be due to abnormalities in the brain structure. Finally, mental illness may be due to micro-organisms. These are all assumptions of the medical model.

> **EXAMINER'S COMMENT:** Sam's answer starts well but then finishes by looking at the biological model in terms of treatments. This material is not relevant to the question. The first two sentences are creditworthy and the third one is a repetition. Some details are included and the answer is generally accurate, but limited, so **3 marks**. All of Chris' answer is relevant and provides sufficient detail for the full **6 marks**.

(c)   "Individuals who are described as abnormal are not that different from the rest of us." Outline and evaluate attempts to define psychological abnormality.   (18 marks)

WATCH OUT FOR: 'Attempts' is in the plural therefore cover more than one attempt for AO1 and AO2, and focus more on evaluation as there are twice as many marks. This is an AO1/AO2 response that should take about 15 minutes to write.

SAM'S ANSWER: One way to define abnormality is the statistical infrequency model. This suggests that what is normal is what is true for most people. The rest is abnormal. The problem with this definition is that some abnormal behaviours are actually desirable. For example, to be a genius is abnormal but still desirable. Another problem is that it is difficult to identify a cut-off point. But this method is useful for some cases, such as defining mental retardation.

A second way to define abnormality is deviance from social norms. In this case it is deviant behaviour that is abnormal. Society sets social norms about what behaviours are deemed to be acceptable. The problem with this definition is that it varies from one society to another so there are no absolutes and it can be misused by tyrants, as it was with Russian dissidents.

A third way to define abnormality is the failure to function adequately. This model makes it easy to objectively identify abnormality because you can have a list of things that count as functioning adequately. But the problem is that the person may be quite happy and think they are coping okay, when it is their family that has a problem.

Finally, there is the ideal mental health model that gives a list of things that are signs of mental health. The problem with this definition is that it is culturally relative and is too ideal—not many of us would be normal according to this list.

In the end we have to say that it is hard to define abnormality.

CHRIS' ANSWER: Psychologists have proposed many different ways to define abnormality. The most obvious way to do this is in terms of statistical infrequency. Any behaviour that occurs rarely is considered to be abnormal (not normal). The main objection to this definition is that it fails to distinguish between desirable and undesirable behaviours. Genius is abnormal but still desirable. Divorce is statistically frequent but undesirable and abnormal (not standard behaviour). Another problem is that statistical infrequency is culturally relative. It is dependant on the norms of a particular culture and, if these norms are used with people from other cultures, then they may be inappropriate.

Another way to define abnormality is with reference to social norms. These are norms that are not established by statistical frequency but instead are established by a social group who dictate what is acceptable behaviour for that society. Anyone who deviates from these norms is seen as abnormal. This again is clearly culturally relative. This definition also has the potential for social abuse. In Russia the government dealt with political dissidents by labelling them as mentally ill and locking them up. In the UK homosexuality was seen as a mental illness because it was socially deviant. It is a potentially dangerous way to define abnormality.

The third way to define abnormality is in terms of a failure to function adequately. This approach takes the individual into account, expressing abnormality in terms of the individual's inability to cope with day-to-day living. It would seem appropriate to suggest that if an individual cannot cope then some form of help is required, but there is the question of who decides when the individual is not coping. In some cases of mental illness the individual is perfectly content, and it is others who say they are not coping. There is also the problem, again, of cultural relativism since one culture's idea of coping is not the same in another culture (e.g. ideas of being punctual or going to the office every day).

The fourth main way to define abnormality is in terms of ideal mental health criteria. We define physical illness as the absence of certain signs of health, so why not do the same for mental illness? Jahoda wrote a list of criteria that represent mental health including high self esteem, capacity for personal growth, autonomy, and mastery of the environment. The list is daunting and one wonders if any of us are normal. The list is also related to one culture—not all cultures would place personal growth on their list. It is more related to individualist rather than collectivist societies.

What this shows us is that no one definition works very well, yet we do need some way of defining abnormality in order to decide when an individual needs treatment. It is not sufficient to wait for people to ask because they might be dangerous to themselves or others.

EXAMINER'S COMMENT: Sam has managed to cover all four of the named definitions in the specification. For some of them a reasonable description is offered, but for the most part it is a list of the models. There is a trade-off between depth (not much given) and breadth (which is comprehensive). The AO1 credit would be **3 marks** because of the lack of detail. For each definition reasonable commentary is given, though the analysis of the comments is somewhat limited. The material has been used effectively, on balance giving AO2 **8 marks**. The last sentence is a rather limp ending and not worth any credit. The total is **11 marks**. Chris' answer goes that extra mile for both AO1 and AO2. There is more detail provided for AO1 and much more elaboration, understanding, and effective use of material for AO2. It is a very long answer but some candidates can manage to write this much in 15 minutes, especially when the question is very straightforward. Notice that there is twice as much AO2 material, which is important in attracting full marks, giving AO1 **6 marks** and AO2 **12 marks**, for a total of **18 marks**.

Sam's total mark for this question would be 17, probably equivalent to a Grade B. Chris' total mark for this question would be 30, equivalent to a Grade A.

We all want to be mentally healthy, but should we all want to be totally "normal"?

(a) Explain what is meant by the terms 'experimental validity' and 'ecological validity'. (3 marks + 3 marks)
(b) Describe the conclusions of **one** study of conformity and give **one** criticism of this study. (3 marks + 3 marks)
(c) To what extent do studies of obedience infringe ethical guidelines? (18 marks)

(a) Explain what is meant by the terms 'experimental validity' and 'ecological validity'. (3 marks + 3 marks)

WATCH OUT FOR: *Describe both terms, explain rather than define. This is an AO1 response that should take about 5 minutes to write.*

SAM'S ANSWER: Experimental validity concerns the extent to which an experiment is valid. Ecological validity is about whether the findings of a study are relevant to all aspects of human behaviour, not just the setting in which the study was conducted.

CHRIS' ANSWER: The term validity refers to whether something is true. There are several kinds of validity. Experimental validity is the extent to which the procedures of an experiment are viewed as real or believable by the participants. For example, in Milgram's experiment there have been questions about whether the participants were behaving like they would in real life because they may not have seen the experiment as real. Ecological validity concerns the extent to which the findings of one study can be generalised to other situations. For example, Milgram's study was conducted in a prestigious university with men. When the setting changed, obedience levels dropped. This means that the original study lacked ecological validity because it applied to a particular set of circumstances.

> **EXAMINER'S COMMENT:** Sam's first explanation is circular, using the same words to provide a definition. As it is not actually wrong it could not receive zero marks. The second explanation is better but Sam's understanding is not very clear. **1(–)** and **1(+) marks** would seem appropriate. Chris has used examples to help explain the concepts, gaining a maximum of **6 marks**.

(b) Describe the conclusions of **one** study of conformity and give **one** criticism of this study. (3 marks + 3 marks)

WATCH OUT FOR: *Describe conclusions only. Criticism may be positive or negative. Only one is required; set it in the context of the study. This is an AO1 response that should take about 5 minutes to write.*

SAM'S ANSWER: Asch did a study of conformity. A number of men were sat around a table and shown a set of three lines. They had to say which line was most similar to the stimulus line. When they gave the wrong answer the true participant was confused but often conformed to the group, even though he knew this was wrong. This shows that people may be quite conformist. One criticism of this study is that it involved all men.

CHRIS' ANSWER: In Asch's study, it was concluded that conformity was demonstrated, as long as all participants were in agreement. In the variations on the study there were other conclusions, for example Asch showed that the presence of one dissenter allows the true participant to stick to their own beliefs, which may be more true to life. Asch also pointed out that even though there was 30% conformity, many participants actually behaved independently when the situation was unambiguous. One criticism of the study was that the sample was biased—it involved only men and students. It may be that other people do not behave the same way.

> **EXAMINER'S COMMENT:** Most of Sam's answer is not creditworthy as it is concerned with the *procedures* of Asch's study. Only the last two sentences would receive credit and both are basic, so **1 mark + 1 mark**. Chris has described an excellent range of conclusions (**3 marks**) but provided slightly less detail for the criticism (**2 marks**).

(c) To what extent do studies of obedience infringe ethical guidelines?   (18 marks)

WATCH OUT FOR: *Only studies of obedience are relevant; these should be described (AO1) and evaluated in terms of ethical infringements. Focus should be on evaluation. This is an AO1/AO2 response that should take about 15 minutes to write.*

SAM'S ANSWER: Many studies of obedience have been accused of being unethical. The best known study is the one by Milgram where he arranged for a participant to think he was drawing lots to see who was the teacher and who was the learner. It was prearranged that the participant was going to be the teacher. He had the task of giving electric shocks to the learner every time the learner made a mistake. The shocks got stronger and stronger each time, and the machine showed descriptions like 'danger level'. The learner started to scream in pain but the 'teacher' was told "you must continue". 65% of them continued to the highest level of shock, which was supposedly fatal.

Milgram repeated this experiment in many different settings, such as in a downtown office where there was less reason for the teacher to obey because the authority (the experimenter) had less prestige.

Other obedience experiments are also unethical. Hofling's study of nurses required them to give a drug to a patient. The instructions were given over the phone by an unknown doctor for an excessive dose. All of this was against the rules, yet 21 out of 22 nurses obeyed. They said they did it because that's what nurses do. In fact, attempts to replicate this study haven't been successful so we don't know how much it tells us about obedience. The study has also been criticised because it lacks ecological validity as it applies to only one particular kind of relationship.

Another obedience study was conducted by Bickman where people in the street were asked to pick up litter or lend someone change. People were more likely to obey someone in a uniform.

In another study of obedience role-play was used, where participants had to interview someone and make them feel uncomfortable during the interview. They continued, even though the person they were interviewing became more and more distressed. This is supposed to be less objectionable than Milgram's study, but it might have been just as distressing as they were face-to-face with the participants.

All of these studies had ethical problems but that is hard to avoid with studies of obedience.

CHRIS' ANSWER: Many studies of obedience have been criticised for infringing ethical guidelines, but is this true? In this essay I will look at several such studies. The best known is Milgram's study. One ethical problem is the question of whether participants did have the right to withdraw. Some would argue that the instruction "You must continue" from the experimenter made it very difficult for the participant to withdraw. On the other hand, participants were told at the start of the experiment that they could stop at any time and they would still be paid. Even so, the participant may feel he has a duty to continue. Milgram could claim that this was not an infringement of guidelines (which weren't in place anyway at the time of this study).

Another ethical issue in Milgram's study is the extent to which participants were psychologically harmed by their experience, another ethical guideline. Milgram did offer them all counselling afterwards. But does this compensate for the real distress that many experienced? They were seen to sweat and dig their fingernails into their palms. Afterwards, some said that they had found the experience valuable.

Psychological harm is also an issue in the study by Meeus and Raaijmakers. Participants had to interview potential job applicants who were told to behave as if they were distressed by the humiliating statements participants were asked to use. Even though participants were told this was a role-playing exercise, the distress they experienced was real, and at the time of this study (1990s) there were ethical guidelines in place.

The study by Hofling et al. may also have caused psychological distress to participants because they must have felt guilty about what they were doing. This study caused a further ethical problem in that the nurses' professional relationships may have been affected by the study. Psychological research should leave things as they were before the study, yet in this study the nurses may have found it difficult to feel the same about doctors.

Finally, the study by Bickman was a field experiment. The ethical problem here is that it was not possible for participants to give their informed consent—which was true of all the studies above because participants had been deceived about the true nature of the experiment. But in Bickman's study it was not possible to compensate for this by debriefing participants afterwards. The excuse is that this kind of infringement is necessary in order to find out about obedience, but does this research really need to be repeated over and over again?

EXAMINER'S COMMENT: Sam has displayed a good knowledge of obedience studies, but that was not what was required by the question. The answer should *use* such material to construct an argument about whether such studies do infringe ethical guidelines. There is minimal reference to the ethical issues, and even these references do not address the actual question. For AO1 the content is accurate but concerned with procedures and therefore limited, verging on basic, so **3 marks**. The AO2 content is just discernible; even though there is commentary and criticism it is not relevant to the question set, so **2 marks**, for a total of **5 marks**. Notice how Chris starts the answer with the question, to ensure that he is answering the question set rather than the question he would like to answer. Chris' answer covers the same studies as Sam's but, first of all, there is no time wasted on describing the studies themselves. It is the ethical issues/guidelines that are described. Second, the material has then been used to consider whether these were infringements and also to question whether they were necessary. No conclusion is offered, which detracts marginally from the analysis, but otherwise this is a balanced and informed essay. AO1 credit would be **5 marks** because the ethical guidelines are not always detailed. AO2 credit would be **10 marks** for the slightly limited analysis; a total of **15 marks**.

Sam's total mark for this question would be 9, possibly equivalent to a Grade E—just. Chris' total mark for this question would be 26, equivalent to a Grade A.

RESEARCH METHODS

A psychology student decides to conduct her coursework study on conformity. She plans to stop people in the street and ask them to estimate the number of jellybeans in a jar. To test participants' conformity she will ask them to respond on a sheet of paper that has the answers of other participants. Some participants will be shown sheet 1, which has answers that are high estimates. These participants would belong to the 'high estimate' group. Other participants (the 'low estimate' group) will be shown sheet 2, which has low estimates. The student prepares 30 sheets—15 for each condition—and hands these out in a random order to participants.

The student's initial hypothesis was that participants would conform to the norm established by the answers on the sheet. The 'high estimate' group should produce a set of higher estimates than the 'low estimate' group.

(a) State a suitable directional hypothesis for this study. (2 marks)

(b) Name the research method used in this study. (1 mark)

(c) Describe **one** advantage and **one** disadvantage of this method in the context of this study. (2 marks + 2 marks)

(d) Identify the research design used in this study and describe **one** limitation of this design. (1 mark + 2 marks)

(e) Describe an example of the kind of data that the student is likely to collect, and describe a suitable measure of central tendency that could be used to represent this data. (2 marks + 2 marks)

(f) Describe **two** methods that you could use to select participants for this study. (2 marks + 2 marks)

(g) Identify **one** ethical problem that may have arisen in this study and suggest a way to deal with it. (1 mark + 2 marks)

(h) The student found no difference between the two groups of participants. What conclusion would you draw from this? (3 marks)

(i) The students decided to conduct some further research into conformity using a questionnaire. Write **two or more** questions that could form part of such a questionnaire on conformity. (6 marks)

WATCH OUT FOR: *Write an appropriate amount for each part in relation to the available marks; set your answer in the context of the study where this is required.*

(a) State a suitable directional hypothesis for this study. (2 marks)

SAM'S ANSWER: The 'high estimate' group should produce a set of higher estimates than the 'low estimate group'.

CHRIS' ANSWER: Participants in the 'high estimate' condition will estimate that there is a greater number of jellybeans in the jar than participants in the 'low estimate' group.

EXAMINER'S COMMENT: Chris' answer is better than Sam's, but both responses are correct and detailed, so **2 marks** each for Sam and Chris.

(b) Name the research method used in this study. (1 mark)

SAM'S ANSWER: A questionnaire.

CHRIS' ANSWER: This is an experiment.

> **EXAMINER'S COMMENT:** It is an experiment. The IV is the estimates on the sheet of paper and the DV is participants' answers. Sam would receive **0 marks** and Chris would receive **1 mark**.

(c) Describe **one** advantage and **one** disadvantage of this method in the context of this study. (2 marks + 2 marks)

SAM'S ANSWER: One advantage is that you can get a lot of answers quickly and easily. A disadvantage is that people may not tell the truth.

CHRIS' ANSWER: An advantage is that you can carefully manipulate the independent variable (the previous bogus estimates) so that the conditions are the same for everyone in each group. A disadvantage is that the context in which conformity is being measured is rather artificial. In real life, people are not often faced with this particular situation, so it is only sampling a very narrow range of conformity behaviour.

> **EXAMINER'S COMMENT:** There is a follow-through issue in this part of the question. As Sam had the wrong answer for part (b), the answers are wrong again for part (c). The advantages and disadvantages of a questionnaire are appropriate but it wasn't a questionnaire, so **0 marks**. Chris has provided an advantage and a disadvantage, and offered sufficient detail in the context of this study for the full **4 marks**.

(d) Identify the research design used in this study and describe **one** limitation of this design. (1 mark + 2 marks)

SAM'S ANSWER: This is an independent groups design. A problem with this is that there are two different sets of people so one group might be more conforming anyway.

CHRIS' ANSWER: It is an independent groups design. The main limitation is that there are individual differences between the two groups of participants. This means that one might be more conforming than the other before the study begins.

> **EXAMINER'S COMMENT:** Both candidates have identified the design correctly (**1 mark** each). Sam's limitation is not very clear (**1 mark**) but Chris has provided a detailed explanation of the limitation (**2 marks**).

(e) Describe an example of the kind of data that the student is likely to collect, and describe a suitable measure of central tendency that could be used to represent this data. (2 marks + 2 marks)

SAM'S ANSWER: The number of jellybeans in the jars. The mean would be a good measure of central tendency because it takes account of all the scores.

176

CHRIS' ANSWER: The data will be the estimates of the number of jellybeans in the jar for each participant. This data is quantitative. A suitable measure of central tendency would be the median, the middle value. This allows for the fact that there might be some extreme scores that would be distorted by using a mean.

> **EXAMINER'S COMMENT:** Sam's answer is incorrect for the data collected and therefore can receive no marks for the second part of the question (**0 marks**). Chris is correct for the kind of data (**2 marks**) and has identified but not described a suitable measure of central tendency. The justification of the choice counts as elaboration (**2 marks**). The mean would also be a suitable answer but it is difficult to see how the mode would be appropriate.

(f) Describe **two** methods that you could use to select participants for this study.

(2 marks + 2 marks)

SAM'S ANSWER: You could use an opportunity sample, just asking your friends and family or people from around college. Or you could use a random sample by choosing people off the registers at college.

CHRIS' ANSWER: Systematic sampling in which, for example, each tenth name is taken from the register in a school or college. Another method would be opportunity sampling in which the researchers use whoever is available and willing.

> **EXAMINER'S COMMENT:** Sam has suggested two appropriate methods but has not fully described the second one (**2 marks + 1 mark**). Chris would get full credit for both answers (**2 marks + 2 marks**).

(g) Identify **one** ethical problem which may have arisen in this study and suggest a way to deal with it.

(1 mark + 2 marks)

SAM'S ANSWER: People may feel a bit silly at filling in the forms if they didn't have a clue about the number of jellybeans—it could embarrass them. You could make sure the results were completely confidential and tell them that from the start. You shouldn't look when they fill in their answers and not have a place for names.

CHRIS' ANSWER: One ethical problem is that the participants may feel awkward and embarrassed at trying to guess the number of jellybeans in case they felt their estimates were too extreme. This could be addressed by ensuring complete confidentiality—participants could put their responses into a box.

> **EXAMINER'S COMMENT:** Again, Chris' answer is more sophisticated, but both answers are correct and detailed (**1 mark + 2 marks** each).

(h) The student found no difference between the two groups of participants. What conclusion would you draw from this?

(3 marks)

SAM'S ANSWER: That there was no conformity. That people took no notice of what had already been put on the sheets and just put what they thought.

CHRIS' ANSWER: That the participants were not affected by the previous estimates and that there was little or no conformity shown by them.

> **EXAMINER'S COMMENT:** Again, both answers are correct but there is more detail in Chris' answer. The conclusion is not just about whether the participants conformed, but whether they were affected by the estimates on the sheet. Sam would get **2 marks** (not muddled or flawed) and Chris would receive **3 marks**.

(i)   The student decided to conduct some further research into conformity using a questionnaire. Write **two or more** questions that could form part of such a questionnaire on conformity.

(6 marks)

SAM'S ANSWER: "Do you usually do what other people tell you to?" Yes/No
"Do you often act on your own accord, regardless of what other people are doing?" Yes/No
"Do you like the same things as other people?" Yes/No

CHRIS' ANSWER: For the following items, please indicate whether you strongly agree, agree, undecided, disagree, or strongly disagree:

> If my friends had all agreed to go to a pub I did not particularly like, I'd go along with them.
> I think on matters of importance you should always state your opinions strongly and honestly, regardless of who may be offended.

> **EXAMINER'S COMMENT:** Both candidates have satisfied the requirement of providing two or more questions. We then must consider the quality of the questions. Sam's questions do not display any understanding of social desirability bias (people would invariably answer 'no' to the questions). The questions are also rather open-ended and do not have clear yes/no answers. The response is basic (**2 marks**). Chris has shown a clearer understanding of how questions need to be more precise, but has used only one kind of question, which is a limited response (**4 marks**).
>
> Sam's total mark for this question would be 14, probably equivalent to a Grade C. Chris' total mark for this question would be 28, equivalent to a Grade A.

Appendix: Key Studies

*By **Clare Charles** (Rutland College, Leicestershire)*

The questions on key studies test your knowledge and understanding (AO1). You must be able to describe the APFCCs:

AIMS	PROCEDURE	FINDINGS	CONCLUSIONS	CRITICISMS

You may be asked to give any two components in any combination. For example, the 'aims and procedure', 'procedure and results', 'procedure and one criticism', and so on.

The question is worth 6 marks and the rule of thumb is to spend approximately 1 minute per mark. Thus, overall your answer should be 120 words per 6 marks/minutes of writing, which means that for every mark you should aim for approximately 20 words. Each of the two components should be approximately 60 words, and 3 minutes of writing. However, as the aims are usually considerably shorter than the procedure or results, the two components do not have to be exactly equal. These suggestions are only approximations.

There are two further types of question based on the key studies:

"Outline the findings of research into…" (6 marks)

This means that you have to know the findings of more than one study, but you do not need to know the other components. This question is also worth 6 marks and so the 120 words/1 minute per mark rule of thumb applies.

"Give **two** criticisms of the study in the above question." (3 marks + 3 marks)

Again, the question is worth 6 marks (3 marks + 3 marks), which works out at approximately 60 words and 3 minutes per criticism. It is useful to remember the MET mnemonic if you forget the criticisms you have revised here. MET stands for methodological, ethical, and theoretical criticisms. *All* studies have methodological criticisms. So, make sure that you have a sound grasp of Unit 3 (Research Methods) as this knowledge is transferable. Also, make sure you clearly relate the criticism to the research. Most of the criticisms included here are methodological, to consolidate your knowledge of Research Methods.

Please organise your answers and focus on the components identified in the question. A way to focus is to note the 'aims', 'procedure', and so on, as headings. If two criticisms are asked for, you should mentally number them to ensure that you do not give more than is necessary, or give too little content to achieve full marks.

The key studies that we are presenting in this Appendix provide examples of relevant studies that you can refer to in the exam; they are not compulsory, so if you feel you know other studies better then use them instead. Do not over-learn, as key studies are based on *specific* parts of the specification, so there is no point learning studies that do not fit into one of the key study topic areas.

At the start of each chapter, these key study topics are presented in a table, so if you do decide to use other studies make sure that they apply to the key study topic areas that are detailed. The appropriate pages for reference are listed below:

- Cognitive psychology key study topics are detailed on page 19.
- Developmental psychology key study topics are detailed on page 41.
- Physiological psychology key study topics are detailed on page 65.
- Individual differences key study topics are detailed on page 89.
- Social psychology key study topics are detailed on page 109.

Finally, do not learn these examples. Use them to help you construct your own 'analysis' of key studies, following the APFCC structure.

COGNITIVE PSYCHOLOGY: HUMAN MEMORY

ENCODING IN SHORT-TERM AND LONG-TERM MEMORY

STUDY: **Baddeley's (1966, see E&F p.36) studies of encoding in short-term and long-term memory**

> **NOTE:** This research was conducted via two studies, one of short-term memory (STM) and one of long-term memory (LTM). The exam question may ask for a study of encoding, in which case all of this is relevant. However, if it asks for a study of encoding in STM you must select from the information below only the content on STM. Do not write about LTM when the question is on STM, and vice versa.

AIMS: Baddeley investigated encoding in STM and LTM, as he predicted that acoustic encoding (based on the sound of the word) would be preferred by STM and semantic encoding (based on the meaning of the word) would be preferred by LTM. This was partly based on past research by Conrad (1964), who suggested that STM encoded information acoustically but did not clarify which code was preferred by LTM. Thus, Baddeley aimed to confirm Conrad's findings and to establish the same level of understanding of LTM.

PROCEDURE: This was a laboratory experiment that used an independent measures design; there were four word lists and participants were presented with one list only. Two lists were the experimental conditions: in one the words were acoustically similar (meet/feet/sweet) and in the other the words were semantically similar (neat/clean/tidy/smart). The other two conditions acted as controls, so one was acoustically dissimilar, and the other semantically dissimilar. Thus, the IV was the form the list of words took (acoustically similar/dissimilar or semantically similar/dissimilar) and the DV was the number of substitution errors made, (when one item is confused with another), which indicated the main form of encoding. To test STM participants were asked to recall the words immediately. To test LTM participants were asked to recall after a timed delay.

FINDINGS: Immediate recall showed the most confusion (substitution errors) between the acoustically-similar words compared to the words that were acoustically dissimilar; there was no difference in recall of the semantically-similar and semantically-dissimilar lists. In the test of later recall the words that were semantically similar showed more confusion than the words that were semantically dissimilar; there was no difference in recall of the acoustically-similar and acoustically-dissimilar lists. Baddeley found that in STM the words that sounded similar were remembered least well, and in LTM the words remembered least well were those with similar meanings.

CONCLUSIONS: The confusion on the semantically-similar list in the test of later recall demonstrates the importance of meaning in LTM and it can be concluded that encoding is mainly semantic in LTM. The confusion on the acoustically-similar list demonstrates the importance of sound in STM and it can be concluded that encoding is mainly acoustic in STM. Thus, STM encodes information based on how it sounds whereas LTM encodes information based on its meaning. There is less confusion on the word lists with distinct sounds and distinct meanings because to is easier to discriminate between them. This has implications for improving memory.

CRITICISMS

- The research lacks mundane realism as in real life people rarely learn word lists and so the recall task is not representative of everyday memory demands. Consequently, the findings cannot be generalised to real-life memory and so ecological validity must be questioned.
- Acoustic and semantic encoding are not the only codes used. Other codes can take precedence depending on the nature of the information being encoded. For example, Posner (1969) has demonstrated that visual coding may take precedence over acoustic in STM, as the letter combination AA was processed before Aa yet there is no difference acoustically, which suggests the data was processed visually before it was processed acoustically. Similarly in LTM information may be encoded acoustically, visually, or by taste and smell. An image can be extremely vivid and long-lasting with little meaning attached to it. Or a song can be encoded based on the sound without any consideration of the meaning.

> **NOTE:** If the question asks for findings or conclusions only, you could include research by Conrad (1964, see E&F p.36), and Posner (1969, see E&F p.36).

CAPACITY IN SHORT-TERM MEMORY

STUDY: **Jacobs' (1887) study of the capacity of short-term memory (see E&F p.33 for other research on the capacity of STM)**

AIMS: To investigate how much information can be held in short-term memory (STM). To do this he needed an accurate measure of STM capacity and so he devised a technique called the 'serial digit span'. His research was the first systematic study of STM capacity.

PROCEDURE: A laboratory experiment using the digit-span technique was conducted. Participants were presented with a sequence of letters or digits, which they were required to serial recall (repeat back to the experimenter in the same order in which they were presented). The pace of the item presentation was controlled to half-second intervals through a metronome. Initially the sequence was three items, which then increased by a single item until the participant consistently failed to reproduce the sequence correctly. This was repeated over a number of trials to establish the participants' digit span. The sequence length that was recalled correctly on at least 50% of the trials was taken to be the participant's STM span (or digit span).

FINDINGS: Jacobs found that the average STM span (number of items recalled) was between 5 and 9 items. Digits were recalled better (9.3 items) than letters (7.3 items). Individual differences were found, hence the range 5–9. Furthermore, STM span increased with age as in one sample he found a 6.6 average for 8-year-old children compared to 8.6 for 19-year-olds.

CONCLUSIONS: The findings show that STM has a limited storage capacity of between 5 and 9 items. The capacity of STM is not determined by the nature of the information to be learned but by the size of the STM span, which is fairly constant across individuals. Individual differences were found as STM span increased with age, which may be due to increasing brain capacity or improved memory techniques, such as chunking.

CRITICISMS
* The research lacks mundane realism as the digit-span task is not representative of everyday memory demands and the artificiality of the task may have biased the results. Letters or digits are not meaningful information and so may be remembered less well than more meaningful information. Thus, the capacity of STM may be greater for more everyday memory. Jacobs' findings cannot be generalised to real-life memory and so ecological validity must be questioned.
* The findings have been usefully applied to improve memory. For example, telephone numbers, post codes, and car registrations are based on this idea of total digit span. Moreover, memory-improvement techniques are based on the findings that digit span cannot be increased; but the size of the bits of information can be. This is what happens in chunking. Chunking is applied very successfully in mnemonics (memory aids), such as acronyms, e.g. ROY G BIV for the colours of the rainbow.

> **NOTE:** If the question asks for findings or conclusions only, you could include research by Miller (1956, see E&F p.34) and Simon (1974, see E&F p.34).

DURATION IN SHORT-TERM MEMORY

STUDY: **Peterson and Peterson's (1959, see E&F p.35) study of the duration of short-term memory**

AIMS: Peterson and Peterson wanted to test their hypothesis that information held in short-term memory (STM) disappears within about 20 seconds if consolidation (rehearsal) is prevented. Thus, they aimed to prove that the duration of STM is limited to approximately 20 seconds.

PROCEDURE: A laboratory experiment using the Brown–Peterson technique was conducted. Participants were presented with sets of trigrams/nonsense syllables (a set of 3 consonants, e.g. BVM, CTG) which they were then asked to serial recall after a delay of 3, 6, 9, 12, 15, and 18 seconds. Participants were tested repeatedly with the different time delays, and so a repeated measures design was used. The IV was the time delay and the DV was number of trigrams recalled. Participants were given an interference task (counting backwards in threes from a random 3-digit number, e.g. 866, 863, 860) between the initial presentation of the word and the time when they were asked to recall it. This controlled for rehearsal, which would have improved recall and so confounded the results. Recall had to be 100% accurate and in the correct order (serial recall) in order to count.

FINDINGS: After 3 seconds 80% of the trigrams were recalled, after 6 seconds delay 50% were recalled and after 18 seconds less than 10% of the trigrams were recalled. Thus, the study demonstrated rapid forgetting. Recall decreases steadily between 3 and 18 seconds suggesting than the duration of STM is not much more than 18 seconds.

CONCLUSIONS: The memory trace in STM has just about disappeared after 18 seconds. Information held in STM is quickly lost without rehearsal and other forms of consolidation. This supports the hypothesis that the duration of STM is limited to approximately 20 seconds if rehearsal is prevented. They also concluded that this is evidence that STM is distinct from LTM as the duration of LTM is much greater.

CRITICISMS

- The research lacks mundane realism as recall of trigrams is not representative of everyday memory demands and the artificiality of the task may have biased the results. The trigrams are not meaningful information and so may be remembered less well than more meaningful information. Thus, the duration of STM may be longer for more everyday memory. This is supported by the case study of "HM" (see E&F p.37) who could form new short-term memories but not long-term memories. He was able to remember information for up to 15 minutes. Consequently, Peterson and Peterson's findings cannot be generalised to real-life memory and so ecological validity must be questioned.
- An advantage of the highly-controlled environment of the laboratory is that the IV is under the direct manipulation of the experimenter. Consequently, cause and effect can be inferred, thus, it can be said that the time delay causes recall to decline.

> **NOTE:** If the question asks for findings or conclusions only, you could include research by Glanzer and Cunitz (1966, see E&F p.34).

ENCODING IN LONG-TERM MEMORY

See the 1966 studies by Baddeley described earlier in this Appendix (under Encoding in short-term and long-term memory).

DURATION IN LONG-TERM MEMORY

STUDY: Bahrick et al.'s (1975, see E&F p.38) study of the duration of long-term memory

AIMS: Bahrick et al. aimed to investigate the duration of very-long-term memory (VLTM). They wanted to demonstrate that memories could endure in order to support the assumption that the duration of memory is infinite, which of course cannot be measured. They aimed to test LTM as a natural behaviour by testing memory of real-life information.

PROCEDURE: An opportunity sample of 392 American ex-high school students aged from 17–74 years was formed. They were tested in a number of ways: 1) Free recall the names of as many of their former classmates as possible. 2) A photo recognition test where they were asked to identify former classmates in a set of 50 photos, only some of which were of their classmates. 3) A name recognition test. 4) A name and photo-matching test. This tested VLTM as time since departing high school varied, but for some it was as long as 48 years. Participants' accuracy, and thus duration of memory, was assessed by comparing their responses with high school yearbooks, which contain pictures and names of all the students in that year.

FINDINGS: 90% accuracy in face and name recognition was found, even in the participants who had left high school 34 years previously. After 48 years this declined to 80% for name recognition and 40% for face recognition. Free recall was considerably less accurate: 60% accurate after 15 years and only 30% accurate after 48 years.

CONCLUSIONS: The findings show that classmates are rarely forgotten once recognition cues have been given. Thus, Bahrick et al.'s aim to demonstrate that people have very-long-term memories was supported. The findings also support the claim that recognition is better than recall. The research demonstrates VLTM for a particular type of information. It cannot be concluded that VLTM exists for all types of information. It can be concluded that that memory may not be as unreliable and subject to confabulation (inaccuracy) as is commonly perceived.

CRITICISMS

- Classmates' faces are a very particular type of information. They might have emotional significance and there will have been opportunity for a great deal of rehearsal given the daily contact classmates will have experienced. The same is not true of other types of information and so the findings on VLTM cannot be generalised to other types of information.
- Compared to the vast majority of memory research, which takes place in the laboratory, Bahrick et al.'s research has high mundane realism. Asking participants to recall their classmates tests real-life memory. Thus, the research is more representative of natural behaviour and so has high ecological validity—that is, it may be possible to generalise the findings to other settings.

> **NOTE:** If the question asks for findings or conclusions only, you could include research by Shephard (1967, see E&F p.38).

REPRESSION

STUDY: **Levinger and Clark's (1961) study of repression as an emotional factor in forgetting (see E&F p.57 for other studies of repression)**

AIMS: To see if there is a difference between participants' recall of their associations to neutral or negative emotionally-charged words. This was based on previous research by Freud (1915), which suggested that forgetting is a motivated process, where information that causes anxiety will be repressed (made inaccessible to the conscious mind) to protect the individual from the emotional threat.

PROCEDURE: An experimental investigation of repression, where the IV is the emotional charge of the words and the DV is speed of recall, which was taken to be an indicator of repression. In part one of the study participants were given word association tests. They were asked to give free associations (to say exactly what came into their minds) in response to neutral words, such as "window", and negative emotionally-charged words, such as "fear". The participants experienced both conditions, and so it used a repeated measures experimental design. In part two of the study participants' recall was tested. They were presented with the original neutral or negative emotionally-charged words as cues and were asked to recall their associations.

FINDINGS: Participants had greater difficulty remembering their associations to the negative emotionally-charged words than to the neutral words. A difference in the speed of recall between negative emotionally-charged words and neutral words was found. It was also found that the negative emotionally-charged words produced higher galvanic skin response, which is a measure of emotional arousal.

CONCLUSIONS: It was concluded that the greater difficulty in the recall of negative emotionally-charged words compared to neutral words was explained by repression. This was supported by the galvanic skin response data, which showed that the emotionally-charged words created more emotional arousal, which may have led to them being repressed into the unconscious to reduce the anxiety. Thus, speed of recall was slower because the emotionally-charged words were made inaccessible due to their emotional threat. Thus, repression as an explanation of forgetting was supported.

CRITICISMS

- One criticism is that the level of arousal may be a confounding variable as whilst immediate tests of recall found the negative emotionally-charged words to be poorly recalled, delayed recall tests have found that the emotionally-charged words are remembered better than the neutral words. This contradicts repression as an explanation of the findings. If repression had occurred the words should still be repressed, and so recall should not improve. Thus, it may be the case that immediate recall is inhibited by the high arousal and this effect (in which repression plays no part) is reversed with delayed recall, meaning Levinger and Clark's research lacks validity.

- The research lacks mundane realism as emotionally-charged words have much lower emotional threat than real-life anxiety-provoking stimuli. For example, a bad argument or personal comment may induce much higher motivation to forget (repression). Thus, the findings are not representative of repression in real-life, which means they lack generalisability, and so ecological validity must be questioned.

FLASHBULB MEMORY

STUDY: **Conway et al.'s (1994, see E&F p.59) study of flashbulb memory as an emotional factor in forgetting**

AIMS: Conway et al. aimed to show that if a public event has a distinctive meaning and emotional impact for the participant, it will be more memorable and thus create a flashbulb memory. They disagreed with the findings of previous research by McCloskey et al. (1988), which had found that flashbulb memories are subject to forgetting in the same ways as other types of memory. Conway et al. predicted that true flashbulb memories are more enduring and so less vulnerable to forgetting than other types of memory.

PROCEDURE: Conway et al. used Mrs Thatcher's resignation as the significant public event. This was a natural experiment, the naturally occurring IV was culturally determined emotional importance and the DV was memorability of the event. An opportunity sample of 923 participants was selected; two-thirds were from the UK and one-third were other nationalities, mainly North Americans. All of the participants were interviewed within a fortnight of Mrs Thatcher's resignation and 369 were interviewed 11 months later. The elapsed time gave opportunity for forgetting. Participants' memories of the event were assessed for accuracy and detail over time as indicative of memorability and thus flashbulb memory.

FINDINGS: At 11 months 86% of the UK participants still had a vivid, detailed, and accurate memory of the event (a flashbulb memory), compared to only 29% of the participants from other countries. The UK participants' memories were very detailed and were consistent over time. Thus, a difference in flashbulb memory was found between UK participants and other nationalities.

CONCLUSIONS: The difference between UK nationals and other nationalities suggests that public events that have cultural relevance are more likely to be remembered by individuals from the culture that the event has meaning and consequence for. The findings suggest that events with distinctive emotional impact are more memorable and create a flashbulb memory. It can also be concluded that flashbulb memories are more enduring and so less subject to forgetting than other types of memory.

CRITICISMS

- A criticism of this study is the sample drop-off, which is a weakness of longitudinal research. The sample drop-off may have left a biased sample for the second interviews, which may have distorted the difference found between the UK nationals and other nationalities. Consequently, the findings may lack validity, which reduces their meaningfulness and generalisability.

- A major concern with this study is that it is difficult to assess whether memorability is due to the distinctiveness and emotional impact of the event or to the fact that important events are often rehearsed. For example, such events are discussed with others, and the subject of repeated news stories on television and in the papers. Such rehearsal would consolidate the memory and explain subsequent recall rather than being due to the fact that a flashbulb memory was created. Thus, the findings may lack validity as the effect may be due to rehearsal rather than the IV.

RECONSTRUCTIVE MEMORY

STUDY: Bartlett's (1932, see E&F p.61) study of reconstructive memory

AIMS: Bartlett aimed to investigate the effect of schema (knowledge of the world) on participants' recall. Schema include prior expectations, attitudes, prejudices, and stereotypes. This was based on Bartlett's schema theory, which states that memory involves an active reconstruction. Thus, some bits of the memory are real but some bits consist of our knowledge of the world, which fill in the gaps in memory. Bartlett intended that this research would support his theory.

PROCEDURE: Twenty English participants took part in a natural experiment. Participants were presented with a range of stimuli, including different stories and line drawings. A serial reproduction method was used as participants were asked to reproduce the stimulus they had seen repeatedly at different time intervals. The time interval varied between days, months, and even years. The story of *The War of the Ghosts* is the best-known example of his materials. This story was selected because it was from a different culture (North American Indian) and so would conflict with the reader's prior knowledge, thus encouraging them to actively reconstruct the story using their schema. Distortions in the participants' successive reproductions were assessed for evidence of reconstruction.

FINDINGS: Bartlett found considerable distortions in the participants' recollections. The distortions increased over successive recalls and most of these reflected the participants' attempts to make the story more like a story from their own culture. Changes from the original included: rationalisations (these made the story more coherent as the story was shortened and phrases changed to be more similar to their own language), flattening (failure to recall unfamiliar details, e.g. the ghosts); and sharpening (elaboration of certain content and altering of its importance). These changes made the story easier to remember.

CONCLUSIONS: Bartlett concluded that accuracy was rare. The changes to the story on recall showed that the participants were actively reconstructing the story to fit their existing schema, so his schema theory was supported. He believed that schema affect retrieval rather than encoding or storage. He also concluded that memory was forever being reconstructed because each successive reproduction showed more changes, which contradicted Bartlett's original expectation that the reproductions would eventually become fixed. This research has important implications for the reporting of events, which require great accuracy, such as in eyewitness testimony.

CRITICISMS

- Demand characteristics may have been elicited by the research stimulus, which resulted in participant reactivity bias. For example, the strangeness of the story may have provided the participants with clues to the research hypothesis. Thus, the distortions are merely the participants' desire to behave in the way expected by the experimenter rather than real distortions. Thus, the research may lack validity, as the distortions were not a genuine effect, and so it did not measure what it set out to.

- A further criticism is that Bartlett's research lacked objectivity, both because his methods of asking participants to recall the stimulus at various intervals were not very rigorous, and the natural experiment lacks control of the variables as any number of factors could also have influenced recall, such as time of day, motivation, and intelligence of the participants. Thus, the research lacks internal validity, but on the other hand these same methods increase the external (ecological) validity as Bartlett's test of memory is more like the memory demands we face in 'everyday memory'.

NOTE: If the question asks for findings or conclusions only, you could include research by Sulin and Dooling (1974, see E&F p.61), Cohen (1981, see E&F p.62), and Bransford and Johnson (1972, see E&F p.62).

EYEWITNESS TESTIMONY

STUDY: **Loftus and Palmer's (1974, see E&F p.65) study of the effects of language on recall in eyewitness testimony**

AIMS: To test their hypothesis that the language used in eyewitness testimony (EWT) can alter memory. Thus, they aimed to show that leading questions could distort EWT accounts and so have a confabulating effect, as the account would become distorted by cues provided in the question. To test this they asked people to estimate the speed of motor vehicles using different forms of questions. Estimating vehicle speed is something people are generally poor at and so they may be more open to suggestion.

PROCEDURE: Forty-five American students formed an opportunity sample. This was a laboratory experiment with five conditions, only one of which was experienced by each participant (an independent measures design). Participants were shown slides of a car accident involving a number of cars and asked to describe what had happened as if they were eyewitnesses. They were then asked specific questions, including the question "About how fast were the cars going when they (hit/smashed/collided/bumped/contacted—the five conditions) each other?" Thus, the IV was the wording of the question and the DV was the speed reported by the participants. A week after the participants saw the slides they were asked "Did you see any broken glass?" There was no broken glass shown in the slides.

FINDINGS: The estimated speed was affected by the verb used. The verb implied information about the speed, which systematically affected the participants' memory of the accident. Those who were asked the "smashed" question thought the cars were going faster than those who were asked the "hit" question. The mean estimate when "smashed" was used was 41 mph versus 34 mph when "hit" was used. Thus, participants in the "smashed" condition reported the highest speeds, followed by "collided", "bumped", "hit", and "contacted" in descending order. In answering the follow-up question, a higher percentage of participants who heard "smashed" said that they did see broken glass than those who heard "hit".

CONCLUSIONS: The questions asked can be termed 'leading' questions because they affected the participants' memory of the event. The answer to a leading question is implicit in the question—that is, the question contains information about what the answer should be. Thus, language can have a distorting effect on EWT, which can lead to confabulated (inaccurate) accounts of the witnessed event. It is possible that the original memory has been reconstructed, but this is impossible to conclude as the original memory may have been replaced or experienced interference. This has important implications for the questions used in police interviews of eyewitnesses.

CRITICISMS
• The research lacks mundane realism, as the video clip does not have the same emotional impact as witnessing a real-life accident. Consequently, the findings may not be representative of real-life EWT and so the research lacks ecological (external) validity.
• The artificiality of the laboratory environment and the task used may have yielded cues to the research hypothesis. These demand characteristics may have resulted in participant reactivity bias. Thus, the distortions in EWT are merely the participants' desire to behave in the way expected by the experimenter rather than real distortions as a consequence of the language used in the question. Thus, the research may lack internal validity as the distortions were not a genuine effect of the IV and so the research did not measure what it set out to.

NOTE: If the question asks for findings or conclusions only, you could include follow-up research by Loftus and Palmer (1974, see E&F p. 65) and Loftus and Zanni (1975, see E&F p.65).

MEMORY FOR FACES

STUDY: **Young et al.'s (1987, see E&F p.66) study of memory for faces**

AIMS: To investigate the relative importance of features versus configuration (overall arrangement) in face recognition. Thus, the aim was to test memory for faces by reconfiguring composite faces to see what effect this had on recognition. If we recognise faces feature by feature then reconfiguration should have no effect on recognition.

PROCEDURE: Laboratory experiment where participants were presented with a visual stimulus of famous peoples' faces that had been artificially constructed so that the top half of one person's face was combined with the bottom half of a different person's face. The pictures fell into two categories (conditions); those where the top and bottom half were closely aligned, and those that were less closely aligned. The IV was how closely aligned the faces were and the dependent variable was speed of face recognition. The repeated measures design enabled features versus configuration to be assessed, because if recognition relied solely on features, there should be no difference between the two conditions. Whereas if configuration played a role the alignment would affect this making closely-aligned composite faces more difficult to recognise than less-closely-aligned ones.

FINDINGS: There was a significant difference in face recognition between the closely-aligned and less-closely-aligned conditions. Participants were slower to identify the two contributing famous faces when the faces were closely aligned. Face recognition was easier and more accurate when the faces were less closely aligned. Thus, it was suggested that alignment produces a new configuration (overall arrangement) of the face, which inhibits recognition of the two components.

CONCLUSIONS: The findings offer insights into the relative importance of features and configuration in memory for faces. Features alone were less effective in eliciting face recognition, as demonstrated when a new configuration was formed due to the close alignment of the two faces. It can be concluded that people do use information on individual features but that the overall configuration may play a more important role. This has implications for eyewitness testimony, which tends to rely on a features approach (Identikit pictures are constructed on a feature-by-feature basis). Such an approach may impede memory for faces if we accept that real-life face recognition relies on a more holistic approach.

CRITICISMS

- The research lacks mundane realism. Whilst configuration may be representative of how faces are perceived in real life, the pictures used to test this are static as the face is motionless, whereas faces seen in real life are in motion. Bruce and Valentine (1988) have demonstrated the importance of face movement as faces have been identified on the basis of movement only, rather than features or overall configuration. Thus, the artificial task is not representative of how faces are witnessed in real life, particularly in eyewitness testimony, where only part of the face rather than the overall configuration may be glimpsed. Thus, the research cannot be generalised to real-life face recognition, and ecological (external) validity can be questioned.

- The materials would have been difficult to standardise, as all faces are unique, and this would have acted as a confounding variable. For example, the widths of faces may have differed. Similarly some faces may have had more distinctive features than others. Both of these effects may have favoured some participants over others if they aided recognition. This may have introduced constant error as the effect on the DV may differ between conditions, or random error where the effect is less systematic. This lack of uniformity means the findings may not be comparable and thus lack validity.

> **NOTE:** If the question asks for findings or conclusions only, you could include follow-up research by Bruce and Young (1986, see E&F p.67) and Bruce and Valentine (1988, see E&F p.67).

DEVELOPMENTAL PSYCHOLOGY: ATTACHMENTS IN DEVELOPMENT
SECURE/INSECURE ATTACHMENTS

STUDY: **Ainsworth et al.'s (1978, see E&F p.88) study of individual differences in types (secure/insecure) of attachments using the Strange Situation**

AIMS: Ainsworth et al. aimed to investigate individual variation in infant attachments; in particular differences between secure and insecure attachments. They hoped that their method of assessing attachments, the Strange Situation test, would prove to be a reliable and valid measure of attachments.

PROCEDURE: The Strange Situation test lasts for approximately 20 minutes and was used on American infants aged between 12 and 18 months. It takes place in the laboratory and the method used is controlled observation. The Strange Situation consists of 7 episodes, which involve the infant being separated from his or her caregiver, being with a stranger, and reunion with the caregiver. There are two separations and reunions. Separation protest, the infant's willingness to explore, stranger anxiety, and reaction to reunion with the caregiver are the key behaviours used to assess the security/insecurity of the attachment relationship.

FINDINGS: The Strange Situation demonstrated considerable individual differences in secure and insecure attachment types. Most of the infants displayed behaviour categorised as typical of secure attachment (70%), whilst 10% were anxious/resistant, and 20% anxious/avoidant. The securely attached infants were distressed when separated from the caregiver, and sought contact and soothing on reunion. Anxious/resistant attachment was characterised by ambivalence and inconsistency, as the infants were very distressed at separation but resisted the caregiver on reunion. Anxious/avoidant attachment was characterised by detachment as the infants did not seek contact with the caregiver and showed little distress at separation.

CONCLUSIONS: The Strange Situation is a good measure of attachment in so far as being able to discriminate between attachment types. It was concluded that secure attachment is the preferred type of attachment. Implications include the linking of secure attachment to healthy emotional and social development and the type of attachment to maternal sensitivity and responsiveness.

CRITICISMS

- The validity of the classification was questioned and a fourth attachment type suggested by Main and Solomon (1986). They found that a small number of infants display disorganised attachment, in which the infants show no consistent pattern of behaviour, and fitting none of the three main attachment types. Thus, on the one hand the validity of the three attachment types is supported as Main and Solomon do not reject any of these as invalid, but the validity of the Strange Situation as a measure must be questioned as it failed to identify the fourth attachment type.

- The Strange Situation was created and tested in the USA, which means that it may be culturally biased (ethnocentric), as it will reflect the norms and values of American culture. The Strange Situation test assumes that behaviour has the same meaning in all cultures, when in fact social constructions of behaviour differ greatly. Thus, the usefulness of the Strange Situation in assessing attachment across cultures may be limited by the subjectivity inherent in observation and interpretation of behaviour. This lack of generalisability means that the ecological validity of the Strange Situation must be questioned.

> **NOTE:** If the question asks for findings or conclusions only, you could include research by Main and Solomon (1986, see E&F p.88), Main and Weston (1981, see E&F p.89), Kagan (1984, see E&F p.89), and Belsky and Rovine (1987, see E&F p.89).

CROSS-CULTURAL VARIATION

STUDY: Van IJzendoorn and Kroonenberg's (1988, see E&F p.91) study of cross-cultural variation in attachment

AIMS: Van IJzendoorn and Kroonenberg aimed to investigate cross-cultural variation in attachment types through a meta-analysis of research, which had studied attachments in other cultures. They compared only the findings of studies that had used the Strange Situation in order to draw inferences about the external validity of this as a measure of attachment to other populations (population validity) and other settings (ecological validity).

PROCEDURE: A meta-analysis was conducted which compared the findings of 32 studies that had used the Strange Situation to measure attachment and to classify the attachment relationship between the mother and the infant. Research from 8 different nations was compared, which included Western cultures (e.g. US, Great Britain, Germany) and non-western cultures (e.g. Japan, China, Israel). Van IJzendoorn and Kroonenberg researched various databases for studies on attachment.

FINDINGS: Considerable consistency in the overall distribution of attachment types was found across all cultures. Secure attachment was the most common type of attachment in all 8 nations. However, significant differences were found between the distributions of insecure attachments. For example, in Western cultures the dominant insecure type is anxious/avoidant, whereas in non-Western cultures it is anxious/resistant, with China being the only exception, as anxious/avoidant and anxious/resistant were distributed equally. One of the most significant findings was that there is one-and-a-half-times greater variation *within* cultures than *between* cultures.

CONCLUSIONS: The overall consistency in attachment types leads to the conclusion that there may be universal characteristics that underpin infant and caregiver interactions. However, the significant variations demonstrate that universality is limited. Implications include the linking of the variation in attachment to child-rearing practices. Also, the greater variation found within cultures suggests that sub-cultural comparison studies may be more valid than cross-cultural comparisons. The significant differences also question the validity of the Strange Situation.

CRITICISMS

- The greater variation found within cultures undermines the cross-cultural research as it shows that it is wrong to think of one culture as a whole, and so cross-cultural comparisons based on this assumption lack validity. It is over-simplistic to view Britain or America as one single culture, as within each country there are many sub-cultures that may differ in the nature of attachment types. This means that the findings may not be representative of the culture they are assumed to represent and will generalise back to only the sub-cultures that were sampled within the various cultures.

- The Strange Situation was created and tested in the USA, which means that it may be culturally biased (ethnocentric), as it will reflect the norms and values of American culture—for example, the belief that attachment is related to anxiety on separation. The Strange Situation test assumes that behaviour has the same meaning in all cultures, when in fact social constructions of behaviour differ greatly. For example, in Japan young infants are very rarely parted from their mother and so the Strange Situation poses more of a threat to them than to Western infants and so their severe distress may not be indicative of insecure attachment. Thus, the Strange Situation lacks ecological and population validity, which means the findings and insights may not be genuine.

> **NOTE:** If the question asks for findings or conclusions only, you could include research by Sagi et al. (1991, see E&F p.90) and Grossmann et al. (1985, see E&F p.91).

SHORT-TERM EFFECTS OF DEPRIVATION/SEPARATION

STUDY: **Robertson and Bowlby's (1952, see E&F p.97) study of the short-term effects of deprivation/separation**

AIMS: Robertson and Bowlby aimed to identify the short-term effects of separation from the caregiver on young children. This was based on Bowlby's theory of attachment and maternal deprivation hypothesis, which predicted that separation from the mother could result in deprivation, particularly if the child was under 5 years. Bowlby intended that this research would support his belief that deprivation would occur if the separation resulted in bond disruption.

PROCEDURE: Naturalistic observation of young children, aged 1 to 4 years, placed in residential nurseries by their parents because their mothers would be absent for some time. In the majority of cases this was because the mother was entering hospital. Films were made using time-sampling methods to avoid observer bias. Behavioural and emotional reactions to this separation were observed to assess the effects of separation on the children.

FINDINGS: There are three progressive reactions to separation (the PDD model), which are evident in a consistent pattern of behavioural and emotional effects.

- *Protest:* The children showed great distress, calling and crying for the absent caregiver, and some appeared panic-stricken. Anger and fear were evident.
- *Despair:* The children became calmer but apathetic as they showed little interest in anything. Self-comforting behaviours were observed such as thumb sucking and rocking.
- *Detachment:* The children appeared to be coping with the separation as they showed more interest in their surroundings, but they were emotionally unresponsive. The children avoided forming new attachments and no interest was shown when the caregiver returned, but most children re-established the relationship over time.

CONCLUSIONS: Bowlby and Robertson concluded that most young children who experience separation suffer distress. The emotional effects during separation can be severe and can result in emotional damage, but rarely bond disruption. Separation was distressing for most of the children but they did resume their attachment on reunion and so the effects are relatively short-term. Greater separation anxiety is the most common long-term effect.

CRITICISMS
- Short-term separation does not necessarily result in distress. Robertson and Robertson (1968) showed that measures could be taken as part of the substitute care to minimise the effects of separation
- The research is correlational; separation cannot be manipulated as an IV, which means cause and effect cannot be inferred. Thus, it cannot be said that separation *causes* emotional damage or deprivation. Other factors may have led to the separation and emotional damage, e.g. the parent's ill-health may have disrupted the attachment bond before the separation took place if it resulted in the parent becoming physically or emotionally detached.

> **NOTE:** If the question asks for findings or conclusions only, you could include research by Barrett (1997, see E&F p.97) and Robertson and Robertson (1971, see E&F p.97).

LONG-TERM EFFECTS OF DEPRIVATION/SEPARATION

STUDY: **Bowlby's (1946, see E&F p.99) study of the long-term effects of deprivation/separation**

AIMS: Bowlby aimed to establish a cause and effect relationship between maternal deprivation and emotional maladjustment based on his observations of patients at his child guidance clinic. He had observed that children showing poor emotional development had often experienced separation/deprivation and suggested that this can result in psychological and behavioural problems in later life.

PROCEDURE: Eighty-eight children forming an opportunity sample were selected from the clinic where Bowlby worked. Of these, 44 were juvenile thieves and had been referred because of their stealing, and 44 'controls' had been referred because of emotional problems. Retrospective and present case studies were used to assess experience of maternal separation and evidence of emotional maladjustment.

FINDINGS: Bowlby diagnosed 32% of the thieves as 'affectionless psychopaths', but none of the controls were. 86% of the thieves diagnosed with affectionless psychopathy had experienced maternal separation before the age of 5 years, whereas only 17% of the thieves who had not been diagnosed had experienced maternal separation.

CONCLUSIONS: Bowlby concluded that the maternal separation/deprivation in the child's early life caused permanent emotional damage. He diagnosed this as a condition and called it affectionless psychopathy, which he concluded was a lack of emotional development, characterised by lack of concern for others, lack of guilt, and inability to form meaningful and lasting relationships. He claimed that that once the attachment bond was broken the negative effects could not be reversed or undone. The implications were that this research could be used to inform on issues concerning parenting; in particular, the potential negative consequences of mothers working.

CRITICISMS

- The research is correlational and separation/deprivation cannot be manipulated as an IV, which means cause and effect cannot be inferred. Thus, it cannot be said that separation/deprivation causes emotional damage or affectionless psychopathy. Other factors may have led to these outcomes, such as conflict within the family. At best we can say that separation/deprivation and affectionless psychopathy are linked. Hence, Bowlby's conclusions were flawed, confusing cause and effect with correlation.
- There was researcher bias. Bowlby conducted the case studies and made the diagnosis of affectionless psychopathy and so his findings may be biased by his own expectations. Bowlby may have unconsciously influenced what he expected to find during the implementation or interpretation of the research, which undermines its validity.

> **NOTE:** If the question asks for findings or conclusions only, you could include research by Bowlby et al. (1956, see E&F p.100) and Rutter (1981, see E&F p.101).

LONG-TERM EFFECTS OF PRIVATION

STUDY: Hodges and Tizard's (1989, see E&F p.105) study of the long-term effects of privation

AIMS: Hodges and Tizard aimed to investigate the permanence of long-term effects of privation due to institutionalisation, including emotional and social effects in adolescence. This followed Bowlby's claim that maternal deprivation would cause permanent emotional damage, and earlier contradictory research by Tizard suggested that the negative effects of privation could be reversed.

PROCEDURE: Sixty-five children who had been taken into care before the age of four months formed an opportunity sample. This was a natural experiment, using a matched pairs design, as the institutionalised children were compared with a control group who were raised at home, and a longitudinal study (age on entering care to 16 years). By the age of 4 years, 24 had been adopted, 15 restored to their natural home, and the rest remained in the institution. The children were assessed at ages 4, 8, and 16 on emotional and social competence through interview and self-report questionnaires.

FINDINGS: At age four the children had not formed attachments. By age 8 significant differences did exist between the adopted and restored children. At age 8 and 16 most of the adopted children had formed close relationships with their caregivers and were as attached as the control group. These attachments were closer than those of the children restored to their natural homes, i.e. the adopted group showed better emotional adjustment. However, negative social effects were evident in both the adopted and restored children at school, as they were attention-seeking and had difficulty forming peer relationships.

CONCLUSIONS: It can be concluded that some of the effects of privation can be reversed, as the children were able to form attachments in spite of their privation. However, some privation effects are long lasting, as shown by the difficulties that the institutionalised children faced at school. This suggests a need for research into possible reasons why the adopted children fared better than the restored children and the importance of high quality subsequent care if the effects of privation are to be reversed. Hence there are practical implications for care home, adoption, and fostering practices.

- Problems of a longitudinal study include sample drop-off. Hodges and Tizard noted that the adopted children who remained in the study had shown better adjustment at age four. Whereas, the restored children who remained in the study had shown more adjustment problems at age four. Thus, sample drop-off left a biased sample, which may have distorted the difference between the adopted and restored children, as the adopted children were better adjusted at the beginning of the study. Consequently, the findings may lack validity, which reduces their meaningfulness and generalisability.

- Lack of control; as this is a natural experiment, the IV cannot be directly manipulated and so cause and effect cannot be inferred. Thus, it cannot be said that privation causes long-term social effects, such as the difficulties the children had forming peer relationships. At best privation is implicated in this effect which means conclusions are limited.

> **NOTE:** If the question asks for findings or conclusions only, you could include research by Rutter (1981, see E&F p.101), Curtiss (1989, see E&F p.102), and Freud and Dann (1951, see E&F p.102).

PHYSIOLOGICAL PSYCHOLOGY: STRESS
STRESS AND CARDIOVASCULAR DISORDERS

STUDY: **Friedman and Rosenman's (1959, 1974, see E&F p.141) study of the association between Type A behaviour and coronary heart disease**

AIMS: Friedman and Rosenman aimed to investigate the hypothesis that Type A individuals (a high-stress personality type) were more likely to develop coronary heart disease (CHD) than Type Bs. This was based on their observations as cardiologists that their patients displayed a common behaviour pattern, which consisted of three key components: impatience, competitiveness, and hostility. Thus, a positive correlation between Type A behaviour pattern and CHD was sought.

PROCEDURE: A self-selected sample of nearly 3200 Californian men aged between 39 and 59 years was used. This was a prospective, longitudinal study, as the participants were healthy at the outset in 1960 and were assessed over a period of eight-and-a-half years. Part one of the study included structured interview and observation, which assessed personality type and current health status. Personality type was determined by the amount of impatience, competitiveness, and hostility reported and observed during the interview. On the basis of this participants were classified as A1 (Type A), A2 (not fully Type A), X (equal amounts of Type A and Type B), or B (fully Type B). Part two of the study was the follow-up eight years later when incidence of CHD was recorded. A correlational analysis was carried out to test the association between Type A/B behaviour pattern and CHD.

FINDINGS: 257 participants had developed CHD during the eight-and-a-half years, 70% of which had been classified as Type A. This was nearly twice as many as were Type B, even when other factors (e.g. blood pressure, smoking, obesity) known to be associated with heart disease were taken into account. Type As were found to have higher levels of cholesterol, adrenaline, and noradrenaline than Type Bs. A significant but moderate correlation was found.

CONCLUSIONS: The research shows that Type A behaviour pattern is strongly linked to CHD. Friedman and Rosenman concluded that the Type A behaviour pattern increases the individual's experience of stress, which increases physiological reactivity, and that in turn increases vulnerability to CHD. The high levels of the stress hormones suggest that they do experience more stress than Type Bs. The stress response stops digestion, which leads to the higher level of cholesterol in the blood, and this places Type As at risk of CHD. Implications include the need to reduce the 'harmful' Type A characteristics.

CRITICISMS

- Type A behaviour pattern involves a number of characteristics and so the variable Type A lacked precision. It is too broad to be useful, as it is not clear which aspect of Type A is most strongly associated with CHD. Consequently, the research lacked validity, as it did not precisely measure what it set out to. Later research by Matthews et al. (1977), who re-analysed the data, found that hostility correlated highest with CHD. Thus, hostility, rather than Type A in general, may explain the findings.

- Weaknesses of the correlational method mean that there is no control over Type A/B behaviour as a variable, which makes interpretations difficult. For example, rather than causing physiological reactivity, the Type A behaviour pattern may be a response to heightened physiological reactivity in some individuals. Thus, the direction of effect can be questioned; does Type A result in increased physiological reactivity or is Type A a result of high levels of physiological reactivity, which may be genetically predisposed? Most importantly, cause and effect cannot be inferred, as the variables are not under the control of the researcher (causation can only be inferred when an IV has been directly manipulated). Thus, it cannot be said that Type A causes CHD and so conclusions are limited.

> **NOTE:** If the question asks for findings or conclusions only, you could include research by Matthews et al. (1977, see E&F p.141) and Ganster et al. (1991, see E&F p141).

STRESS AND THE IMMUNE SYSTEM

STUDY: Kiecolt-Glaser et al.'s (1984, see E&F p.128) study into the effects of stress on the immune system

AIMS: Kiecolt-Glaser et al. aimed to establish a link between stress and reduced immune functioning. This was based on the assumption that the body's response to stress decreases immune functioning (immunosuppression). They aimed to establish a difference in immune response between conditions of high and lower stress. They also aimed to see if other factors such as psychiatric symptoms, loneliness, and life events were associated with immune functioning.

PROCEDURE: Seventy-five first-year medical students (49 males and 26 females) volunteered (a self-selected sample). This was a natural experiment as the independent variable (the level of stress due to the imminence of exams) was naturally occurring and a repeated measures design was used as participants' blood samples were taken one month before their final exams (lower stress condition) and again on the first day of their final exams (high stress condition). The number of natural killer cells and T cells were measured as indicators of immune functioning (the DV), where a high number indicated better immune functioning. Students were also issued with questionnaires on both occasions, which measured psychiatric symptoms, loneliness, and life events.

FINDINGS: Natural killer and T cell activity did decline between the lower stress and high stress conditions. Thus, the findings confirm the assumption that stress is associated with reduced immune functioning. The findings from the questionnaires revealed that immune responses were particularly suppressed in participants who reported that they were also experiencing psychiatric symptoms, loneliness, or stressful life events.

CONCLUSIONS: The research shows that stress is associated with immunosuppression and that the effect is stronger when there are multiple sources of stress. A number of different sources of stress were shown to contribute to reduced immune functioning—exams, psychiatric symptoms, loneliness, and life events were all implicated. An association only has been identified, as causation cannot be concluded due to the fact this is not a true experiment. Implications include the importance of stress management to good immune functioning.

CRITICISMS

- This is not a true experiment; it is a natural experiment. This means the IV was not under the control of the experimenter. This lack of control also makes the experiment highly vulnerable to confounding variables such as participant variation; that is, individual differences in physiological reactivity, diet, lifestyle, stressful personality type, and so on; all of which could affect immune functioning. This means that cause and effect cannot be inferred as the IV is neither controlled nor isolated (causation can only be inferred when an IV has been directly manipulated). Thus, it cannot be inferred that stress causes the immunosuppression, and at best stress and immune response are negatively correlated.
- The measure of immune function (the number of natural killer and T cells) is objective and so cannot be biased by investigator effects or participant reactivity. The participants cannot control their immune response and so it cannot be biased by subjectivity. Similarly, neither can the investigator influence the immune response and so the findings cannot be biased by experimenter expectancy. This increases the validity of the measure, but does not rule out other sources of bias such as the confounding variables mentioned above.

> **NOTE:** If the question asks for findings or conclusions only, you could include research by Cohen et al. (1991, see E&F p.126), Riley (1981, see E&F p.127), and Schliefer et al. (1983, E&F p.128).

LIFE CHANGES

STUDY: Rahe et al.'s (1970, see E&F p.132) study of the correlation between life events and susceptibility to stress-related illnesses

AIMS: Rahe et al. aimed to test the hypothesis that the stress of life events was correlated with illness. This followed up research by Holmes and Rahe (1967) who had observed that patients tended to have experienced critical life events in the months prior to the onset of illness. Life events were defined as positive or negative events, which disrupted normal routines and so required social readjustment.

PROCEDURE: An investigation of 2500 male US naval personnel took place over a period of 6 months. A self-report questionnaire measured the number of life events, which was based on the social readjustment rating scale (SRRS) constructed by Holmes and Rahe. This consisted of 43 life events, each of which had assigned to it a value (or life change unit, LCU) based on how much readjustment the event would necessitate. Participants were asked to indicate how many of the life events they had experienced in the past 6 months. A total life change unit (stress score) was calculated for each participant by adding up the LCUs of each life event. A health record was also kept of each participant during the six months tour of duty. A correlational analysis was carried out to test the association between total LCUs and incidence of illness.

FINDINGS: A significant positive correlation of 0.118 was found between the total LCU score and illness (as total LCUs increase so does incidence of illness). The direction of the correlation was positive and the strength of the relationship was weak. The association was small but significant.

CONCLUSIONS: The findings suggest that the stress of life events is correlated with physical illness. The correlation appears weak: if the total LCU score was always associated with illness a perfect positive correlation of +1 would have been found. If there were no association the correlation coefficient would have been 0. The correlation coefficient of 0.118 is closer to 0 than +1, but in a sample of 2500 this is a significant correlation. Implications include the importance of using stress management techniques when experiencing life events.

CRITICISMS

- Weaknesses of the correlational method mean other factors besides those taken into account could be involved in the correlation. For example, individual differences may contribute to illness such as the participant's personality or coping skills. The direction of effect must also be questioned: do life events cause stress and subsequently illness, or does stress cause life events? Most importantly, cause and effect cannot be inferred, as the variables are not controlled (causation can only be inferred when an IV has been directly manipulated). Thus, it cannot be said that life events cause illness and so conclusions are limited.

- The sample was biased because only American men were investigated. This means the sample was ethnocentric (as only one culture was sampled) and androcentric (as only males were sampled). The fact that such a restricted sub-group was sampled means the findings are not representative of the wider population as they are not necessarily representative of other cultures or women. The findings may not even be representative of the target population; as a random sample of American naval men was not taken. Thus, the research may lack population validity.

> **NOTE:** It is tempting to criticise the SRRS as there are many criticisms of this. However, it is better to focus on criticisms of this piece of research rather than the general criticisms of the SRRS.

> **NOTE:** If the question asks for findings or conclusions only, you could include research by Rahe and Arthur (1977, see E&F p.133).

WORKPLACE STRESSORS

STUDY: Marmot et al.'s (1977, see E&F p.137) study of the association between workplace stress and stress-related illness

AIMS: Marmot et al. aimed to investigate the association between workplace stress and stress-related illness in male and female civil servants. This was part of the Whitehall studies where a number of different psychosocial characteristics of work were investigated to test their association with illness. This particular investigation focused on the negative correlation between job control and stress-related illness.

PROCEDURE: A sample of 10,308 civil servants aged 35–55 (6895 men—67%, and 3413 women—33%) were investigated in a longitudinal study over three years. Research methods included questionnaires and observation. Job control (an aspect of workplace stress) was measured through both a self-report survey and by independent assessments of the work environment by personnel managers. Job control was assessed on two occasions, three years apart. Records were also kept of stress-related illness. A correlational analysis was carried out to test the association between job control and stress-related illness.

FINDINGS: Participants with low job control were four times more likely to die of a heart attack than those with high job control. They were also more likely to suffer from other stress-related disorders such as cancers, strokes, and gastrointestinal disorders. These findings were consistent on both occasions that job control was measured and the association was still significant after other factors, such as employment grade, negative attitude to employment, job demands, social support, and risk factors for CHD had been accounted for.

CONCLUSIONS: The findings show that low job control is associated with high stress, as indicated by the number of stress-related illness. There is an inverse social gradient in stress-related illness among British civil servants: i.e. as illness increases job control decreases—in other words, the variables are negatively correlated. Implications include the responsibility of employers to address job control as a source of stress and illness. Giving employees more autonomy and control may decrease stress-related illness, which would increase the efficiency and productivity of the workforce.

CRITICISMS

- The self-report method is vulnerable to investigator effects and participant reactivity bias. The questions may give cues as to the aim of the research and so create an expectancy effect. Or demand characteristics may be evident which influence the participants to behave in ways that support the research aims/hypothesis as participants are usually co-operative and try to 'help' the researcher by conforming to the demand characteristics. Thus, participants may guess that an association between job control and stress-related illness is being sought and so report low job control if suffering from illness and high job control if not. Similarly, the observations made by the personnel managers could be biased by an expectancy effect.

- Weaknesses of the correlational method mean that there is no control over job control as a variable, which makes interpretations difficult as cause and effect cannot be inferred (causation can only be inferred when an IV has been directly manipulated). Thus, it cannot be said that low job control causes stress-related illness, only that an association can be inferred, which means conclusions are limited. This lack of control also means that other factors may be involved in the association, which were not considered or taken into account in the research. For example, individual differences such as personality, coping skills, or number of life events experienced are also implicated in stress-related illness, so there is no clear-cut association between job control and illness.

> **NOTE:** If the question asks for findings or conclusions only, you could include research by Shirom (1989, see E&F p.137), Czeisler et al. (1982, see E&F p.138), and Matteson and Ivancevich (1982, see E&F p.138).

INDIVIDUAL DIFFERENCES: ABNORMALITY

BIOLOGICAL EXPLANATIONS OF ANOREXIA

STUDY: **Holland et al.'s (1988, see E&F p.187) study of genetic vulnerability in anorexics**

AIMS: Holland et al. aimed to investigate whether there was a higher concordance rate of anorexia nervosa for monozygotic (MZ) than dizygotic (DZ) twins. This was based on past research, which suggested that abnormality might have a genetic basis. A difference is being sought between MZ and DZ twins because MZ are 100% genetically identical whereas DZ have only 50% in common. Thus, it follows that there should be higher concordance for MZ than DZ if there is a genetic basis to anorexia nervosa.

PROCEDURE: An opportunity sample of 34 pairs of twins (30 female and 4 male) and one set of triplets was selected because one of the pair (or triplet) had been diagnosed with anorexia. This was a natural experiment as the IV (genetic relatedness) is naturally occurring and cannot be controlled by the experimenter. A physical resemblance questionnaire established genetic relatedness, that is, whether the twins were MZ or DZ (16 were MZ and 14 were DZ). Usually MZ twins have greater physical resemblance but if there was any uncertainty a blood test was carried out. This was a longitudinal study; the researchers checking over time to establish whether the other twin went on to develop anorexia (the DV). A clinical interview and standard criteria were used for diagnosis of anorexia.

FINDINGS: A significant difference was found as there was a much higher concordance rate of anorexia for MZ (56%—9 of 16) than DZ (7%—1 of 14) twins. Further findings were that in three cases where the non-diagnosed twin did not have anorexia they were diagnosed with other psychiatric illnesses, and two had minor eating disorders.

CONCLUSIONS: The results suggest a genetic basis for anorexia and general psychiatric illness. The percentage suggests that genes are not wholly responsible and so they constitute a predisposition; that is, they make the individual vulnerable but do not trigger the disorder. Implications include the need to identify the precipitating factors i.e. environmental triggers, which interact with the genetic predisposition.

CRITICISMS

- The study ignores any role nurture may play in causing anorexia, that is, the environmental explanations for the disorder. Certainly nurture plays a role, as the concordance rates are only 56%. They would have to be 100% if anorexia was exclusively due to genetic factors. Furthermore, the 56% concordance may be due to nurture as MZ twins may experience a more similar environment and may be treated more similarly than DZ twins due to the fact that they look and behave more alike. Whilst this does not account for the considerable difference found between

MZ and DZ twins, it does show that it is difficult to separate out the influence of nature and nurture. Thus, it is over-simplistic and reductionist to consider only one factor, genes, as a basis for anorexia.

- The natural experiment lacks control of the variables. The IV, genetic relatedness, is not isolated, as multiple other factors (confounding variables) may be implicated, for example, environmental factors (as identified above), individual-specific experiences, and socio-economic factors. Consequently, internal validity is low, as factors other than the IV may have resulted in anorexia. Also the IV is not controlled and so causation cannot be inferred. This means conclusions are limited as it cannot be said that genes cause anorexia, at best they are strongly implicated.

> **NOTE:** If the question asks for findings or conclusions only, you could include research by Strober and Humphrey (1987, see E&F p.186), Park et al. (1995, see E&F p.186), Barlow and Durand (1995, see E&F p.188), and Garfinkel and Garner (1982, see E&F p.188), all of which offer further insights into biological explanations.

BIOLOGICAL EXPLANATIONS OF BULIMIA

STUDY: **Kendler et al.'s (1991, see E&F p. 187) study of genetic vulnerability in bulimics**

AIMS: Kendler et al. aimed to investigate whether there was a higher concordance rate of bulimia nervosa for monozygotic (MZ) than dizygotic (DZ) twins. This was based on past research, which suggested that abnormality might have a genetic basis. A difference is being sought between MZ and DZ twins because MZ are 100% genetically identical whereas DZ have only 50% in common. Thus, it follows that there should be higher concordance for MZ than DZ if there is a genetic basis.

PROCEDURE: A sample of 2163 female twins was selected, based on one of the pair being diagnosed with bulimia. This was a natural experiment as the IV (genetic relatedness) is naturally occurring and cannot be controlled by the experimenter. This was a longitudinal study: the researchers checked over time to establish whether the other twin went on to develop bulimia (the DV). The clinical interview and standard criteria were used for diagnosis of bulimia.

FINDINGS: There was a higher concordance rate of bulimia for MZ (23%) than DZ (9%) twins and the difference was statistically significant. Overall, 123 cases of bulimia were reported. Furthermore, significant evidence of other mental disorders was also reported: 10% of the non-bulimic twins reported anorexia, 5% a phobic disorder, and 11% an anxiety disorder.

CONCLUSIONS: The results suggest a genetic basis for bulimia, but the evidence is less strong than that for anorexia. The percentage concordance suggests that genes are not wholly responsible but constitute a predisposition for the disorder. That is, they make the individual vulnerable but do not trigger the disorder. Implications include the need to identify the precipitating factors (environmental triggers), which interact with the genetic predisposition.

CRITICISMS

- The study ignores any role nurture may play in causing bulimia; that is, the environmental explanations for the disorder such as any shared dysfunctional environment. Certainly nurture plays a role, as the concordance rates are only 23%. They would have to be 100% if bulimia was exclusively due to genetic factors. Furthermore, the 23% concordance may be due to nurture as MZ twins may experience a more similar environment and may be treated more similarly than DZ twins due to the fact that they look and behave more alike. Whilst this does not account for the considerable difference found between MZ and DZ twins it does show that it is difficult to separate out the influence of nature and nurture. Thus, it is over-simplistic and reductionist to consider only one factor—genes—as a basis for bulimia.
- The natural experiment lacks control of the variables. The IV (genetic relatedness) is not isolated, as multiple other factors (confounding variables) may be implicated, e.g. environmental factors (as identified above), individual-specific experiences, and socio-economic factors. Consequently, internal validity is low, as factors other than the IV may have resulted in bulimia. Also the IV is not controlled and so causation cannot be inferred. This means conclusions are limited, as it cannot be said that genes cause bulimia, at best they are strongly implicated.

> **NOTE:** If the question asks for findings or conclusions only, you could include research by Strober and Humphrey (1987, see E&F p.186), Barlow and Durand (1995, see E&F p.188), and Garfinkel and Garner (1982, see E&F p.188), all of which offer further insights into biological explanations.

PSYCHOLOGICAL EXPLANATIONS OF ANOREXIA AND BULIMIA

STUDY: **Behar et al.'s (2001) study of a psychological explanation for the eating disorders anorexia and bulimia (see E&F pp.191–192 for further studies on role models and eating disorders)**

AIMS: Behar et al. aimed to investigate the effect of gender identity on eating disorders. This was based on behavioural explanations that gender differences exist because women experience more pressure to be thin than men do, for example, women are presented with more 'idealised' body images in the media. The hypothesis is that the existence of these role models can lead to the development of eating disorders if women model themselves on these examples of female 'perfection'. Thus, they aimed to see if acceptance of the female gender role, as indicated by feminine gender identity, was higher in females with eating disorders than in controls.

PROCEDURE: 126 participants—63 patients with eating disorders (anorexia and bulimia) and 63 comparison subjects—were selected. This was a natural experiment as the IV (presence/absence of eating disorder) cannot be controlled by the experimenter. Further procedures included a structured clinical interview for diagnosis of eating disorders using standardised (DSM-IV) criteria, and a self-report survey to measure gender identity, the Bem Sex Role Inventory (BSRI), which is accepted as a valid measure of gender identity.

FINDINGS: Significant differences were found in gender identity. More eating disorder patients were classified as feminine gender identity; 43% compared to only 23.8% of controls. Whereas more controls were classified as androgynous (showing a mixture of feminine and masculine traits); 31.7% of controls compared to only 19% of patients. Also more controls were classified as undifferentiated (fitting neither masculine, feminine nor androgynous category); 43% compared to 27% of patients.

CONCLUSIONS: Feminine gender identity was significantly more prevalent in eating disorder patients than 'normal' controls, which supports the behavioural explanation for eating disorders, i.e. that women face greater pressure than men from society (in particular the media) to conform to 'idealised' body images, which may place them at greater risk for eating disorders. Implications include the positive applications of androgyny as a defence against eating disorders.

CRITICISMS

- The study ignores any role nature may play in causing eating disorders. Certainly nature plays a role, as there is strong evidence for genetic involvement. It is difficult to separate out the influence of nature and nurture, but it is over-simplistic and reductionist to consider only one explanation—the behavioural explanation—as a basis for eating disorders when there are many other explanations, e.g. biological, cognitive, and psychodynamic.
- This is not a true experiment; it is a natural experiment. This means the IV (presence/absence of eating disorder) was not under the control of the experimenter. Causation cannot be inferred if the IV is not directly manipulated and so it cannot be said that eating disorders and gender identities are causally related. Furthermore, the direction of effect is wrong as gender identity has been measured after eating disorders have developed, when the explanation being sought is that gender identity predisposes eating disorders. Thus, a prospective study (gender identity would be the IV, participants would be initially eating disorder free, and then monitored to see if this develops) would need to be carried out to establish gender identity as a cause of eating disorders.

> **NOTE:** This research investigated anorexia and bulimia and so could be used as a psychological study of either disorder. Remember to focus on the disorder asked for in the question. So indicate that it was an investigation of both eating disorders and so offers insight into anorexia/bulimia, but then refer to the disorder specified in the question for the rest of your answer.

> **NOTE:** If the question asks for findings or conclusions only, you could include research by Lee et al. (1992, see E&F p.192), Cooper (1994, see E&F p.191), and Nasser (1986, see E&F p191), all of which offer further insights into behavioural explanations.

PSYCHOLOGICAL EXPLANATIONS OF BULIMIA

STUDY: Jaeger et al.'s (2002) study of cross-cultural differences in body dissatisfaction, a risk factor for bulimia (see E&F pp.191–192 for other studies of psychological explanations of bulimia)

AIMS: Jaeger et al. aimed to investigate body dissatisfaction because it is identified in past research as being a risk factor for bulimia and dependent on cultural factors. It is suggested that eating disorders are in fact Western culture-bound syndromes. However, few past studies have compared cultures using rigorous methodology. Thus, this research aims to gather reliable information about body dissatisfaction and interrelated factors (self-esteem and dieting behaviour), and consequent cultural differences in vulnerability to bulimia.

PROCEDURE: 1751 medical and nursing students were sampled across 12 nations, including both Western and non-Western countries. This was a natural experiment as the IV (culture) cannot be controlled by the experimenter. A self-report method was used to obtain data on body dissatisfaction, self-esteem and dieting behaviour. A series of 10 body silhouettes, which were designed to be culture-free, as far as is possible, were shown to the participants to assess body dissatisfaction. Body mass index (BMI) measures were also taken.

FINDINGS: Significant differences between cultures did exist. Most extreme body dissatisfaction was found in Mediterranean countries followed by northern European countries. Countries in the process of Westernisation showed an intermediate amount of body dissatisfaction. Non-western countries showed the least amount of body dissatisfaction. Body dissatisfaction was the most important influence in most countries on dieting behaviour. Body dissatisfaction was found to be independent of self-esteem and BMI.

CONCLUSIONS: The significant differences between cultures support behaviourist explanations of bulimia; that is, the disorder is due to the 'idealised' body images portrayed in the media, which encourage distorted views and consequently body dissatisfaction and dieting behaviour. Western countries are more exposed to these images and they do show higher body dissatisfaction than non-western cultures. Perhaps even more significant is the increase in body dissatisfaction in cultures undergoing Westernisation, where exposure to idealised images will be increasing. Implications are that explanations of the disorder must be considered at a macro-level (society) rather than as originating solely within the individual (micro-level).

CRITICISMS
- The study ignores any role nature may play in causing bulimia. Certainly nature plays a role, as there is strong evidence for genetic involvement. It is difficult to separate out the influence of nature and nurture, but it is over-simplistic and reductionist to consider only one explanation, behavioural, as a basis for eating disorders when there are many other possible explanations, e.g. biological, cognitive, and psychodynamic.
- This is not a true experiment; it is a natural experiment. This means the IV (culture) was not under the control of the experimenter. Causation cannot be inferred if the IV is not directly manipulated and so it cannot be said that culture causes differences in body dissatisfaction and the subsequent risk for bulimia, at best they are strongly implicated.

NOTE: If the question asks for findings or conclusions only, you could include research by Lee et al. (1992, see E&F p.192), Cooper (1994, see E&F p.191), and Nasser (1986, see E&F p191), all of which offer further insights into behavioural explanations.

SOCIAL PSYCHOLOGY: SOCIAL INFLUENCE
CONFORMITY/MAJORITY INFLUENCE

STUDY: **Zimbardo et al.'s (1973, see E&F p.204) study of conformity in the Stanford prison experiment**

AIMS: To investigate conformity to social roles through the role-playing of either a prisoner role or guard role. Zimbardo et al. also aimed to find out if the conforming behaviour was due to the nature of the person (dispositional factors) or the prison context (situational factors) and hoped to apply this knowledge to real-life prison behaviour and the abusive interrelations that existed between the prisoners and guards.

PROCEDURE: Twenty-four male American undergraduate volunteers formed a self-selected sample. They were randomly allocated to either the role of prisoner or guard. This was a controlled observation study, which was made as realistic as possible. For example, 'prisoners' were arrested at their homes and taken to a police station before transfer to the 'prison'. Once at the mock prison they were deloused, issued with a prison uniform, and an ID number (and they were then addressed by this instead of their name). The guards were also issued with uniforms and 16 rules, which they were asked to enforce to maintain a 'reasonable degree of order'. The interaction between prisoners and guards, mood state, self-perception, and coping behaviour were observed as indicators of conformity. Data was collected via videotape, audiotape, direct observation, questionnaires, and interviews.

FINDINGS: An extremely high level of conformity to social roles was observed in both the guards and the prisoners. The 'guards' conformed to a sadistic role, e.g. they readily issued punishments for prisoner misbehaviour. At first punishment took the form of loss of privileges, however, later punishments included food and sleep deprivation, solitary confinement, and humiliation, e.g. cleaning toilets with their bare hands. Their aggression was out of proportion to the threat to prison order posed by the prisoners who, after some initial resistance, became passive, excessively obedient, showed flattened mood, and distorted perception of self. Some prisoners conformed to their role by becoming 'sick', and five prisoners had to be released early because of extreme emotional disturbance. Further evidence of prisoner conformity was that five experienced a parole board! The study was stopped on the sixth day instead of running for two weeks as planned as a result of the extreme pathological behaviour.

CONCLUSIONS: The research shows the strength of conformity as a form of social influence. The participants showed 'public conformity' as many reported afterwards that they felt they had acted out of character and so there was no lasting change in private opinion. Personality tests indicated no significant differences between the guards' and prisoners' personalities, which supports a situational explanation of social influence. Thus, the conformity is due to the situation rather then the personal characteristics of the participants. The prison environment is the main cause of the abusive interrelations, which means that this research has significant implications for the running of real-life prisons.

CRITICISMS

- The artificial set-up and consequent demand characteristics resulted in participant reactivity bias. The guards and prisoners were play-acting rather than genuinely conforming to their roles. The guards reported afterwards that they were influenced by the film *Cool Hand Luke*, which stereotyped prison guards as tough and aggressive. Thus, the research may lack validity as the conformity to roles was not a genuine effect and so the research did not measure what it set out to.
- The findings have been positively applied to real-life prisons as the insights revealed have been incorporated into guards' training. Thus, the research has been instrumental in improvements in the American prison system. However, the current prison system is increasingly impersonal and brutal and so the value of this extrapolation and the ecological validity of the research can be questioned.

> **NOTE:** This is a study of conformity so do not forget to relate the procedures and findings to conformity. If the question asks for findings only, you could include research by Asch (1951, 1956, see E&F p. 202), Perrin and Spencer (1980, see E&F p. 208), and Smith and Bond (1993, see E&F p. 209).

MINORITY INFLUENCE

STUDY: Moscovici et al.'s (1969, see E&F p.207) study of minority influence

AIMS: To determine whether a minority can influence a majority of naïve participants and thus reverse the usual direction of social influence. Moscovici et al. aimed to determine the conditions necessary for this to occur, in particular, the importance of consistency to the influence of the minority.

PROCEDURE: Participants were pre-tested to check for colour blindness. A laboratory experiment was carried out where participants were randomly allocated to either a consistent, inconsistent, or control condition. Each condition consisted of six participants; four naïve participants (the majority), and two confederates (the minority). Participants were asked to describe the colour of 36 slides, all of which were blue, but which varied in brightness due to different filters. In the consistent condition the two confederates described all 36 slides as green. In the inconsistent condition the two confederates described 24 of the 36 slides as green and the remaining 12 slides as blue. In the control condition there were no confederates. Minority influence was measured by the percentage of naïve participants who yielded to the confederates by calling the blue slides green.

FINDINGS: In the consistent condition 8.42% of the participants' answers were green and 32% conformed at least once. In the inconsistent condition 1.25% of the participants' answers were green. In the control condition only 0.25% of the participants' answers were green. Thus, the consistent condition showed the greatest yielding to minority influence. In a follow-up study both experimental groups were more likely to report ambiguous blue/green slides as green compared to the control group.

CONCLUSIONS: The minority does have influence over the majority and this influence is more effective when the minority is consistent. This shows that minorities are more persuasive when they are consistent, which has implications for people in leadership positions who are hoping to influence the majority.

CRITICISMS

- The research lacked experimental realism, which means that the experimental set-up was simply not believable. The slide test was artificial and may have yielded demand characteristics because it was not believable. Thus, the research lacked internal validity, as the conversion was not a genuine effect. It was due to demand characteristics (the cues that revealed conversion was expected), which resulted in participant reactivity bias.
- The research lacked mundane realism; that is, the research set-up had no relevance to real-life as it took place in a controlled environment with an artificial task that is not representative of minority influence in real-life social situations. Identifying the colour of a slide is trivial compared to real-life instances of minority influence such as the views of political leaders or decision-making by juries. Consequently, the findings have low ecological (external) validity as they cannot be generalised to real-life settings.

> **NOTE:** If the question asks for findings only, you could include research by Nemeth et al. (1974, see E&F p.207).

OBEDIENCE

STUDY: Milgram's (1963, 1974, see E&F p.213) study of obedience, the 'remote victim' condition

AIMS: Milgram aimed to test the hypothesis "Germans are different" which was based on the atrocities committed during the Second World War. Milgram was sceptical that these atrocities were due to a national character defect and so he aimed to investigate how the situational context could lead to ordinary people inflicting harm on others.

PROCEDURE: Forty male volunteers (a self-selected sample) took part in a controlled observational study, which they were deceived into thinking was a test of learning. The naïve participant was always assigned the role of 'teacher' and a confederate, Mr Wallace, played the role of 'learner'. A word association test was the learning task and the naïve participant was instructed to deliver an electric shock to the learner for each incorrect answer. The teacher and learner were in separate rooms with no voice contact. The measure of obedience was the strength of the electric shock administered by the participants, which was on a scale of 15 to 450 volts with 15-volt increments for each wrong answer. Unbeknownst to the participant, the shocks were not real.

FINDINGS: All participants continued to give shocks up to the 300-volt level, and 65% of participants continued to the highest level, 450 volts. This completely contradicted the predicted results that 3% or less would reach 450 volts. Marked effects in the naïve participants' behaviour were observed, as most showed signs of extreme tension. For example, they trembled, sweated, stuttered, groaned, dug their fingernails into their flesh, and three had uncontrollable seizures.

CONCLUSIONS: The research demonstrated that obedience was due more to situational factors (the experimental setting, the status of the experimenter, and the pressure exerted on the participant to continue) than to 'deviant' personality, which contradicts the "Germans are different" hypothesis. Implications include the relevance of this research to the real-life atrocities of the Second World War.

CRITICISMS

- Orne and Holland (1968) claim the research lacked experimental realism, which means that the experimental set-up was simply not believable. They thought the participants were alerted to the fact that the electric shocks were not real, because electric shocks were not a believable punishment for making a mistake on a test. Thus, the research lacked internal validity, as the obedience was not a genuine effect. It was due to demand characteristics (the cues that revealed the shocks were not real and that obedience was the expected behaviour), which resulted in participant reactivity bias. However, the participants' stress reactions contradict this.

- Orne and Holland (1968) also claim that the research lacked mundane realism. The research set-up is unlike real life as it was an artificial, controlled, environment. Consequently, the findings have low ecological (external) validity as they lack generalisability to real-life settings. Thus, the explanations of obedience may not be true for real-life social situations, such as obedience within the family or obedience at work. However, experimental realism can compensate for a lack of mundane realism, which it could be argued is the case with this study.

> **NOTE:** If the question asks for findings or conclusions only, you could include research by Hofling et al. (1966, see E&F p.216) and Bickman (1974, see E&F p.216).

Glossary

The following list is a glossary of the key terms and concepts that are presented on the second page of each chapter. It is important that you are able to define the key terms (listed in blue), as many questions will ask you for definitions. The key term definitions provided are 3 marks-worth each, and this is usually the detail that is required to get full marks in the exam. The remainder of the terms (listed in black) are for your information only, and you will not be asked to define these in the exam. Each term has been presented so you can test yourself by covering the definitions up and trying to define the terms. Try to focus on the distinction between similar-sounding terms, for example, the difference between 'anorexia nervosa' and 'bulimia nervosa'. Working through and self-testing the blue key terms in this glossary should complete your revision and give you confidence that you are well prepared for the exam.

Abnormality	Behaviour that is considered to deviate from the norm (statistical or social), or ideal mental health. It is dysfunctional because it is harmful or causes distress to the individual or others and so is considered to be a failure to function adequately. Abnormality is characterised by the fact that it is an undesirable state that causes severe impairment in the personal and social functioning of the individual, and often causes the person great anguish depending on how much insight they have into their illness.
Acoustic coding	The memory's way of automatically encoding information by its sound.
Adrenal glands	The endocrine glands that are located adjacent to, and covering, the upper part of the kidneys.
Adrenaline	One of the hormones (along with noradrenaline) produced by the adrenal glands, which increases arousal by activating the sympathetic nervous system and reducing activity in the parasympathetic system.
Affectionless psychopathy	A condition where individuals appear to experience little guilt or emotion, lack normal affection, and are unable to form permanent relationships.
Agentic state	A state of feeling controlled by an authority figure, and therefore lacking a sense of personal responsibility.
Anaclitic depression	A severe form of depression in infants who experience prolonged separations from their mothers. The term 'anaclitic' means 'arising from emotional dependency on another'.
Anorexia nervosa	An eating disorder characterised by the individual being severely underweight; 85% or less than expected for size and height. There is also anxiety, as the anorexic has an intense fear of becoming fat and a distorted body image. The individual does not have an accurate perception of their own, or 'normal', body size, has a distorted belief in the importance of body size, and may minimise the dangers of being severely underweight.
ANS (autonomic nervous system)	That part of the nervous system that controls vital body functions, which is self-regulating and needs no conscious control (automatic).

Articulatory-phonological loop	The part of working memory that holds information for a short period of time in a phonological (sound) or speech-based form.
Attachment	This is a strong, reciprocal, emotional bond between an infant and his or her caregiver(s) that is characterised by a desire to maintain proximity. Attachments take different forms, such as secure or insecure. Infants display attachment through the degree of separation distress shown when separated from the caregiver, pleasure at reunion with the caregiver, and stranger anxiety.
Aversion therapy	A form of treatment based on the principles of classical conditioning in which undesirable behaviour is eliminated by associating it with severe punishment, such as electric shocks.
Avoidant attachment (type A)	An insecure attachment of an infant to its mother. The child avoids contact on reunion.
Bar chart	Like a histogram, a representation of frequency data but the categories do not have to be continuous; used for nominal data.
Barbiturates	Drugs that used to be widely used to treat anxiety disorders.
Behavioural model of abnormality	A model of abnormality that considers individuals who suffer from mental disorders possess maladaptive forms of behaviour, which have been learned.
Benzodiazepines	Anti-anxiety drugs such as Valium and Librium. They work by reducing serotonin levels and are more effective than barbiturates.
Biofeedback	A technique that aims to control involuntary (autonomic) muscles through the use of feedback about current physiological functioning. Relaxation is an important aspect of its success when used in the context of stress.
Bond disruption	When a child is deprived of their main attachment object, in the short or long term, and receives no substitute emotional care.
Bonding	The process of forming close ties with another.
Buffers	Term used to refer to aspects of situations that protect people from having to confront the results of their actions.
Bulimia nervosa	An eating disorder in which excessive (binge) eating is followed by compensatory behaviour such as self-induced vomiting or misuse of laxatives. It is often experienced as an unbreakable cycle where the bulimic impulsively overeats and then has to purge to reduce anxiety and feelings of guilt about the amount of food consumed, which can be thousands of calories at a time.
Burnout	Physical and/or emotional exhaustion produced especially by stress.
Capacity	A measurement of how much is held in memory.
Cardiovascular disorders	These are disorders of the cardiovascular system, which includes the heart and it's supporting systems. An example is atherosclerosis, which is the thickening of the arteries due to high levels of cholesterol in the bloodstream. Another disorder is hypertension or high blood pressure, which puts pressure on the heart as it has to work harder to beat at high pressure.
Caregiving sensitivity hypothesis	Secure attachments are due to a caregiver's sensitivity and responsiveness, which creates independence in the infant.
Chunking	The process of combining individual letters or numbers into larger, meaningful units.
CNS (central nervous system)	Part of the nervous system that consists of the brain and the spinal cord.

Cognitive development	The development of the child's mental processes such as thought, reasoning, and memory. IQ tests and the child's academic performance at school are used to assess cognitive development. Cognitive development is determined by an interaction of biological predisposition and the environment.
Cognitive model of abnormality	A model of abnormality which considers that individuals who suffer from mental disorders have distorted or irrational thinking.
Cognitive restructuring	The technique used by cognitive therapists to make distorted and irrational beliefs more rational.
Compliance	Conforming to the majority view in order to be liked, avoid ridicule or social exclusion. Compliance occurs more readily with public behaviour than private behaviour, and is based on power.
Conformity/ majority influence	This occurs when people adopt the behaviour, attitudes, or values of the majority (dominant or largest group) after being exposed to their values or behaviour. In this sense they publicly yield to group pressure (compliance), although in some cases they yield privately (internalisation). The majority is able to influence because of other people's desire to be accepted (normative) or their desire to be right (informational).
Confounding variables	Variables that are mistakenly manipulated or allowed to vary along with the independent variable and therefore affect the dependent variable.
Context dependency	The reliance on context as a cue to recall.
Control	This refers to the perception of being in command (control) of one's responses to stimuli, such as stressors. Self-perception is the crux of this, as according to the transactional model, a lack of control and consequently stress may be experienced when there is a mismatch between the perceived demands of the situation and the individual's perceived ability to cope. Perception of control gives the individual a sense of self-efficacy, that is, they perceive that they can cope with the stressor.
Correlational analysis	Testing a hypothesis using an association that is found between two variables.
Critical period	A biologically determined period of time during which an animal is exclusively receptive to certain changes.
Cross-cultural variations in attachments	Cross-cultural variations refer to the fact that behaviour, attitudes, norms, and values differ across cultures. This is because cultures socially construct different values and norms, etc. Thus, the relationships between infants and caregivers vary across cultures because of different childrearing styles and beliefs about which qualities should be nurtured. This is evident in the cross-cultural differences that research has suggested between individualistic and collectivist cultures.
Cue-dependent forgetting	Forgetting that occurs because of the absence of a suitable retrieval cue.
Cultural relativism	The view that one cannot judge behaviour properly unless it is viewed in the context from which it originates. This is because different cultures have different constructions of behaviour and so interpretations of behaviour may differ across cultures. A lack of cultural relativism can lead to ethnocentrism, where only the perspective of one's own culture is taken.
Day care	This refers to care that is provided by people other than the parent or relatives of the infant. It can take different forms, for example, nurseries, childminders, play groups, etc. It is distinct from institutionalised care, which provides permanent substitute care; day care is a temporary alternative to the caregiver.

Debriefing	Attempts by the experimenter at the end of a study to provide detailed information for the participants about the study and to reduce any distress they might have felt.
Deception	This is an ethical guideline, which states that deception of the participants during the research process should be avoided wherever possible. Deception refers to the withholding of information that might affect the participant's decision to take part in the research. It is an issue because this might lead to psychological harm. Deception is a particularly common issue because the withholding of the research hypothesis is often considered necessary in order to avoid demand characteristics.
Defence mechanisms	Strategies used by the ego to defend itself against anxiety.
Demand characteristics	Features of an experiment that help participants to work out what is expected of them, and lead them to behave in certain predictable ways.
Deprivation	To lose something, such as the care of an attachment figure for a period of time.
Deprivation dwarfism	Physical underdevelopment found in children reared in isolation or in institutions. Thought to be an effect of the stress associated with emotional deprivation.
Deviation from ideal mental health	Deviation from optimal psychological well-being (a state of contentment that we all strive to achieve). Deviation is characterised by a lack of positive self-attitudes, personal growth, autonomy, accurate view of reality, environmental mastery, and resistance to stress; all of which prevent the individual from accessing their potential, which is known as self-actualisation.
Deviation from social norms	Behaviour that does not follow socially accepted patterns; violation of them is considered abnormal. These unwritten social rules are culturally relative and era-dependent. For example, homosexuality was once illegal and considered to be a mental disorder because it deviated from the social norm. Now there are campaigns for gay marriages to be recognised and afforded the same benefits as heterosexual marriages, and this shows the extent to which this definition of abnormality is subject to change.
Directional (one-tailed) hypothesis	A prediction that there will be a difference or correlation between two variables and a statement of the direction of this difference.
Disorganised attachment (type D)	The infant shows no set pattern of behaviour at separation or reunion (thus "disorganised"). This kind of behaviour is associated with abused children or those whose mothers are chronically depressed.
Displacement	The pushing out of information from short-term memory by new information before it has been processed for long enough to pass on to long-term memory.
Dispositional explanation	Deciding that other people's actions are caused by their internal characteristics or dispositions.
Dissociation	Minority ideas absorbed into the majority viewpoint without anyone remembering where they came from.
DSM-IV	The most recent version of the *Diagnostic and Statistical Manual of Mental Disorders* published by the American Psychiatric Association, provides a means of classifying and diagnosing mental disorders.
Duration	This refers to how long a memory lasts. The existence of two distinct memory stores is supported by duration because this differs between STM and LTM. STM has a very limited duration of 18–30 seconds, whereas LTM potentially lasts forever and so a memory may endure permanently.

DV (dependent variable)	An aspect of the participant's behaviour that is measured in the study.
Eating disorder	A dysfunctional relationship with food. The dysfunction may be gross under-eating (anorexia), binge–purging (bulimia), over-eating (obesity), or healthy eating (orthorexia). These disorders may be characterised by faulty cognition and emotional responses to food, maladaptive conditioning, dysfunctional family relationships, early childhood conflicts, or a biological and genetic basis, but the nature and expression of eating disorders show great individual variation.
Ecological validity	The validity of the research outside the research situation itself; the extent to which the findings are generalisable to other situations, especially 'everyday' situations. The question is whether you would get the same findings in a different setting or whether they are they limited to the original research context. If the latter is true then there is a lack of external validity.
Encoding	The transfer of information into code, which creates a memory trace, which can be registered in the memory store. STM and LTM are dependent on different codes, as in STM encoding is primarily acoustic (based on the sound of the word) and in LTM encoding is primarily semantic (based on the meaning of the word).
Endocrine system	A system of a number of ductless glands located throughout the body that produce the body's chemical messengers, called hormones.
Enmeshment	A situation in which all of the members of a family lack a clear sense of their own personal identity.
Ethical guidelines	A written code of conduct designed to aid psychologists when designing and running their research. The guidelines set out standards of what is and is not acceptable. The code focuses on the need to treat participants with respect and to not cause them harm or distress. For example, the BPS code of conduct advises of 'the need to preserve an overriding high regard for the well-being and dignity of research participants' (BPS 1993).
Ethical issues	Ethical issues arise in the implementing of research when there is conflict between how the research should be carried out (e.g. with no deception to the participants) and the methodological consequences of observing this (e.g. reduced validity of the findings). Another issue is that of participants versus society. Is it justifiable to infringe upon the rights of participants if the research will be of benefit to society? Such issues are an inevitable consequence of researching people and resolving the issues can be difficult.
Ethnocentrism	The belief that one's own ethnic or cultural group is superior to others.
Ethological approach	The study of animal behaviour in natural environments; this approach emphasises the importance of inherited capacities and responses.
Experiment	A procedure undertaken to make a discovery about causal relationships. The experimenter manipulates one variable to see its effect on another variable.
Experimental validity	The extent to which research has internal and external validity. Internal validity refers to the extent to which the experiment measured what it set out to, i.e. is the observed effect in the DV a result of the manipulation of the IV? External validity refers to the generalisability of the findings to other settings (ecological), or populations and periods in time (temporal). Any threats to internal or external validity reduce the meaningfulness of the findings.
External validity	The validity of an experiment outside the research situation itself; the extent to which the findings of a research study are applicable to other situations, especially 'everyday' situations.

Eyewitness testimony	Evidence supplied by people who witness a specific event or crime, relying only on their memory. Statements often include descriptions of the criminal (facial appearance and other identifiable characteristics) and subsequent identification, and details of the crime scene (e.g. the sequence of events, time of day, and if others witnessed the event, etc).
Failure to function adequately	A model of abnormality based on an inability to cope with day-to-day life caused by psychological distress or discomfort.
Field experiment	A study in which the experimental method is used in a more naturalistic situation.
Flashbulb memory	A long-lasting and vivid memory of a specific event and the context in which it occurred, that is important and emotionally significant. This could be a national or personal event. The term 'flashbulb' refers to the fact that it is as if a photographic image of the event and setting has been encoded, as the memory is so detailed and accurate. Examples include the atrocities of September 11th 2001, and the deaths of Princess Diana and John F. Kennedy.
Forgetting	This is the inability to recall or recognise information. Forgetting may occur because the information no longer exists in memory and so is not available for retrieval or because it cannot be found and so is not accessible. Forgetting is more likely with information that needs to be recalled, as recognition is generally greater than recall.
Frequency polygon	A graph showing the frequencies with which different scores are obtained by participants in a study.
General adaptation syndrome (GAS)	The body's non-specific response to stress that consists of three stages: the alarm reaction, when the body responds with the heightened physiological reactivity of the 'fight or flight' response to meet the demands of the stressor; resistance, when the body tries to cope with the stressor and outwardly appears to have returned to normal but inwardly is releasing high levels of stress hormones; and exhaustion, where resources are depleted and the body's defence against disease and illness is decreased.
Groupthink	Conformity to group opinion.
Hardiness	A cluster of traits possessed by those people best able to cope with stress.
Histogram	A graph in which the frequencies of scores in each category are represented by a vertical column; data on the y-axis must be continuous with a true zero.
Homeostasis	The process of maintaining a reasonably constant environment.
Hypothalamus	The part of the brain that integrates the activity of the autonomic nervous system. Involved with emotion, stress, motivation, and hunger.
Ideal mental health	A state of contentment that we all strive to achieve.
Identification	Conforming to the demands of a given role because of a desire to be like a particular person in that role.
Immune system	A system of cells (white blood cells) within the body that is concerned with fighting disease. The white blood cells, called leucocytes, include T and B cells and natural killer cells. They help prevent illness by fighting invading antigens such as viruses and bacteria.
Independent groups design	A research design in which each participant is in one condition only. Each separate group of participants experiences different levels of the IV. Sometimes referred to as an unrelated or between subjects design.
Informational social influence	This occurs when someone conforms because others are thought to possess more knowledge.

Informed consent	This is an ethical guideline, which states that participants' agreement to take part in research should be based on their full knowledge of the nature and purpose of the research. Thus, they should be made aware of any tasks required of them and their right to withdraw and any other aspects of the research that might affect their willingness to participate.
Insecure attachment	The attachment bond is weaker in insecure attachments and this may result in an anxious and insecure relationship between the infant and caregiver, such as avoidant and resistant attachments. Insecure attachments are assessed by the infant's separation distress, lack of stranger anxiety, and either avoidant or resisitant reactions when reunited with the caregiver. The insecure attachment has a poor effect on development, as the infant has a negative working model of themselves and others.
Internalisation	Describes an individual adhering to the ideas, values, and behaviour of the majority because they accept and agree with their world view.
Internal validity	The validity of an experiment in terms of the context in which it is carried out. Concerns events within the experiment as distinct from external validity.
Interview	A verbal research method in which the participant answers a series of questions.
Investigator effects	The effects of an investigator's expectations on the response of a participant. Sometimes referred to as experimenter expectancy effect.
IV (independent variable)	Some aspect of the research situation that is manipulated by the researcher in order to observe whether a change occurs in another variable.
Laboratory experiment	An experiment conducted in a laboratory setting or other contrived setting away from the participants' normal environments. The experimenter is able to manipulate the IV and accurately measure the DV, and considerable control can be exercised over confounding variables.
Legitimate authority	The assumption that people in positions of power have earned the right to tell others what to do because they have superior expertise, knowledge, or ability.
Levels of processing	The extent to which something is processed, not in terms of how much processing is done (as in repetition), but in terms of how much meaning is extracted. Shallow processing focuses on the superficial features of the information, such as whether a word is in upper or lower case, whilst deep processing focuses on the meaning of the information and is thought to lead to better retention.
Life changes	Life changes require some degree of social readjustment or alteration in the individual's current life patterns (life change), which is the response to a significant life event. For example, death, divorce, a change of job, marriage, vacation, or Christmas. Each life event is assigned a life change unit (LCU) based on how much readjustment the change would necessitate. The adaptation needed to cope with the life change absorbs energy, and so depletes the body's resources, and thus life changes are a source of stress.
Long-term memory	A relatively permanent store, which has unlimited capacity and duration. Different kinds of long-term memory have been identified, including episodic (memory for personal events), semantic (memory for facts and information), and procedural (memory for actions and skills).
Maltreatment	Physical or psychological harm directed at participants during psychological research.
Matched pairs (matched participants) design	A research design that matches participants on a one-to-one basis rather than as a whole group.

Maternal deprivation hypothesis	The view, suggested by Bowlby, that separation from the primary caregiver (maternal deprivation) leads to bond disruption and possibly the breaking of the attachment bond. This has long-term effects on emotional development. Bowlby believed that once broken the attachment bond could not be fixed and so the damage would be permanent.
Mean	An average worked out by dividing the total of participants' scores by the number of participants.
Median	The middle score out of all the participants' scores.
Medical/biological model of abnormality	A model of abnormality that regards mental disorders as illnesses with a physical cause.
Memory	The mental processes used to encode, store, and retrieve information. Encoding takes many forms; visual, auditory, semantic, taste, and smell. Storage refers to the amount of information that can be held in memory. Retrieval refers to the processes by which information is 'dug out' of memory, and includes recognition, recall, and reconstruction. It is useful to distinguish between two types of memory: short-term or immediate memory and long-term or more permanent memory.
Memory for faces	This relies on the accurate recognition and recall of faces. Face recognition seems to rely on a combination of factors such as the features, configuration (overall arrangement) and movements of the face. Identification of the criminal means memory for faces provides key information in eyewitness testimony. However, memory for faces is subject to the same distortions due to reconstructive memory and emotional factors as other types of memory.
Minority influence	A majority being influenced to accept the beliefs or behaviour of a minority. This usually involves a shift in private opinion, as the majority needs to accept the minority as 'right' if they are to reject the dominant majority. This private change involves a process of conversion, which is more likely to occur when the minority is consistent and flexible, as this is more persuasive.
Mode	The most frequently occurring score among participants' scores in a given condition.
Modelling	A form of therapy based on observing a model and imitating that behaviour.
Monotropy hypothesis	The notion that infants have an innate tendency to form strong bonds with one caregiver, usually their mother.
Multi-store model	The concept that memory is divided into several kinds of store (sensory, short- and long-term) and data are passed from one to the other because of verbal rehearsal.
Mundane realism	The use of an artificial situation that closely resembles a natural situation.
Natural experiment	A type of experiment where use is made of some naturally occurring variable(s).
Naturalistic observation	An unobtrusive observational study conducted in a natural setting.
Negative correlation	As one co-variable increases the other decreases. They still vary in a constant relationship.
Non-directional (two-tailed) hypothesis	A prediction that there will be a difference or correlation between two variables, but no statement about the direction of this difference.
Noradrenaline	One of the hormones (along with adrenaline) produced by the adrenal glands which increases arousal by activating the sympathetic nervous system and reducing activity in the parasympathetic system.
Normative social influence	This occurs when someone conforms in order to gain liking or respect from others.

Norms	Cultural expectations, standards of behaviour.
Null hypothesis	A hypothesis that states that any findings are due to chance factors and do not reflect a true difference, effect, or relationship.
Obedience to authority	Behaving as instructed, usually in response to individual rather than group pressure. This usually takes place in a hierarchy where the person issuing the order is of higher status than the person obeying the order. Obedience occurs because the individual feels they have little choice; they cannot resist or refuse to obey. It is unlikely to involve a change in private opinion.
Opportunity sampling	Participants are selected because they are available, not because they are representative of a population.
Pilot study	A smaller, preliminary study that makes it possible to check out standardised procedures and general design before investing time and money in the major study.
Physiological approaches to stress management	Techniques that try to control the body's response to stress by reducing physiological reactivity. For example, anti-anxiety drugs decrease the 'fight or flight' response such as high blood pressure, increased heart rate, etc. Biofeedback is another technique, which works by training the participant to recognise their heightened physiological reactivity and reduce it though relaxation exercises.
PNS (peripheral nervous system)	Part of the nervous system that excludes the brain and spinal cord, but consists of all other nerve cells in the body. The PNS is divided into the somatic nervous system and the autonomic nervous system.
Positive correlation	When two co-variables increase at the same time.
Privation	The lack of any attachments, as distinct from the loss of attachments (deprivation). This is due to the lack of an appropriate attachment figure. Privation is more likely than deprivation to cause permanent emotional damage or 'affectionless psychopathy'; the condition diagnosed by Bowlby as involving permanent emotional damage.
Proactive interference	Current learning and memory being disrupted by previous learning.
Protection of participants from psychological harm	An ethical guideline, which states that participants should be protected from psychological harm, such as distress, ridicule, or loss of self-esteem. The risk of harm during the research study should be no greater than the participant would experience in their everyday life. Debriefing can be used to offer support if a study has resulted in psychological harm.
Psychodynamic model of abnormality	A model of abnormality that regards the origin of mental disorders as psychological rather than physical, and suggests that mental illness arises out of unresolved unconscious conflicts.
Psychological approaches to stress management	Techniques that try to control the cognitive, social, and emotional responses to stress. They attempt to address the underlying causes of stress, such as faulty thinking and disproportionate emotional responses (overreactions and underreactions). Psychological techniques work by changing the person's perception of the stressor and/or increasing the individual's perception of control.
Psychoneuroimmunology	The study of the effects of both stress and other psychological factors on the immune system.
Qualitative data	Concerned with how things are expressed, what it feels like, meanings or explanations; i.e. the quality.
Quantitative data	Concerned with how much. Data is presented in numerical terms.

Quasi-experiment	Research that is similar to an experiment but certain key features are lacking, such as the direct manipulation of the independent variable by the experimenter and random allocation of participants to conditions.
Questionnaire survey	A survey requiring written answers.
Random sampling	Selecting participants on some random basis (e.g. numbers out of a hat). Every member of the population has an equal chance of being selected.
Range	The difference between the highest and lowest score in any condition.
Reconstructive memory	This is a form of recall which involves an active process whereby the memory is reassembled with some pieces of 'real' information and some pieces that are 'made-up' to fill in the gaps in memory. The gaps are filled in based on our existing knowledge and experience of the world, called schema. Schema include stereotypes, prejudices, and our expectations of the world. Consequently, the memory recalled is not an accurate reproduction of the original stimulus; it is distorted by the schema that have filled in the gaps.
Rehearsal	The verbal repetition of information, which strengthens its memory trace.
Reliability	The extent to which a method of measurement or test produces consistent findings.
Repeated measures design	A research design where the same participants are used for all conditions in the experiment.
Repression	This is a defence mechanism suggested by Freud whereby memories that cause anxiety are kept out of conscious awareness as a means of protecting the individual. This is also called motivated forgetting. An example of this could be when you do not want to do something particularly tiresome (such as homework!) and so you forget all about it.
Research	The process of gaining knowledge and understanding via either theory or empirical data collection.
Research/experimental/ alternative hypothesis	A statement put forward at the beginning of a study stating what you expect to happen, generated by a theory.
Resistant attachment (type C)	An insecure attachment of an infant to its mother. The child resists contact on reunion.
Retrieval	Recovering stored information. Essentially, remembering it.
Retroactive interference	Subsequent learning disrupting memory for previous learning.
Right to withdraw	The basic right of participants in a research study to stop their involvement at any point, and to withdraw their results if they wish to do so.
Scattergraph/scattergram	Two-dimensional representation of all the participants' scores in a correlational study.
Schema	An 'organised' packet of information that is stored in long-term memory.
Secure attachment (type B)	A strong contented bond between the infant and caregiver. The secure infant shows distress at separation but is easily comforted by the caregiver when reunited. This characterises the majority of attachments and is related to healthy development as the infant has a positive working model of relationships.
Semantic coding	The memory's way of automatically encoding information by its meaning.
Sensitive period	A looser interpretation of the concept of a critical period—changes are more likely during the period of time rather than being exclusive to it.

Separation	This refers to the absence of the caregiver (e.g. due to work commitments, divorce, or hospitalisation), which usually causes great distress, but not necessarily permanent bond disruption. Separation has a number of effects, such as protest, despair, or detachment, and if prolonged it may result in deprivation.
Separation anxiety	The sense of concern felt by a child when separated from their attachment figure.
Separation protest	The infant's behaviour when separated—crying or holding out their arms. Some insecurely attached infants show no protest when left by their attachment figure, whereas securely attached children do.
Serial reproduction	A method used by Bartlett to show how information changes as it passes between different people. Bartlett read a story to an individual, who then told their version to another participant, who in turn passed the information onto the next participant, and so on. This method allows us to see what changes take place with each reproduction.
Set point	The ideal or most appropriate value of the system variable.
Short-term memory	A temporary place for storing data where they receive minimal processing. Short-term memory has a very limited capacity and short duration, unless it is maintained through rehearsal.
Situational explanation	Deciding that people's actions are caused by the situation in which they find themselves rather than by their personality.
Social contract	This describes an unwritten contract between people that is difficult to break because of social pressure. Thus, having agreed to take part in a study or to help someone, it is difficult to withdraw.
Social development	The development of the child's social competence includes social skills, ability to relate and empathise with others, and formation of close and meaningful relationships. Social development is determined by an interaction of biological predisposition and the environment.
Social influence	The influence of a group (majority influence) or individual (minority influence or obedience) to modify the thinking, attitudes, and/or behaviour of others. For example, fashion trends are a consequence of majority influence; political and religious leaders are an example of minority influence; and complying with the demands of an authority figure, such as an employer, is an example of obedience.
Standard deviation	A measure of the spread of the scores around the mean. It is the square root of the variance and takes account of every measurement.
State dependency	The reliance on a match of emotional or physical state at the time of an event and at the time of retrieval as a cue to recall.
Statistical infrequency/ deviation from statistical norms	Behaviours that are statistically rare or deviate from the average/statistical norm as illustrated by the normal distribution curve, are classed as abnormal. Thus, any behaviour that is atypical of the majority would be statistically infrequent, and so abnormal (e.g. schizophrenia is suffered by 1 in 100 people and so is statistically rare).
Strange situation	An experimental procedure used to test the security of a child's attachment to a caregiver. The key features are what the child does when it is left by the caregiver and the child's behaviour at reunion, as well as responses to a stranger.
Stranger anxiety	The distress experienced by a child when approached by a stranger.

Stress	A state of psychological and physical tension produced, according to the transactional model, when there is a mismatch between the perceived demands of a situation (the stressor[s]) and the individual's perceived ability to cope. The consequent state of tension can be adaptive (eustress) or maladaptive (distress).
Stress inoculation training	A technique to reduce stress through the use of stress-management techniques and self-statements that aims to restructure the way the client thinks.
Stress management	Stress management is the attempt to cope with stress through reduction of the stress response. This may be aimed at the physiological effects of stress (e.g. anti-anxiety drugs or biofeedback) and the psychological effects of stress (e.g. stress inoculation training or hardiness training). Stress management is often based on changing the person's perception of the stressor and/or increasing the individual's perception of control.
Stressor	An event that triggers the stress response because it throws the body out of balance and forces it to respond. For example, life changes (e.g. divorce, bereavement), daily hassles (e.g. traffic, lost keys), workplace stressors (e.g. role strain, lack of control) and environmental stressors (e.g. noise, temperature, overcrowding). Stressors are not objective in that they do not produce the same response in all people as this depends on the individual's perception of the stressor. Thus, nothing is a stressor unless it is thought to be so!
System variable	The characteristic that needs to be regulated in order to maintain a reasonably constant environment.
Systematic desensitisation	A form of treatment for phobias, in which the fear response to a threatening stimulus is replaced by a different response such as relaxation.
Temperament hypothesis	The view that a child's temperament is responsible for the quality of attachment between the child and its caregiver, as opposed to the view that experience is more important.
Token economy	Institution-based therapy based on the principles of operant conditioning. Desirable behaviours are encouraged by the use of selective reinforcements.
Trace decay	The physical disappearance of a memory trace.
Type A personality	In biopsychology, a personality type who is typically impatient, competitive, time pressured, and hostile.
Validity	The soundness of the measurement tool, the extent to which it is measuring something that is real or valid.
Visual spatial coding	The memory's way of automatically encoding information by its appearance.
Visuo-spatial sketch pad	A system within working memory designed for spatial and/or visual coding.
Working memory model	A model of memory proposed by Baddeley and Hitch as an alternative to the multi-store model. The model consists of a central executive (an attentional system, which has a limited capacity, and which is involved in decision-making), together with two slave systems (the articulatory-phonological loop, and visuo-spatial sketch pad). This model is concerned with both active processing and the brief storage of information.
Workplace stressor	Factors in the work environment or aspects of the job that cause stress. For example, overcrowding, noise, and temperature are factors in the environment. Lack of control, interpersonal relationships, role ambiguity, and work overload, are all examples of work pressures that cause stress.